Written for Our Learning

Written for Our Learning

The Single Meaning of Scripture in Christian Theology

Benjamin Sargent

CASCADE *Books* • Eugene, Oregon

WRITTEN FOR OUR LEARNING
The Single Meaning of Scripture in Christian Theology

Copyright © 2016 Benjamin Sargent. All rights reserved. Except for brief quotations in critical publications or reviews, no part of this book may be reproduced in any manner without prior written permission from the publisher. Write: Permissions, Wipf and Stock Publishers, 199 W. 8th Ave., Suite 3, Eugene, OR 97401.

Cascade Books
An Imprint of Wipf and Stock Publishers
199 W. 8th Ave., Suite 3
Eugene, OR 97401

www.wipfandstock.com

PAPERBACK ISBN: 978-1-4982-7856-0
HARDCOVER ISBN: 978-1-4982-7858-4
EBOOK ISBN: 978-1-4982-7857-7

Cataloguing-in-Publication data:

Names: Sargent, Benjamin.

Title: Written for our learning : the single meaning of Scripture in Christian theology / Benjamin Sargent.

Description: Eugene, OR: Cascade Books, 2016 | Includes bibliographical references.

Identifiers: ISBN 978-1-4982-7856-0 (paperback) | ISBN 978-1-4982-7858-4 (hardcover) | ISBN 978-1-4982-7857-7 (ebook)

Subjects: LCSH: Bible—Hermeneutics. | Hermeneutics—Religious aspects—Christianity. | Polysemy.

Classification: BS476 S19 2016 (print) | BS476 (ebook)

Manufactured in the U.S.A.   JULY 21, 2016

With gratitude to Tony Thomson, librarian at Moorlands College,
for so much help and encouragement.

Contents

Abbreviations | viii

Introduction: Determinacy, Polysemy, and Single Meaning | 1

1. Written for Us: Single Meaning in the Use of Scripture in the New Testament | 24
2. Written for Christ: Single Meaning in the Fathers | 95
3. Written for Correction: Single Meaning in Medieval Theology | 121
4. Written for You: Single Meaning in Renaissance and Reformation | 134
5. Written for Them: Single Meaning in Modernity | 151
6. Written at All? Single Meaning after Modernity | 177

Conclusion: Single Meaning and Theological Interpretation | 189

Bibliography | 193

Abbreviations

ABC	Anchor Bible Commentary
AJBI	*Annual of the Japanese Biblical Institute*
ANTC	Abingdon New Testament Commentaries
ASNU	Acta Seminarii Neotestamentici Upsaliensis
AsSeign	*Assemblées du Seigneur*
AUSS	*Andrews University Seminary Studies*
BBR	Bulletin for Biblical Research
BECNT	Baker Exegetical Commentary on the New Testament
BeO	*Bibbia e Oriente*
BEvT	Beiträge zur Evangelischen Theologie
Bib.	*Biblica*
BIS	Biblical Interpretation Series
BSac.	*Bibliotheca Sacra*
BZ	*Biblische Zeitschrift*
BZNW	Beihefte zur Zeitschrift für die neutestamentliche Wissenschaft
CBOTS	Coniectanea Biblica: Old Testament Series
CBQ	*Catholic Biblical Quarterly*
CI	*Critical Inquiry*
DSD	Dead Sea Discoveries

ErIsa	ארץ ישראל
EvQ	*Evangelical Quarterly*
ExpTim	*Expository Times*
HBT	*Horizons in Biblical Theology*
HeyJ	*Heythrop Journal*
HThKNT	*Herders Theologische Kommentar zum Neuen Testament*
HTR	*Harvard Theological Review*
IBS	*Irish Biblical Studies*
ICC	International Critical Commentary
IJST	*International Journal of Systematic Theology*
JAAR	*Journal of the American Academy of Religion*
JBL	*Journal of Biblical Literature*
JETS	*Journal of the Evangelical Theological Society*
JJS	*Journal of Jewish Studies*
JQR	*Jewish Quarterly Review*
JSNT	*Journal for the Study of the New Testament*
JSNTSup	*Journal for the Study of the New Testament Supplement*
JSOTSup	*Journal for the Study of the Old Testament Supplement*
JSS	*Journal of Semitic Studies*
JTS	*Journal of Theological Studies*
LD	Lectio Divina
LHBOTS	Library of Hebrew Bible/Old Testament Studies
LNTS	Library of New Testament Studies
NA 27	Nestle and Aland Ed., *Novum Testamentum Graece, 27 revidierte Auflage* (Stuttgart: Deutsche Bibelgesellschaft, 2001).
NIDNTT	The New International Dictionary of New Testament Theology
NIGTC	*The New International Greek Testament Commentary*

NovT	*Novum Testamentum*
NovTSup	Supplements to Novum Testamentum
NTL	New Testament Library
NTS	*New Testament Studies*
PMLA	*Proceedings of the Modern Language Association of America*
RB	*Revue Biblique*
ResQ	*Restoration Quarterly*
RevQ	*Revue de Qumran*
RHPhR	*Revue d' Histoire et de Philosophie Religieuses*
RThL	*Revue Theologique de Louvain*
SBLSCS	Society of Biblical Literature Septuagint and Cognate Studies
SBLSP	Society of Biblical Literature Seminar Papers
SBLWGRW	Society of Biblical Literature Writings of the Greco Roman World
SDSSRL	Studies in the Dead Sea Scrolls and Related Literature
SPA	*Studia Philonica Annual*
SJT	*Scottish Journal of Theology*
SwJT	*Southwestern Journal of Theology*
TDNT	*Theological Dictionary of the New Testament*
TLNT	*Theological Lexicon of the New Testament*
TS	*Theological Studies*
TynBul	*Tyndale Bulletin*
WBC	Word Biblical Commentary
WUNT	Wissenschaftliche Untersuchungen zum Neuen Testament
ZECNT	Zondervan Exegetical Commentary on the New Testament
ZCP	*Zeitschrift für celtische Philologie*
ZNW	*Zeitschrift fur Neutestamentliche Wissenschaft*

Introduction
Determinacy, Polysemy, and Single Meaning

A vicar in a rural parish in the south of England stands up in his study to place a commentary on the Greek text of Philippians back on an overburdened bookshelf. The sermon preparation for the week is over and the inevitable loss of the knowledge of Greek gained at Theological College is deferred for another week. He feels confident that his sermon will be a faithful presentation and modern day application of what Paul intended his first hearers to grasp. With what he understands to be the meaning of the lesson from Philippians still circling in his mind, he jumps on his bicycle to take communion to the local care home. There, he reads the lesson from Philippians and gives a distilled version of his sermon in fewer than ten sentences. After the care home, the vicar cycles to the hospital to visit a parishioner about to undergo surgery. As he arrives, the parishioner is very distressed. The vicar quietly reads the lesson from Philippians and, without relating everything he plans to say on Sunday, chooses a few choice words of encouragement derived from what he understands to be the meaning of the lesson. That evening, the vicar begins the Church council meeting with a verse from the lesson and a prayer based on its message as guidance for the meeting to follow. That night, as he prays, the lesson from Philippians is still in mind and influences the concerns and requests he brings to God.

In this single, hypothetical day, a passage from Philippians is interpreted for a variety of contexts by the hypothetical vicar. By way of apology for introducing a study of an issue in biblical hermeneutics with such a mundane scenario, it ought to be noted that this scenario is a contemporary, if idealized, rewriting of a similar illustration given by David Steinmetz and developed by Stephen Fowl.[1] In Steinmetz and Fowl's mundane scenario, a medieval monk studies and lectures on the psalms within an academic context. He then prays them as part of the daily office in chapel. At another point in the day he spends time illuminating a psalter on vellum. On Sunday, he preaches on the psalms to a mixed congregation of local people. This scenario is given as evidence of indeterminate or polysemic meaning. The psalms have significance for monastic prayer and yet are also interpreted in a different way for the lecture hall and for the parish pulpit. The illumination of the manuscript suggests yet another level of significance. Likewise, the rural vicar interprets the same text for a variety of contexts as diverse as the hospital visit and the business meeting. The question to be asked is whether or not these interpretative contexts and the different role the scriptural text has in each are evidence of interpretive plurality or indeterminate meaning. Does the text possess a scholarly level of meaning, a devotional level of meaning, a pastoral level of meaning, and a practical level of meaning? Or is it that a single meaning guides diverse applications of the text for a variety of contexts as is perhaps evident in the example of the vicar?

Ideas of polysemy, determinacy, and indeterminacy are far from clearly defined. For some, determinate meaning is the opposite of any kind of plurality in interpretation of a single text, even to the point of denying multiple applications or uses of a single meaning, as in the examples above. For others, determinate meaning is a quality which governs and limits variety in interpretation, while clearly permitting a degree of that variety. For some, determinate meaning is exclusively associated with historical criticism, to the extent that the often projected end of historical criticism as the dominant scholarly approach to the Bible is at the same time the end of determinate meaning. For some, polysemy knows clear interpretive limits while, for others, it represents a total interpretive free-for-all. What is perhaps clear to those familiar with contemporary biblical interpretation, whether in the academy or the Church, is that polysemy and indeterminate meaning are in vogue, whereas determinate meaning is treated with suspicion.

The current lack of regard for determinate meaning within Christian theology is particularly interesting. The seemingly inevitable death of historical criticism has been greatly trumpeted but slow in coming and

---

1. Steinmetz, "Superiority of Pre-Critical Exegesis," 28; Fowl, *Engaging Scripture*, 37.

is an important factor in relation to the status of determinate meaning. As many have sought to provide new approaches to Scripture, defined not by the concerns of modernity but by those of Christian doctrine, various forms of theological interpretation of Scripture have emerged. These reflect a variety of concerns, one of which is the necessity of interpreting texts with the assumption that meaning can be more than simply what an historical author wished to convey to a single historical audience.

For the most part, theological interpretation of Scripture vigorously asserts polysemy. It does so for a variety of reasons. For some, theological interpretation of Scripture is a doctrinal supplement to biblical criticism, not seeking to replace it but to provide another alternative. Because of this, it must operate upon an assumption of indeterminate meaning, since both routes might yield startlingly different interpretations of the same passage. This can be seen in some works of canonical interpretation, such as that of Brevard Childs, in which theological reading is understood to be something of a supplement to historical-critical reading. This approach to reading the Bible is often influenced by the work of the Germa hermeneutical theorist Hans Georg Gadamer, particularly his interest in interpretation as expanding the horizon of a text's meaning. For others, theological interpretation of Scripture seeks a return to pre-critical modes of biblical interpretation, eschewing the anti-theological tendencies of modernity's approaches to the Bible. Often such interpreters find inspiration in Patristic and medieval exegesis in which polysemy is an important element. For yet others, theological interpretation of Scripture is a response to philosophies that have emerged at the end of modernity. Stephen Fowl's appropriation of American Literary Pragmatism for Theological Exegesis is a good example of this. Fowl's hermeneutic might at first appear to stress the determinate nature of meaning, since each of his "interpretive communities" is likely to demand a single interpretation of a particular text. But because interpretation only serves a particular community, there are naturally endless possible meanings for the same text.

For each of these approaches to theological interpretation, polysemy or indeterminate meaning is an important principle. Yet, polysemy is not simply a principle governing theological reading of the Bible in the academy: it makes a strong impression upon the use of the Bible in local churches, in some cases to the point where it is given the status of the foundational ideal from which biblical interpretation proceeds. Just as Scriptural Reasoning proceeds from the assumption that the meaning of texts is indeterminate, so a local church study group might lay down a ground rule that no interpretation within the group can be wrong, arguably transforming the object of study from the meaning of a biblical text to the interpretations of individual members of the group.

While the view that the meaning of Scripture is polysemic certainly does reflect the reality of the vast majority of pre-critical, theological interpretation of the Bible, there have always been Christian voices claiming that the meaning of the Scripture is determinate, also from a theological perspective. The purpose of this book is to explore various theological accounts of and approaches to determinate or single meaning from the reception of Scripture in the New Testament to theological interpretation of Scripture in the present day. It will be argued that determinate meaning is not a straightforwardly anti-theological concept, but one which has endured in various guises throughout much of the history of Christian scriptural interpretation. Because of this long association with Christian doctrine, determinate meaning must still be considered worthy of a future in biblical scholarship and theological interpretation. But before this case can begin to be made, some analysis is needed of what is meant by terms seeking to express limitation or expansion of meaning.

Defining Determinate Meaning

Very little work has been done to define what is meant by "polysemy," "determinate" or "indeterminate" meaning. The meaning of these terms appears to be more-or-less assumed, even by some of the most prominent twentieth century and contemporary hermeneutical theorists, both within Christian theology as well as outside it. Of the three terms, "polysemy" appears to have received the most attention. In general, polysemy is taken to be synonymous with indeterminacy, both of which are seen to be the opposite of determinate meaning. Therefore, an understanding of polysemy is of great importance to understanding determinate meaning. Some of the most substantial work on the nature of polysemy has been within the confines of academic theology and religious studies: in particular, within literary criticism of the Hebrew Bible and within Jewish Studies. Much of this work focuses upon polysemy which is intentional: polysemy that is a literary feature of a text and is deliberately created by an author or redactor. Here it has been possible to define various sorts of polysemy. *Contronymic polysemy*, for example, refers to terms that can mean two opposing things, whereas *antanaclasis* features the repetition of an identical phrase in such a way as it means something different when it is repeated.² *Unidirectional polysemy* refers to terms which offer two meanings in relation to a referent further ahead in the text, whereas *Janus parallelism* offers a meaning to a referent further ahead as well as to a referent prior to the term.³ *Bilingual polysemy* refers to terms which can be read as possessing an additional meaning when a language other than Hebrew is known, whereas *amphiboly* refers to deliberately ambiguous grammar that might be interpreted in more than one way.⁴ In addition to this, some terms are explained with a variety of philological and etymological arguments that indicate their ambiguity and offer multiple interpretive possibilities.⁵ There is some evidence to suggest that each of these forms of polysemy are deliberate literary features of the Hebrew Bible. Of course, there are other forms of polysemy which are not created with the text but created in the act of reading. One example of this within rabbinic literature is the practice of *gematria*: reading consonants as though they are numbers, something that is possible to do with Hebrew since consonants may also represent numbers. There is no evidence that this particular sort of polysemic reading was intended by authors or redactors, even though a developed numerical interest is a feature of some elements of Hebrew literature within the biblical canon. One can see similar exegetical practices in the sectarian scriptural interpretation of Qumran. Though the famous *pesher* interpretation of the Dead Sea Scrolls is remarkable for the way it assumes determinate meaning and scriptural texts are seen to have a single and simple prophetic referent, there is evidence of the polysemic interpretation more familiar in rabbinic literature. As Michael Fishbane has shown, 1QpHab 2.1–10 features multiple interpretations of a single phrase from Hab 1:5, 1QpHab 11.8ff. employs paranomasia, or wordplay, on "staggering" and "uncircumcised," which both look and sound similar. CD 10.1 uses *notrikon*, the individual

---

2. Noegal, "Polysemy," 178–86.

3. Noegal, *Janus Parallelism*.

4. An example of the former is the use of the Hebrew *rā'āh* ("wickedness," "evil") in Exod 10:10 which sounds a great like the name of the Egyptian god *Ra'*. Rendsburg, "Word Play in Biblical Hebrew," 137–62.

5. Malachi, "Creative Philology," 269–87.

interpretation of the letters in a word, similar to *gematria*.⁶ Fishbane suggests that these modes of interpretation have a common origin in ancient dream interpretation.⁷

It is not simply within rabbinic interpretation of texts that polysemic meaning is encountered. Certain biblical texts appear to be rife with ambiguous terms inviting polysemic interpretation. As Doug Ingram has shown in a study that includes one of the most sophisticated analyses of the terminology of determinate/indeterminate meaning, Ecclesiastes contains terms and phrases that can be seen as deliberately ambiguous.⁸ Ingram argues this ambiguity of meaning is a form of indeterminacy, encouraging the reader to play a significant part in identifying meaning. For example, even the term *Qohelet*, variously translated "prophet," "teacher," or "gatherer," is ambiguous and necessarily open to a variety of interpretations. Likewise the superscription invoking Davidic sonship is open to an extraordinary variety in interpretation when it could have been composed much more straightforwardly, avoiding this ambiguity.⁹

In addition to these types of polysemy observed in Hebrew and Rabbinic literature, the sheer fact that multiplicity of meaning is recounted in the Talmud, for example, is seen as an assertion of Scripture's polysemic meaning by many. Rather than claiming a single meaning for a given scriptural text, or indeed a single answer to an interpretive problem, the Talmud lists multiple authoritative interpretations. Polysemy does indeed appear to be the intent behind the classical Talmudic expression of "seventy-two modes of interpretation." The thought here is that, since the Torah was given to the nations, of which there are understood to be seventy-two, Scripture has a meaning for each.¹⁰ But whether these are distinct meanings that exist simultaneously is beyond the scope of the phrase and its explanation. In any case, it is unclear whether the polysemy implied by the collection of interpretations in the Talmud is a typical feature of rabbinic hermeneutics, or simply a creation of the Talmudic redactors, as argued by Daniel Boyarin.¹¹

---

6. Fishbane, "Qumran Pesher," 97–114.

7. Cf. Fishbane, *Biblical Interpretation in Ancient Israel*, 443–44; and Rabinowitz, "Pesher/Pittaron," 219–32.

8. Ingram, *Ambiguity in Ecclesiastes*, 1–43.

9. Ibid., 75–90.

10. Bacher, "Seventy-Two Modes," 509.

11. Boyarin, *Border Lines*, 151–201. Against this position, see Fraade, "Rabbinic Polysemy," 1–40.

The ambiguity of whether polysemy is a definite feature of rabbinic hermeneutics has not stopped so-called rabbinic polysemy becoming something of a *cause célèbre* amongst literary theorists such as Frank Kermode. For Kermode, the apparent indeterminacy of rabbinic scriptural interpretation gives a pre-critical foretaste for the sort of indeterminacy favoured by scholars at the end of Modernity.[12] This association has been firmly rejected by David Stern and others from within the guild of Jewish Studies.[13] Stern draws a distinction between the apparently limitless indeterminacy of recent hermeneutics and the tightly limited range of interpretative approaches witnessed in rabbinic literature. Stern suggests that literary theorists have sought a hermeneutic of alterity, or otherness, in rabbinic scriptural interpretation: a hermeneutic that seeks to keep the question of meaning eternally open. Yet Stern argues that multiple interpretation in rabbinic literature bares little relation to this indeterminacy. As an example, Stern examines the treatment of Jer 23:29 in b. Sanh. 34a. According to the School of Rabbi Yishmael recounted here, Jeremiah's double simile of God's word as both hammer and fire is an image of forged metal being beaten by a blacksmith: just as the hammer produces many sparks, so the word of God has several meanings. Interpretation here is certainly multiple, but not inherently boundless. The hammer does not produce an endless quantity of sparks. Polysemy in Midrash is tightly limited by convention. Something of this convention can be seen in the exegetical *middoth*, or rules, ascribed to Hillel and detailed in b. Sanh. 7:11. Stern also argues that rabbinic midrash is also distinct because of the "formal resistance to closure" in contemporary indeterminacy. Where multiple readings are offered in midrash, the student should follow the majority, suggests the Talmud (y. Sanh 4:2, 22a—b). According to Stern, Midrash is unique and ought not to be seen as offering a hermeneutical precursor to contemporary notions of indeterminate meaning.[14] The distinction Stern appears to make is that polysemic meaning is limited and bound by convention and the limits of practice, whereas indeterminate meaning is a conception of meaning as resistant to ultimate closure. However, it is not clear that this distinction holds in the way that others use the terms "polysemy" and "indeterminacy." The terms appear to be

12. Kermode, "Plain Sense of Things," 179–94.

13. Stern, *Midrash and Theory*, 15. This chapter is also published as Stern, "Midrash and Determinacy," 132–61. Cf. Fraade, "Rabbinic Polysemy," 1–40.

14. The same is argued by Longxi, "Tao and the Logos," 385–98 in respect of another supposed precursor of indeterminate meaning.

synonymous. For example, as will be seen below, Paul Ricoeur and Wolfgang Iser both treat polysemy as something potentially limitless.

The work of scholars in the field of Jewish Studies draws attention to another important distinction regarding polysemic and determinate meaning. In some cases, polysemic meaning is created by the authors of ambiguous text, such as Ecclesiastes. In other cases, polysemic meaning is read into a text, such as in examples of *gematria*, or numerical interpretation of Hebrew consonants. This seems to be the sense of polysemy understood by some scholars of linguistics. Charles J. Fillmore and Beryl T. S. Atkins define polysemy in relation to the potential of words or phrases to have multiple meanings. The various senses of a polysemic word have a common origin, either in the sound or lexical meaning of the word itself. Similarly, these multiple senses are related within a network such that understanding the "inner" meaning of the word helps to understand the "outer" meanings of its interpretation.[15] Yet the sort of polysemy which is deliberately created and encouraged by an author who employs ambiguous words is not what most theologians and philosophers mean when they discuss polysemic meaning. One might be unlikely to regard writing such as George Orwell's *Animal Farm* as an example of deliberately polysemic writing, though it is both a story about animals and a story about revolutionary communism. The political reading of this text is, in a sense, its true meaning. We know this because we understand George Orwell to be a political writer, rather than a children's author. The farm story simply exists to support the political story. It would be incorrect to define the meaning of texts designed to support another reading as polysemic, since the apparent authorial control over the other reading makes meaning determinate, albeit in a less obvious way.

Polysemy is typically understood as a quality of a text's meaning that is distinguished by its independence from a single controlling influence upon that text which makes its meaning determinate. At the same time, there is little agreement as to the degree of flexibility or limitation of meaning polysemy permits. For instance, polysemy as a description of rabbinic or medieval views of biblical meaning is not the same as polysemy as applied to American Literary Pragmatism. The former operates with a relatively limited view of what is interpretively possible, whereas the latter allows for any reading that can be received as being persuasive in a specific interpretive context.

---

15. Fillmore and Atkins, "Describing Polysemy," 91–110.

For some, polysemy is a feature of the text itself as a product of human language. Against structuralism's attempt to make meaning determinate within a fixed and closed system of language, Jacques Derrida explored the extent to which language endlessly defers meaning beyond itself. One word evokes another which, in turn, evokes others in an inexhaustible chain of reference. This opens the meaning of a text up to seemingly endless possibilities of meaning. The term *différance*, coined by Derrida, is itself an example of a term which apparently polysemic meaning, as a homophone with *difference*.[16] *Différance* signifies the deferral of meaning elsewhere within a web of language. Because of this essential element in interpretation, meaning can never be truly determinate because the relationship between the signifier in text or speech and the signified referent can never be fixed, nor can the search for meaning ever be complete: words will never fail to defer their meaning. Kevin J. Vanhoozer credits Derrida with the destruction of the idea of determinate meaning.[17] As Derrida emphasized the linguistic nature of thought, he called into question the simple Aristotelian relationship between thoughts and words, insofar as the latter can adequately represent the former, just as thought can adequately represent reality. Because of this, language cannot represent thought and reality perfectly and determinately. Vanhoozer suggests that Roland Barthes, Ferdinand de Saussure, along with Reader-Response critics and Canonical Interpretation within Biblical Interpretation, never really depart from an assumption of determinate meaning, though for them it is established on the basis of the text itself rather than the author of the text.

For others (and possibly the majority today), polysemy is a feature of the reader and his or her interpretive context. This is largely because the text is not understood as owning any inherent properties of meaning, or possessing any sort of agency upon the reader. Meaning is created as a text is read: it is not a latent quality within the text, waiting to be discovered. The text itself may be understood in a purely materialist sense: as a sequence of signs on a page. For this reason, meaning utterly depends upon the concerns and questions with which a reader approaches the text. Regardless of whether there is a correct way of reading which makes meaning determinate, this is the polysemic reality of interpretation. Something like this position is taken by Paul Ricoeur. Ricoeur argues

---

16. Derrida, "Différance," 3–27.
17. Vanhoozer, *Is There a Meaning in This Text?* 37–196.

that interpretation of any text must aspire to hear the text as discourse, as properly interpersonal communication set within a meaning-limiting context. Indeed, in a sense, the discernment of context is the act of interpretation. Interpretation of a written text is somewhat harder because the personal interplay of discourse within a particular context is not as readily available as it is with speech.

> [Polysemy is] the feature by which our words have more than one meaning when considered outside their use in a determinate context.... Sensitivity to context is the necessary complement and ineluctable counterpart of polysemy....[Interpretation] consists in recognising which relatively univocal message the speaker has constructed on the polysemic basis of the common lexicon. To produce a relatively univocal discourse with polysemic words, and to identify this intention of univocity in the reception of messages: such is the first and most elementary work of interpretation.[18]

Likewise, Geoffrey H. Hartman prefers polysemy to be understood as a product of reading, rather than the deferring web of meaning provided by language. Whereas polysemy is understood by some as limited by convention or by the interpreted word or phrase itself, Hartman claims that polysemy is potentially limitless.

> [Polysemy] suggests ... that where there is a conflict of interpretations or codes, that conflict can be rehearsed or reordered but not always resolved, and ... that even where there is no conflict we have no certainty of controlling implications that may not be apparent or articulable at any one point in time.[19]

A similar position is taken by Wolfgang Iser who also understands polysemy to be a result of the reader's reception of the text. Ricoeur urges readers to reimagine a text as discourse to enable a sense of its alterity within their understanding, so that it is not utterly overwhelmed by the act of interpretation. In contrast, Iser argues that written texts have a sort of fixity by virtue of being meaningful collections of meaningful words. Polysemy is a feature of how individual readers respond to those fixed signs in particular ways.

> Two people gazing at the night sky may both be looking at the same collection of stars, but one will see the image of a plough,

---

18. Ricoeur, *From Text to Action*, 52–53
19. Hartman, *Criticism in the Wilderness*, 265.

and the other will make out a dipper. The 'stars' in a literary text are fixed; the lines that join them are variable.[20]

Compared to the understandings of polysemy as defined within Jewish Studies, this position locates multiplicity of meaning exclusively in the response of the reader to the text rather than the craft of an author. In addition to this, polysemy here is notably less limited than it might be within rabbinic exegesis. Whereas rabbinic polysemy is limited by the conventions of an interpretive community, the response of Ricoeur's reader is limited only by his or her ideas about the context in which a text can be realized as discourse.

As subsequent chapters of this book will detail, there are also specifically theological understandings of polysemy. These are typically grounded in a theory of the Bible's inspiration. Because God is the author of Scripture in some manner and because he is understood to be sovereign, nothing can limit or contain the meaning God intends for Scripture. In theory, this results in completely endless possibilities of meaning, though in practice theological polysemy is limited either grammatically (because the words cannot be made to support a meaning) or theologically (because God would not want some meanings that went against his character or the truth of Christian doctrine). Perhaps the best way to understand the nature of theologically conceived polysemy is to witness it in practice as it exists in medieval exegesis. The contention of the classic four-fold levels of meaning is that a text may contain multiple distinct meanings, perhaps with no obvious relation between them. The anagogical or moral meaning of a passage may not necessarily be derived from its literal meaning. Likewise, the tropological or eschatological meaning might be quite distinct from the allegorical meaning. Yet each of these separate meanings can be regarded as true and faithful interpretations. Typological interpretation is quite different in that it must be established in some way upon another prior interpretation.

Polysemy within the special hermeneutic of Christian theological reading of the Bible can be more expansive than the limited concepts within rabbinic exegesis, scholarship on the Hebrew Scriptures, and, indeed in the hermeneutical tradition of continental philosophy. Whereas polysemy can be a feature of language, either intended or unintended, in Christian Theology polysemy can be grounded in the inspiration of either text or reader to such an extent that an apparently determinate text

20. Iser, *Implied Reader*, 282.

can always be read in another way in spite of its apparent determinacy. Whereas Ricoeur charges the reader of written texts to choose a context in which that text can be received as determinate discourse, allegorical interpretation for example, depending on the interpreter, may exhibit an even more tenuous relationship to the commonly understood lexical meaning of a texts words or any of its perceived authorial or literary contexts.

As has been noted, what determinate meaning actually is is rarely articulated or reflected upon. If it were, it would be clear that a number of ideas are meant by this terminology. Perhaps this is appropriate. All who use this terminology use it to imply some degree of limited meaning. The extent to which determinate meaning is limited varies from one commentator to another, as does the extent to which it is a feature deliberately written into texts by an author rather than a feature of texts and their meaning generally. For example, if one associates determinate meaning with some form of authorial intent, a text that is meant by its author to be ambiguous might be regarded as genuinely polysemic, though that polysemy is only an aspect of the determinate meaning originating from the idea of the author. The distinctions draw by Stern in relation to rabbinic polysemy serve as well as any, if such distinction is necessary. One might regard indeterminate meaning as such meaning which is not circumscribed in any way, in contrast to polysemic meaning which might be limited in some way. One might therefore regard determinate meaning as meaning which is in some way limited, whether by authorial intent, grammatical sense or the norms of an interpretive community. Yet, as has been noted, this idea of determinate meaning does not rule out the possibility of polysemic meaning: an author, for example, may well intend specific multiple meanings and shape his or her text in such a way as urges multiplicity of meaning upon interpreters. Determinate meaning may be understood, then, simply as meaning which is theoretically limited by something.

Because of this ambiguity, a simpler notion of "single meaning" will be the subject of investigation here. This is the claim that a text means one thing and one thing alone, universally. This is the claim that a text has a single unified referent: that the signifier that is the text refers to a single signified object. The idea of single meaning will be used here because it is simple, in comparison to the language of determinate and indeterminate meaning, and because it embraces all that the very different interpreters of the Bible discussed below might have thought about Scripture. The use of this terminology also avoids the assumption that interpreters of Scripture from the Christian past held to more complex and contemporary ideas about meaning than historically plausible, or than that the detail of their use of Scripture will permit. Because of the complexity of what is understood by the designation "determinate meaning," this study will concentrate on the use of one interpretation of the concept. While determinate meaning has often been seen intrinsically linked to authorship and the intentions of authors in modernity, this relationship will not be considered necessary to an understanding of single meaning. As will be shown, single meaning is just as closely related to some allegorical interpretation and some eschatological interpretation as it is to the historical and grammatical interpretation with which it is often associated.

While this study will seek to demonstrate that an emphasis upon the scriptural texts as bearing a single meaning is far from alien to Christian theology, it will also seek to foster an appreciation of the value of biblical interpretation which proceeds from an assumption that it is possible both to get a text "wrong" as well as to get it "right." Reading which assumes that Scripture's meanings are in some way determinate can be virtuous reading. It is all too easy for readers of the Bible, especially scholarly readers, to posit interpretations which aspire to plausibility or attractiveness rather than truthfulness. Determinate meaning enables biblical interpretation to be theoretically accountable to other interpreters: it prevents it from becoming a sheer act of will or imagination. Determinate meaning fosters reverence for the text of Scripture as an object of study, taking some of the emphasis away from the readers' choice to create a meaning that suits their concerns. Determinate meaning enables a sense that the meaning of a text might be something other than what a reader can say that it is. As naïve as it sounds, determinate meaning assumes the possibility of agreement about interpretation. This was the great aim both of Irenaeus and Tertullian in asserting a "rule of faith," as it was for Spinoza and Gabler at the birth of supposedly scientific biblical interpretation. This was the aim of Zwingli as he sought to reunite the fragmenting Zurich reformation with the foundation of the *Prophezei*.

It must be acknowledged first, however, that determinate meaning is a deeply unpopular and, indeed, problematic idea, both theologically and philosophically. Before an analysis of the single meaning of Scripture in Christian theology, the case against it must be heard.

The Case Against Determinate or "Single" Meaning

For Ricoeur and Iser, the meaning of a text is limited in some way by the intention of the reader to find a determinative context in which to realize the text as discourse, or by the text itself as it exercises some sort of agency upon the reader. Like Ricoeur, Edward Said also sees the interpretive contexts or "worlds" of the text (behind the text, of the text, and in front of the text) as limiting interpretation.[21] Yet it would be a mistake to suggest these thinkers were claiming a single determinate meaning for text. As Iser himself argues,

> Interpretation is an act of translation, the execution of which depends on the subject matter to be interpreted as well as on the context within which the activity takes place. Consequently, there are only variables of interpretation, conceived as iterations of translatability, and there can never be such a thing as the interpretation.[22]

These changing variables in interpretation include perceptions of authority, literary canon and the hermeneutic cycle. For Iser, the text interpreted by a reader is somewhere in virtual reality between what is written and the act of reading itself. Meaning is built up by an interaction of both sides, neither of which owns the meaning. The text gives instructions to the reader to create what is signified. Because of this essential contingency upon a reader, meaning must be understood as a transitory event, not a fixed thing in itself.[23] This view is seen as deeply problematic by Stanley Fish, particularly because of the kind of agency it attributes to the text. For Fish, there is no real way to claim that a text can do anything to the reader: it has no meaningful existence outside of the perception of the reader who can make of it whatever he or she will. According to Fish, Iser's theory fails because of its distinction between the determinate and the indeterminate. For Iser, the text's instruction to the reader must be determinate. It is only able to be so because Iser sees the text as part of the world: the world which is determinate. But nothing in reality truly has this degree of fixity in relation to its meaning and interpretation, argues Fish.[24]

21. Said, *The World, the Text, and the Critic*, 39–40.
22. Iser, *Range of Interpretation*, 145.
23. Iser, "Talk Like Whales," 82–87.
24. Fish, "Why No One's Afraid," 2–13.

To many theologians and biblical scholars, the notion of determinate meaning has been thoroughly discredited. The reasons for this rejection are numerous. For some, determinate meaning has no proper philosophical basis in authorship or the structure of language following the work of Jacques Derrida and, where it is retained, depends on redundant hermeneutical myths, such as authorial intent, vigorously defended by an earlier generation of thinkers including, most notably, E. D. Hirsch.[25] For others, there are empirical reasons for rejecting the notion of determinate meaning: that it is simply not the case, according to observation, that texts yield limited meaning. For others, there are ethical reasons: that determinate meaning arrogantly assumes the normativity of a certain worldview or hermeneutic. At the most sophisticated level, determinate meaning is rejected because of its position in the story of biblical interpretation and the associated belief that it is the product of an anti-theological tendency within modernity and modernity's biblical hermeneutic: historical criticism.

According to John Milbank, perhaps representative of a much broader post-liberal tendency, determinate meaning is a feature of the limitation of theological meaning urged by early modern thinkers who wished to carve out a secular space for biblical interpretation, free from the influence of the Church. In their new vision of society, the state would replace the Church as the interpreter of Scripture. From Milbank's point of view, the scriptural hermeneutics of the state proclaimed an idea of language as only humanly contingent, apparently following the rejection of divine participation in human language understood as beginning with Duns Scotus.

> Both allegory and "scholastic" interpolations were banished by Hobbes and Spinoza because they implied an uncontrollable proliferation of Christocentric meaning which inserted divine communication into the process of human historical becoming and must forever escape from sovereign mastery.[26]

This loss of medieval Christianity's theological proliferation of meaning is also lamented by Rowan Williams in his analysis of the hermeneutical tradition of historical criticism, beginning in early modernity.

> The classical historico-critical approach, with its interest in origins and its compulsive tendency to reduce textual material

---

25. Hirsch, *Validity in Interpretation*.
26. Milbank, *Theology and Social Theory*, 22. Cf. Sargent, "John Milbank," 253–63.

to evidence for a developmental narrative, misses something of [the] complexity [of textual representation]. Texts are preserved because they speak of more than the circumstances that produced them; to see this, we also need as a full a conspectus as possible of those circumstances—but we need a sensitivity to what in the text is "excessive" and therefore unsettled, to its representation of a question, of a tension for which the words are not yet clear.[27]

The problem with historical criticism, according to Williams, is its exclusive location of meaning with the origins of a text. This is a betrayal of the synchronic aspect of the text's meaning: the meanings it had for the countless generations who preserved the text who undoubtedly had more than simply an interest in the original world behind the text.

Part of the problem with determinate meaning has been its association with the supposedly "literal" meaning or sense of a text. Yet the concept of literal meaning is really quite ambiguous and not necessarily to be thought of as pertaining purely to historical and grammatical meaning. As Hans Frei argues, literal meaning is conditioned by the theological emphases of the particular Christian community reading the Bible. Literal meaning can be spiritual or figurative if that meaning is most obvious to the interpreter. Literal meaning is the meaning given authority by the emphases of the interpreter and his or her community. Frei argues that through the Reformation, this authority to determine meaning ceased to come from the Church but from an understanding of plain meaning in relation to perspicuity.[28] Historical critical interpreters of the Bible have their own view of literal meaning which privileges a view of the text's historical contingency. If literal meaning is to have a future, argues Frei, it will be on the basis of theological narrative definition as before, not because of a theory of meaning divorced from theology, as he argues was the case with historical criticism.[29] The issue for Frei is that no apparently literal meaning can claim universality. Childs also draws attention to the variety of views within Jewish and Christian biblical interpretation as to what constitutes "literal" meaning.[30] Childs contends that an exclusive emphasis upon a single "literal" meaning of scriptural texts is feature of biblical interpretation introduced in modernity. He notes that the idea of

27. Williams, "Historical Criticism," 223.
28. Frei, "Literal Reading," 41. Cf. Williams, "Literal Sense of Scripture," 121–34.
29. Frei, "Literal Reading," 61–62.
30. Childs, "Sensus Literalis," 80–94. Cf. Loewe, "'Plain' Meaning," 140–85.

plural meanings was almost unheard of by the end of the eighteenth-century, except in some Roman Catholic theology. Historical criticism, both liberal and conservative, urged a single "literal" meaning as historical meaning. This was something of a disaster for theological interpretation of the Bible. Not only did the meaning of Scripture become highly speculative, the association of literal meaning with the distant past created a heightened sense of the Bible's historical distanciation and remoteness from the modern reader.[31]

Brian H. McLean rejects determinate meaning as a philosophically implausible feature of historical criticism.[32] While historical criticism is to be lauded for making the biblical text less familiar to its readers, it has reduced study of the Bible to the study of ancient history, argues McLean. Its claim to objective interpretation and its assumption of the determinate meaning of texts is no longer warranted. The subject-object distinction, as well as the idea of the rational and sovereign subject, is difficult to maintain after the work of Martin Heidegger and a growing recognition of the historical contingency of the human subject. No longer can the interpreter see himself or herself as standing outside of his or her own historically mediated concerns. At the same time, language can no longer be thought of as able to adequately and univocally convey truth following the work of Ferdinand de Saussure. As a result, McLean argues that interpreters need to acknowledge their own existential situated-ness and the necessary limitation of their interpretations of Scripture.

Anthony C. Thiselton rejects total indeterminacy of meaning as the result of a neo-pragmatic overemphasis on the authority of the reader to freely determine meaning without reference to the truth of Christian doctrine. However, Thiselton also regards determinate meaning as somewhat anti-theological, insofar as it restricts the text in the variety of responses it is intended to evoke.

> We cannot conceivably find ways in which a consumer philosophy or consumer hermeneutic of indeterminate meaning open to the shaping of ethnocentric communities may be regarded as compatible with Christian theism, which asserts certain universal truth claims about "how things are" (against Rorty). Nevertheless, we must also concede that any approach that limits textual meaning to either a *single* meaning or a *tightly determinate* meaning *in all genres of Scripture in every case* will reduce

---

31. Childs, "Sensus Literalis," 89–91.
32. McLean, *Biblical Interpretation*, 13 and 302–8.

and emasculate the capacity of Scripture to act *transformatively and creatively*. The proof of this is that even when we accord to authorial agency the indispensable role which Vanhoozer (rightly) gives to it, authors *choose* sometimes to communicate in terms of a goal of matching codes through closed texts, for example in cases where information or description is more important and more primary than creative shaping or transformation. On the other hand, they sometimes *choose* "open" texts or a "switching" of codes, when creative transformation or iconoclasm becomes their aim.[33]

Thiselton's version of legitimate indeterminate meaning never departs from what might plausibly be understood as the intention of an author and is therefore limited to such an extent that one might want to call it determinate meaning. However, the necessity of admitting and indeed permitting indeterminate meaning is also evident from the actual practice of interpretation, suggests Thiselton. Thiselton sees interpretation as governed in different ways by the Habermasian *life-world* of readers, who may employ texts in different ways as the contextual and existential situation of reading changes. Within a life-world, the meaning of a text may appear to be determinate, but this determinacy is illusory. "All the while we remain at the level of the life-world alone, the transcending of pluralism will remain relative and temporary."[34] It is the changing context of reading that claims new horizons of meaning for the text. Yet despite this, Thiselton contents that certain features of Christian theology are "transcontextual" and challenge the indeterminacy demanded by the life-world of readers. But even these ideas are to be understood within a certain theological framework which gives them the power to be received as determinate in their meaning.[35] The cross, for example, though universal and transforming for both Jew and Greek, male and female, is properly understood within the specific salvation historical narrative of the story of Israel, without which it can be interpreted differently. Likewise, the illocutionary force of Scripture as divine speech-act, which enables texts to be understood as direct discourse with determinate meaning, can only be received as such, argues Thiselton, from within a theological narrative in which God speaks. Additionally, the apparently fixed interpretative horizon of Christian eschatology as representing the ultimate and

---

33. Thiselton, "'Behind' and 'In Front Of,'" 115.
34. Thiselton, *New Horizons in Hermeneutics*, 613.
35. Ibid., 613–19.

unsurpassable meaning of texts is likewise a feature of a purely theological life-world, with no claim to limit meaning outside of the perspective given by this life-world. Yet this analysis implies that determinate meaning is possible and, indeed, is to be expected within the theological narrative of the Christian Gospel. As will be demonstrated in subsequent chapters of this book, some sort of single meaning for Scripture has been claimed again and again throughout the history of Christian biblical interpretation, by Christians set within vastly different cultural, intellectual and theological contexts.

Stephen Fowl's reasons for rejecting determinate meaning in theological interpretation reflect a variety of theological and ethical concerns. According to Fowl, determinate meaning attempts to make the very process of interpretation pointless since it assumes that meaning ought to be obvious.[36] This seems to confuse claims about the perspicuity of Scripture, often associated with determinate meaning, with determinate meaning itself. A text can potentially be quite confusing and require detailed interpretation, while still believing that the meaning of the text, whatever that might be, is determinate. This is certainly the working hypothesis of many scholars employing historical-critical research methods on difficult texts. Of course this association of determinate meaning with modernity's historical criticism is grounds itself for reconsidering the value of determinate meaning.[37] This association provides certain ethical difficulties for determinate meaning. It encourages interpreters to see the text as a problem to be solved or a difficulty to be mastered. It encourages interpreters to see themselves as neutral and makes them unaware of how their interests and prejudices relate to the interpretations they provide. Because of this, theological interpretation becomes a one-way street in which meaning is permitted to inform doctrine, but doctrine is never able to inform meaning or aid reflection on the nature of that meaning.[38] For the most part, these are difficulties with determinate meaning as understood from the perspective of historical criticism. It is hard to see how some of them relate to other forms of determinate meaning. For example, as will be seen in chapter two, when Justin Martyr argues that the Jewish reading of the Scriptures is wrong and his is right, he gives no indication that he understands himself as a neutral interpreter with no

---

36. Fowl, *Engaging Scripture*, 32.
37. Ibid., 183.
38. Ibid., 34.

theological agenda: nor does he make the claim that his interpretation is obvious once theological prejudice is put to one side. Justin's reading is committed. While Fowl's criticisms of determinate meaning within an historical critical framework are significant, do they apply to determinate meaning per se?

Similar to Fowl's rejection of determinate meaning is that of the feminist theologian, Sallie McFague. Whereas early feminist biblical criticism can be understood as related to the historical critical enterprise of establishing the true meaning of the ancient and historically contingent text, McFague offers a pragmatic assessment of various metaphors for God in Scripture. McFague's criteria for judging the "goodness" of doctrines of God is purely functional, related to the usefulness of the idea within the contemporary context, rather than how historically appropriate they might be.[39] McFague shares with Fowl the neo-pragmatic view of interpretation as *use* of texts, following Stanley Fish and, to a lesser extent, Richard Rorty.[40] The idea of meaning as something single and universal is dismissed in favor of a positive functional meaning within a specific interpretive context. As will be argued below, this can imply a form of single meaning in practice, since the interpretive community will typically have a quite defined view of what constitutes the best use of a text.

The single meaning of Scripture as understood from the perspective of historical criticism is also rejected within canonical interpretation, as typified by the work of Brevard Childs. Childs argues that even literary approaches to the Bible assume the hermeneutics of historical criticism, particularly in the severance of exegesis from dogmatics and the exclusive location of meaning with the historical location of the text within an ancient literary context.[41] In a post-holocaust context, the Old Testament must be read simultaneously both as Jewish and Christian Scripture: both as testimony to Israel's past and prophetic witness to Christ and the Church.[42] What enables this potential multiplicity of meaning is a recognition of the different contexts in which theological interpretation takes place, whether Synagogue or Church.

---

39. McFague, "Mother God," 324–29.
40. Cf. Fish, *Is There a Text*, 15; and Rorty, *Philosophy and Social Hope*, 144.
41. Childs, "Theological Exegesis," 16.
42. Ibid., 20.

> When proposing a multi-level approach to Scripture I am suggesting a single method of interpretation which takes seriously both the different dimensions constituting the biblical text and the distinct contexts in which the text operates. There is no single hermeneutical principle which would establish a fixed temporal order in exegesis or which would prioritize one entrance into the text. The test of success lies in the ability of exegesis to illuminate the full range of the sense of the text while holding together witness and subject matter in a unity commensurate with its canonical function.[43]

The different dimensions of biblical interpretation include historical, literary and canonical contexts. Like the definition of polysemy offered by Fillmore and Atkins, the level of meaning in each interpretive context is related to a prior meaning and typically derived from it. For example, typological comparison of content, based on the two part canon, is a form of theological reading derived from historical and literary meaning.[44] Childs does not seek to deny the primacy of historical criticism, simply to express its theological limitations.

The rejection of single and determinate meaning is also a feature of Scriptural Reasoning: an interfaith movement of Scripture reading. The aim of Scriptural Reasoning is to enable participants to encounter the deep reasoning of another person's faith tradition through a reading of their sacred texts with them. An important tenet is the potential plurality of meaning of each participant's Scriptures. As David F. Ford argues,

> The "native speakers" hosting a scripture and its tradition need to acknowledge that they do not exclusively own their scriptures—they are *not experts on its final meaning;* guests need to acknowledge that hosts are to be questioned and listened to attentively as the *court of first (but not last) appeal.*[45]

The thought here is that a fixed view of a sacred text's single meaning implies the end of meaningful dialogue about that text. However, as will be argued below, the idea of a single meaning can foster rigorous debate as much is it can remove the potential for debate. Believing that there is such a thing as a single determinate meaning is not the same as believing that that meaning is so well established that it cannot be challenged.

---

43. Ibid., 22.
44. Ibid., 23.
45. Ford, "Interfaith Wisdom," 349.

The case against single meaning is very strong, both from theological and philosophical perspectives. Yet the fact remains that the assumption of scriptural texts' single meaning is far from absent within the history of Christian biblical interpretation. While it has by no means been the dominant assumption with which the Bible has been approached by Christians throughout the ages, it is certainly well attested both during modernity as well as before it. This is significant, because much of the debate about determinate meaning focuses upon its association with modernity and historical criticism. This book provides an account of this important undercurrent of biblical interpretation that can be seen again and again, in quite different forms, throughout the history of the Church's reading of Scripture. For some first-century Christians, the single meaning of Scripture was a feature of its orientation towards themselves as an eschatologically significant community. For some third-century Christians, the single meaning of Scripture was a feature of its own grammatical and linguistic limitations. For some fourteenth-century Christians, the single meaning of Scripture was assumed from the way in which Scripture directly addressed contemporary concerns. For some sixteenth-century Christians, the single meaning of Scripture was a consequence of the intent of the Holy Spirit. For some eighteenth-century Christians, the single meaning of Scripture was a feature of its contingency upon an historical process. While there have been many frameworks from which the single meaning of Scripture has been articulated, this book will show that Christians have often approached biblical texts seeking a single, determinate meaning. This is by no means to suggest that assumptions of single meaning are more prominent than assumptions of polysemy: Christian biblical interpretation of Scripture has overwhelmingly tended towards the latter. However, the regular occurrence of interpretation which proceeds from assumptions about single meaning is enough to show that such thought is not alien to Christian theology. Moreover, it cannot be regarded simply as a feature of biblical interpretation in modernity, predicated upon a worldview which itself is a denial of Christian doctrine.

A Comment On the Titles for the Chapters of This Study

It is impossible to neatly define the basis of understandings of determinate or single meaning in the vast historical and cultural periods explored in each chapter. None of these periods are utterly distinct from those which precede or follow them. However, the chapter titles attempt to offer a broad indication of some of the principal emphases or characteristics that make reading of Scripture as owning as single meaning possible. "Written for Us" reflects the primarily eschatological framework within which Scripture is received in the earliest Church, as witnessed in the New Testament documents. Scripture is understood to have a single meaning because it is orientated towards the Church for whom it was written. "Written for Christ" reflects the change from an overtly eschatological basis for single meaning to a more theological basis in patristic exegesis. "Written for Correction" attempts to express the dominant mode in which Scripture is read as having a single meaning in medieval biblical interpretation: polemic. "Written for Us" relates to the importance of the perspicuity of Scripture in the biblical hermeneutics of the European Reformation, both as a general approach to the Bible as well as the basis for a determinate meaning which permitted popular interpretation. "Written for Them" attempts to express the historical orientation of biblical hermeneutics and ideas of single meaning in modernity. It also hints at the new sense of historical distanciation introduced within this period as a feature of this account of single meaning. "Written at All?" reflects attempts after modernity, historical criticism and, indeed, structuralism to ground determinate meaning in a understanding of the biblical text as direct discourse, either through the influence of speech-act theory or the work of Paul Ricoeur. All of these titles are imperfect reflections of the real complexity of how single meaning has been understood within Christian theology, though they may be helpful in giving a sense of the historical distinctives of the different periods explored. What is most important to grasp is that there is no single approach to single meaning in Christian theology, but that single meaning is a recurring, if minority and often eccentrically conceived, theme within Christian biblical hermeneutics.

1

Written for Us

Single Meaning in the Use of Scripture in the New Testament

The New Testament represents a profound movement of scriptural interpretation. No New Testament text can be said to exist without some implied or explicit relation to the story of God's redeeming work in the Scriptures of Israel. Whether such books explicitly quote or allude to Scripture, the narrative substructure of each piece of writing is fundamentally scriptural. This is as true for the Epistle to the Hebrews with its extensive commentary on Ps 110:4 as it is for Paul's Epistle to Philemon which contains no obvious references to Scripture. Because of this, the New Testament itself is an appropriate place to begin an exploration of the hermeneutical theme of the single meaning of Scripture in Christian thought.

Attempts to articulate the scriptural hermeneutics of New Testament literature are a relatively recent addition to the field of the use of Scripture in the New Testament, partly because hermeneutical ideas are rarely articulated within New Testament literature itself. For the most part, early scholarship on the use of Scripture in the New Testament concentrated upon the nature and number of references, as well as the possible sources of quotations and their variance from extant versions of the same texts. With the growth of interest in theological interpretation towards the end of the twentieth century, attention has increasingly been given to the hermeneutical ideas which provide the basis for the interpretation of Scripture in the New Testament. Within this context, it would be most difficult to argue that any New Testament writer entertained a hermeneutical theory of indeterminate or polysemous meaning. Instead, ideas of the single meaning of Scripture appear to dominate the way in which Scripture is interpreted. However, as noted already, the New Testament does not abound with hermeneutical statements. Because of this, scholarly accounts of the earliest Christian biblical hermeneutics are often expressions of the assumed hermeneutical theory behind actual interpretations of Scripture within the New Testament. So it is the case that, while some "hermeneutical statements" in the New Testament claim forms of single meaning for Scripture, most often single meaning can simply be identified as a probable hermeneutical idea governing a New Testament writer's interpretation of a scriptural text.

Single Meaning Articulated

In certain places, New Testament literature comes close to offering ideas on biblical hermeneutics. Of course, biblical interpretation is never taken up as a subject for discussion in itself. Instead, there are a number of places in which an author makes statements about the nature of Scripture: what it is about and why it exists. Such statements can be useful in determining an author's approach to biblical interpretation, assuming that the "hermeneutical statement" itself corresponds with the manner in which Scripture is actually interpreted by that author. These "hermeneutical statements" include Rom 15:4; 1 Cor 10:6–11; 2 Cor 3:12–16; Gal 3:19–26; 1 Pet 1:10–12; and 2 Pet 1:19–21. These texts can be regarded as "hermeneutical" because they make claims which are intended to have a direct influence upon how scriptural texts are understood and interpreted, though the designation is clearly anachronistic insofar as there is no evidence that the theory of interpretation was conceived of as an independent object of inquiry, as is now implied by the term "hermeneutics." The discussion of these statements begins here with Paul and Rom 15:4, from which the title of this book is derived.

Paul's Use of Scripture

Of course, the analysis of Paul's use of Scripture has not yielded a single, dominant account of Pauline scriptural hermeneutics. E. Earle Ellis argues that Paul's interpretation of Scripture is "grammatical-historical plus."[1] According to Ellis, Paul does not deny the historical and grammatical meaning of scriptural texts text but builds on it. This analysis suggests that Paul's interpretation, insofar as it differs from what one might consider to be the historical or grammatical meaning of a text, supplies the *sensus plenior*, or full meaning of that text. From this perspective, Paul's interpretation deliberately supplements a prior interpretation or meaning, admitting a degree of polysemic meaning. According to Ellis, Rom 15:4 and 1 Cor 10:11 are evidence of Paul's belief that the significance of Scripture overwhelms its original use. But where is the evidence that Paul is interested in the grammar and history of texts? Perhaps the most notable and notorious Pauline use of grammar in the interpretation of a scriptural text is the interpretation of "seed" (*sperma*) from the old Greek of Gen 12:7 in Gal 3:15–18. This use of grammar appears to deliberately undermine the apparently historical interpretation of Gen 12:7 as referring to Abraham's direct descendants, including Isaac. Historical meaning appears to be undermined here so as to promote a single Christological meaning. Indeed, one of the only clear instances of Pauline interest in the "historical" setting of a scriptural text is part of the same argument of Gal 3:15–18, in v.17: that the law came 430 years after the Abrahamic covenant and thus does not annul it.[2] The explanation of the law enables the law to be contained within a Christological narrative in which it functions simply and singly in Gal 3:24 as *peidogogus*: leading the children of the covenant to justification by faith with the coming of Christ. There is no evidence that Paul sustained a belief in grammatical and historical interpretation as distinct from theological interpretation as Ellis contends. Indeed, such a distinction reflects the biblical hermeneutics of modernity, more than it does the biblical hermeneutics of Paul. As Francis Watson suggests,

> Paul has no independent interest in the meaning of scripture as such: the meaning of scripture is identical to its significance, and both are to be found in its manifold, direct and indirect testimony to God's saving action in Christ. Scripture is not a secondary confirmation of a Christ-event entire and complete in itself; for scripture is not external to the Christ-event but is constitutive of it, the matrix within which it takes shape and comes to be what it is. Paul proclaims not a pure, unmediated

---

1. Ellis, *Paul's Use of the Old Testament*, 147–48.
2. Jeremias, "Paulus als Hillelit," 94; Cohn-Sherbok, "Paul and Rabbinic Exegesis," 130.

experience of Christ, but rather a Christ whose death and resurrection occur "according to the scriptures" (1 Cor. 15.3-4).[3]

As will be discussed below, discussion of the use of Scripture in the New Testament, particularly in relation to issues surrounding the extent and nature of meaning, has been significantly influenced by desire to make early Christian use of Scripture acceptable to contemporary audiences. This is perhaps the case with regards to Ellis's analysis of Paul's interpretation of Scripture.

Perhaps the two most prominent contemporary schools of thought in the area of Paul's use of Scripture are those of Richard B. Hays and Christopher D. Stanley. For Hays, Paul's use of Scripture is sophisticated. As Paul employs Scripture in his arguments there is often some indication that he is aware of the literary context of his reference, a context with which he interacts. The position of Hays and others is that not only was Paul interested in original context, but his audiences too would have recognized scriptural references and would have understood them in relation to where they come from. From this perspective, the simple use of Scripture in an argument by Paul may have theological or narrative overtones which would have been obvious to an early audience, but may be missed if one assumes that Paul is not interested in the context from which he has taken references. This assessment of Paul's use of Scripture has led to a significant amount of research into particular uses of Scripture by Paul and Paul's use of particular books of Scripture, with some arguments for detail interest in context more convincing than others. The other hermeneutical aspect of Hays's analysis is the importance of the Christian community as the true referent of the Scriptures of Israel. For Paul, argues Hays, Scripture is orientated towards the Church and must be interpreted in relation to it.

> What Paul finds in Scripture, above all else, is a prefiguration of the *church* as the people of God. (By *church*, I mean, of course, not the institutional hierarchy that took shape over time but the community of people who confess that Jesus Christ is Lord.) This way of reading is not just a contingent effect of the problems addressed in Romans. In other letters also, Paul uses Scripture primarily to shape his understanding of the community of faith; conversely, Paul's experience of the Christian community—composed of Jews and Gentiles together—shapes

---

3. Watson, *Hermeneutics of Faith*, 16–17.

his reading of Scripture. In short, Paul operates with an *ecclesiocentric* hermeneutic.[4]

This orientation is a significant feature of the assumed single meaning of scriptural texts in Paul and other New Testament literature. Single meaning appears to be stated as part of Scripture's purpose in Rom 15:4 and 1 Cor 10:6–11 and is evidenced in Paul's actual use of Scripture in relation to the communities for whom we writes, though, as Francis Watson contends, does not explain all of Paul's use of Scripture.[5]

The opposing view to that of Hays is typically identified with the work of Christopher D. Stanley. Stanley argues that Paul's use of Scripture is predominantly rhetorical. Because of this, Paul is less interested in the details of original literary context than what can be achieved for his argument by the use of a scriptural reference.

> When Paul quotes from the Jewish Scriptures in his letters, he invariably has a rhetorical purpose. Usually this means drawing on the authority of the biblical text to extend or seal an argument. In these cases the biblical quotation carries weight regardless of whether the recipients fully understand the reference, since the quotation shows the God of Israel is firmly on the side of the speaker. The ability to quote and interpret Scripture is a potent weapon within a religious community, especially when the skill is limited to a few practitioners, and Paul did not hesitate to wield this weapon in his letters.[6]

The accompanying assumption, in contrast to Hays, is that Paul's audiences would have been unaware of the earlier contexts of the references Paul makes to Scripture and would receive them simply as authoritative proofs of Paul's assertions.

> Although it is certainly possible that Paul thought that his readings of Scripture were so obvious as to require no justification, it seems more likely that he was aware that any serious effort at justification would have been useless because of the limited biblical knowledge of his intended audience. In other words, instead of assuming that his audience knew the context of his quotations and could evaluate his interpretations accordingly,

---

4. Hays, *Echoes of Scripture*, 86.
5. Watson, *Hermeneutics of Faith*, 21.
6. Stanley, *Arguing with Scripture*, 52. Cf. idem., "'Pearls Before Swine,'" 124–44.

Paul seems to have crafted his quotations for an audience with relatively little knowledge of the biblical text.[7]

This element of using Scripture as simple and incontestable proof of an argument or proposition is also an important feature of the assumed single meaning of Scripture in Paul and other New Testament literature. While this in not the place to decide between Hays and Stanley's analyses of Paul's use of Scripture, it must be noted that both contribute to an understanding of how Paul understands plurality or singularity of meaning in Scripture. Whether Paul intended his audiences to be attentive to specific intertextual features of his use of Scripture and, therefore, understand his references in a specific way, or whether Paul intended his audiences simply to hear his scriptural references as authoritative proofs, a single meaning is assumed. In Hays's account, single meaning is determined by knowledge of the context Paul draws upon. In Stanley's account, single meaning is determined by interpretative assertion.

Other elements of scholarly analysis of Paul's use of Scripture also have a bearing on the idea of single meaning. As J. Louis Martyn argues, most of Paul's sustained exegetical passages are polemics against someone else's teaching of the Scriptures.[8] He argues that this is particularly evident in 1 Cor 10:1–13 which demonstrates an unusual familiarity with his opponents' treatment of specific texts. However, Martyn also notes that there is generally little evidence to make it clear that Paul is arguing against specific interpretations of the same texts he uses. Mishandling of Scripture and its message are more generally addressed. Yet the implication is that Paul's interpretation cannot sit side by side with a false one. The Gospel is far too important for that. When engaging in exegetical controversy, whether explicit or implicit, Paul presents a stark choice between truth and falsehood, faithfulness and faithlessness. There is no sense that Paul's interpretation of Scripture permits multiplicity of meaning when it comes to the contrast between his use of Scripture and that of his opponents. Indeed, as Martyn argues, there is a sense in which the meaning of Scripture is quite closed apart from the revelation of Jesus Christ. According to Martyn, the apocalyptic relation of the Gospel to Scripture is seen in the dichotomy of foolishness and revelation in 1 Cor 17:24.[9] Here, the wisdom of the wise is proclaimed as foolishness with

---

7. Stanley, *Arguing with Scripture*, 56–57.
8. Martyn, *Theological Issues*, 159.
9. Ibid., 217–21.

the help of a reference to Isa 29:14. But the eventual comparison between the Gentile perception of the Gospel as foolishness and the perception of those who are being saved that it is the power of God is surprising. Paul's Corinthian audience would expect to hear that the Gospel is *wisdom* to those who are being saved since it is *foolishness* to everyone else. According to Martyn, this dichotomy claims that the Gospel is not something discerned by the wise through reflection on Scripture, but is something that reveals its own authority through apocalyptic revelation: the power of God.

> What brought Paul to the gospel was not his decision about God, based on criteria learned in his scribal study of scripture, but rather what one might call God's apocalyptic decision about him: "But when [God] was pleased to apocalypse his Son to me...." (Gal 1:15–16). For Paul, then, there are no through-trains from the scriptural, patriarchal traditions and their perceptive criteria to the gospel of God's Son. Taking a final glance at 1 Cor 1:17–24, we can be certain, that Paul did not make his way *from* Isaiah's words about God's destroying the discernment of the discerning *to* the foolish word of the crucified Messiah. His hermeneutic worked exactly the other way around, from the previously unknown and foolish gospel of the cross to the previously known and previously misunderstood scripture.[10]

Single meaning in this sense is related to the apocalyptic nature of the Gospel of Jesus Christ. There can be no alternative understanding of Scripture than that disclosed through the unveiling of Jesus Christ to those who are being saved, according to Paul. As will be seen below, the single meaning of Scripture in the Pauline corpus is related to a variety of factors, including the perceived eschatological orientation of Scripture towards the Church, the rhetorical function of Scripture as proof, and the apocalyptic nature of faith in Christ vis-à-vis the interpretation of Scripture.

Rom 15:4

The first of these ideas behind the single meaning of Scripture in Paul is witnessed in Rom 15:4.

---

10. Ibid., 221.

> For everything that was written in the past was written beforehand for our learning, so that by endurance and by the comfort of the Scriptures we might have hope.

Paul's claim, within the context of a closing paraenetic and following a scriptural reference from Ps 69:9, is that Scripture, though written in the past was written for "us." More precisely, Scripture is seen to have been written for the purpose of providing early Christian communities with the learning and comfort that leads to hope. As Dunn remarks, "Paul does not hesitate to describe the reason why the scriptures were written: not as a source book for all sorts of information, historical or scientific, but "for our instruction," to sustain faith and renew hope."[11] Douglas J. Moo connects the statement in 15:4 to the interpretation of the law in the earlier chapters of the epistle, arguing that the statement gives a sense of Scripture's moral purpose.

> The OT, though no longer a source of direct moral imperative (6:14, 15; 7:4), continues to play a central role in helping Christians to understand the climax of salvation history and their responsibilities as the New Covenant people of God.[12]

Though the law of Scripture functions to make sin known and cannot of itself give rise to righteousness, it nonetheless offers learning leading to hope. Paul's interest seems to be the whole of the Scriptures (*graphē*) here, while other statements examined below can be seen to apply to specific elements within Scripture, the prophets and the law in particular.[13] Indeed, there seems to be some agreement that this statement offers some explanation of the use of Scripture quite generally in the Pauline corpus, as well as the use of the quotation from Ps 69:9.[14] Indeed, Hays suggests that pre-Pauline interpretation of lament psalms, such as Ps 69, would have taken them to be statements about Jesus' death to be fulfilled as if spoken by him. Here Paul does not do this with the psalm but rather holds up the image of Christ's suffering in the lament psalm as a "paradigm for Christian obedience." Because this is unusual, Paul interjects to explain that this is what Scripture is for.[15] According to Hays, the Scriptures are

---

11. Dunn, *Romans 9–16*, 843.

12. Moo, *Epistle to the Romans*, 869.

13. Ellis, *Use of the Old Testament*, 21; Dunn, *Romans 9–16*, 839; Morris, *Epistle to the Romans*, 499–500.

14. Dunn, *Romans 9–16*, 839; Cranfield, *Epistle to the Romans*, 2:734.

15. Hays, *Conversion of the Imagination*, 113.

understood by Paul to give hope because they enable a Christological and eschatological perspective on life, taken from the psalms expression of the suffering of Christ and identification with him. Though hope is absent from Psalm 69, it is a consistent feature of the lament psalms, as in Psalm 22, argues Hays. This analysis is quite typical of Hays: Paul and his audience have a detailed understanding of references to Scripture and recognise the context from which references are drawn. Though Hays agrees that a single meaning is being claimed for Scripture in Rom 15:4, particularly in its possible denial of a dominant interpretive tradition for the lament psalms, one must ask whether Paul's audience would recognise that Psalm 69 is a royal lament psalm and ask the implied question Hays thinks Rom 15:4 answers? Would Paul's readers really be worried by Paul's use of the psalm as a paradigm for Christian obedience, thus departing from prior early Christian interpretation of such psalms? Is there any evidence that Rom 15:4 is anything more than an interpolation, with no real value for the psalm reference?[16] While this may be difficult, Hays agrees that 15:4 represents more than just a justification of the use of Psalm 69. It is possible that this was an established Pauline hermeneutical statement as many suggest.[17]

Comparison is often made between the statement in Rom 15:4 and the treatment of Abraham in Rom 4:23–24. Here God's declaration of Abraham's righteousness was "written not for his sake alone ... but for us to whom God will count as righteous, to we who believe in the one who raised Jesus our Lord from the dead." In terms of the nature of the meaning of Scripture, as that which has been written, Rom 4:23–24 and 15:4 appear to be quite different. Though both claim that Scripture exists for Paul's audience, 4:23–24 suggests that it was not written for the audience's sake alone, implying a degree of multiplicity of meaning insofar as Gen 15:6 is taken to refer both to Abraham and to the Church in Rome.[18] The possibility of multiple meaning is completely absent in Rom 15:4. Yet to what extent does Rom 4:23–24 claim that Gen 15:6 meant something *for* Abraham in the past and now means something else for the church in the eschatological present? C. E. B. Cranfield notes that the Gen 15:6 phrase "and he counted it to him as righteousness" is not *for* Abraham but *about* Abraham. Of course, this makes some sense: Abraham would

---

16. Keck, "Romans 15:4," 125–36.
17. Hays, *Conversion of the Imagination*, 114; Keck, "Romans 15:4," 125–36.
18. Morris, *Romans*, 214.

not have read Gen 15:6, even in Paul's understanding of the text, so it is hard to explain how it was written *for* him as it is for those who would one day believe in the God who raised Jesus from the dead. It makes more sense to say that Gen 15:6 is simply about Abraham. Consequently it was not written as a memorial to him but to instruct a later generation: the Church.[19] If this is the case, the meaning of Gen 15:6 is singular: it describes the past for the purpose of instructing those who would hear it in the future. It is *about* Abraham but *for* the Church. This exclusive orientation of meaning towards the eschatological reality of the Church certainly agrees with the use Paul goes makes of Gen 15:6 as a proof for the righteousness of faith through Christ. The difficulty with Cranfield's analysis, though it is most plausible, is that it is hard to fit with the parallelism of Rom 4:23-24, which claims Gen 15:6 as *for* Abraham and *for* "us."

The eschatological orientation of Scripture towards the Church in Rom 15:4 agrees with the broader characterisation and use of Scripture in the epistle. Mark A. Seifrid summarizes the latter thus:

> The incarnate, crucified and risen Christ is the center and end of Scripture. Paul's interpretation of Scripture arises from this confession. As the apostle makes clear at decisive points in his argument (1:1-7; 10:1-4; 15:4; 16:25-27), the letter is a lesson in hermeneutics for his readers. The "gospel of God, concerning his son" in the fulfilment of prophetic promise, and thereby of the message of the whole of Scripture (1:2; 16:25-27). The law along with the prophets bears witness to the righteousness of God manifest in Jesus Christ (3:21; see 10:4). This lesson is no mere intellectual exercise but a witness given for exhortation, comfort, and faith (see 1:12; 15:4, 14-15). The message of Scripture has been hidden in the past, not because it has not been announced, but because faith alone opens the Scripture to us (1:1-7). The once-hidden mystery of the Gospel now has been made known through the "prophetic scriptures" themselves for the "obedience which is faith" (*hypakoē pisteōs*; 16:25-26; see 1:5).[20]

Seifrid suggests that 15:4 is something of a "counterpart" to Rom 1:1-2, which also uses a *pro* compound: the Gospel was "written before/ promised before" through the prophets in the Holy Scriptures. These two statements reveal Paul's hermeneutic for Scripture. Scripture is written in the

---

19. Cranfield, *Commentary on the Epistle to the Romans*, 1:250.
20. Seifrid, "Romans," 607.

past, but it is not for the past.[21] Scripture is focused upon the present reality of the Gospel and the Church: Scripture in Paul is ecclesiological and Christological in nature. Even when Scripture records something from the past, it does so for the Church (Rom 4:23–24). This purpose for the Church is yet more explicit in the next Pauline text to be discussed.

1 Cor 10:1–11

A similar "hermeneutical statement" to Rom 4:23–24 and 15:4 can be found in 1 Cor 10:1–11. Here Paul, drawing upon episodes during the wandering of Israel in the wilderness, emphasises the eschatological orientation of Scripture as intended for the community to whom he writes.

> Now these things happened as examples for us, so that we might not desire evil as they desired it. Do not become idolaters as some of them were, as it is written, "the people sat down to eat and drink and rose up to play." We must not get into sexual immorality as some of them did, and twenty-three thousand fell in a single day. We must not put Christ to the test, as some of them tested and were destroyed by snakes. Nor must we grumble, as some of them grumbled and were destroyed by the destroyer. Now these things happened to them as examples, but they were written down for our instruction, on whom the end of the ages has come.

Paul draws a distinction between what "happened to them" in the past and the purpose for which these events were written down as Scripture. While the content of Scripture relates to the past, inasmuch as it describes what took place in the history of Israel, the meaning of Scripture relates completely to the present. Scripture is imbued with a sense of purpose, and that purpose is to warn those "on whom the fulfilment of the ages has come." The scriptural narrative of the wilderness generation has one purpose, according to Paul: to warn the Church. The orientation of Scripture is made very specific indeed. It is not enough for Paul to say that these events were written down as warnings: they were written down as warnings for *us*. This "us" is certainly an explicitly eschatological "us." Here Paul goes beyond Rom 15:4 to draw attention to the specificity of the people in their own moment for whom Scripture was intended, the moment in which the whole of history would find its completion.

---

21. Ibid., 686–87.

Because of the importance of the Church's situation in salvation history, it is clear to Paul that those who wrote Scripture had nothing else in mind: the wilderness generation was recorded in Scripture for the benefit of the Church.[22] The reference to the wilderness generation draws upon a number of texts with allusions to Exod 14:21–22 (the cloud); 15:21–22 (the division of the Red Sea); 17:6 (manna in the wilderness); Num 20:2–13; and possibly Ps 95:7–8 (the waters of Meribah); probably Num 25:1–9 (the plague killing twenty four thousand); 21:4–6 (the plague of serpents); 14:1–3 and 16:41, etc. (grumbling); and 16:31–35 (the destruction of Korah's rebellion). The admonition also features a quotation from Exod 32:6, "the people sat down to eat and drink and rose up to play." All of these events and the quotation are understood in 1 Cor 10:6 and 11 to be "types," "examples," or "warnings" for the Church. The definition of the interpretation of Scripture here as simply typological is difficult. Roy E. Ciampa and Brian S. Rosner argue that 1 Cor 10:1–11 must be regarded as typological interpretation of the wilderness generation, partly on account of the use of *typoi* in 10:6.

They suggest that the wilderness generation's redemption, idolatry, and punishment are a "lens" through which to understand the situation of the Corinthian church:

> Paul clearly establishes a typological relationship between Israel and Christian experience in 10:1–4. It could be argued, however, that in 10:5–11 he points not to divinely established patterns, but rather to patterns which the Corinthians must avoid fulfilling.[23]

The difficulty here is that this level of sophistication is somewhat difficult to prove. It is hard to see how the wilderness generation could be a type of something that might not happen if the implied warning is observed: that is not the way in which typology generally functions. On one hand, as Goppelt notes, 1 Cor 1:11 is a clear example of Pauline typological interpretation. Situations from the past are seen as figuratively corresponding to events in the present. For example, the water-producing rock understood by Paul to have accompanied Israel in the wilderness is identified as Christ (10:4). The manna and water provided for Israel in the wilderness is identified as spiritual food and drink, associating them with the Lord's supper (10:3). Similarly, the cloud and the sea are given Christian

---

22. Conzelmann, *1 Corinthians*, 168.
23. Ciampa and Rosner, "1 Corinthians," 724. Cf. Garland, *1 Corinthians*, 459.

"sacramental" significance in 10:2, as through them Israel was "baptised into Moses."[24] These interpretations of scriptural ideas are typological in the most uncomplicated sense: events of the past that are seen to correspond to events of a later time. But this is not all that takes place with Scripture in 1 Cor 10:1–11, nor indeed is it obviously an act of scriptural interpretation. In these instances identified by Goppelt, Paul is interested in *events* rather than things that are explicitly textual. His understanding of how Scripture, as the written record of Israel in the wilderness, corresponds to the present reality of the Church is quite different. As Thiselton argues, the *events* are formative for Israel while the narrative of the events is formative for the Church.[25]

In what sense is the claim of 10:6 and 11 typological? Here the words *typoi* and *typikōs* ought not to be seen as technical exegetical terms indicating a very clear sense of typological interpretation, but, as many commentators argue, as much simpler terms meaning "example" or "warning."[26] An example is quite different to a type in the hermeneutical sense of the term.[27] This non-technical use of the term is also witnessed in 1 Thess 1:7 and Phil 3:17 where it most naturally has the sense of a moral example. In its later technical usage, type implies that the significance of something is, at the very least, dual: it is both *that* and *this*, a signifier of the past and of something later. An *example* in this case, written for a particular setting, has just one purpose. It is not that Scripture is being interpreted typologically, it is that Scripture itself, according to Paul, identifies the wilderness generation as a type or example for the Church. Because this is Paul's claim about why the wilderness generation was recorded in Scripture, his interpretation follows the only legitimate use of this record: to warn the Church. In this respect, Gardner argues this claim is similar to Rom 15:4 in that Scripture is designed to instruct and teach the Church as it bears witness to the past.[28] While typology is a feature of what Paul does with events of the past in 1 Cor 10:1–11, the

---

24. Goppelt, *Typos*, 218–19.

25. Thiselton, *First Epistle to the Corinthians*, 732.

26. Robertson and Plummer, *First Epistle of St. Paul*, 202–3; Thiselton, *1 Corinthians*, 732; Garland, *1 Corinthians*, 459; Barrett, *First Epistle to the Corinthians*, 227; Perrot, "Les examples du desert," 437–52; and Conzelmann, *1 Corinthians*, 167. Cf. readings in KJV; Philips; RSV; NIV 2011; JB; TNIV; ESV and NRSV.

27. As Conzelmann (*1 Corinthians*, 167) notes, the use of *typoi* here is moral rather tha hermeneutical.

28. Garland, *1 Corinthians*, 459 and Rosner, "Written for Us," 100.

only claim he makes about Scripture is that it records the past for the single purpose of warning the Church in the last days. As James A. Sanders contends, Scripture is understood here simply as a record of the past written to instruct those living in the present.[29] Again, it must be stressed that this is part of a single purpose. It is not as though Paul understands the witness to Scripture to the past to be both a source of purely historical knowledge and a source of moral warnings for the present. The past is recorded in Scripture purely for the benefit of the Church. As Rosner argues, 1 Cor 10:11 claims that the deeds of the wilderness generation were written down with the purpose of ethical instruction. Interestingly, this shows that Paul does indeed try to derive his ethical teaching from Scripture, albeit not directly from the law.[30]

To many scholars, the significance and similarity of the wilderness generation to the Church is very specific indeed. In two separate articles, Hays suggests that Paul's Corinthian audience would have seen the particular relevance of Paul's references to Israel through their knowledge of the narrative context of the wilderness generation. In the earlier of the two articles, Hays argues that the use of the wilderness generation in 1 Cor 10:1–11 would have implied a special significance to the Corinthian debate about idol sacrificed to meat in a sort of "double exposure" with Israel's idolatry in the wilderness.[31] Here, the audience's understanding of a broader theological theme uniting the wilderness events referred to by Paul is essential to see the aptness of Israel as an example pertaining to the idolatry of eating food sacrificed to idols. In a later article, Hays argues that Paul employs the wilderness generation to encourage the Corinthian Church to understand its status eschatologically.[32] The Corinthians, who are gentiles, are invited into the narrative of Israel's history with "our fathers," reinforced with a reference to their former idol worship. They stand in a "typological relationship to Israel": as Israel was purged of wrongdoing in the wilderness, so the Church in the last days must be purged of wrongdoing. This identification with Israel in the wilderness requires a "conversion of the imagination" in order for Corinthian Christians to see themselves inside the narrative of Scripture.

---

29. Sanders, "Paul and Theological History," 54.
30. Rosner, "Written for Us," 98.
31. Hays, "Christology and Ethics," 268–90.
32. Hays, "Conversion of the Imagination," 391–412.

> Here we see how Paul's eschatological hermeneutic informs his reading and application of Scripture. He calls his converts to understand that they live at the turning point of the ages, so that all the scriptural narratives and promises must be understood to point forward to the crucial eschatological moment in which he and his churches now find themselves. His eschatological reasoning calls upon the Corinthians to perform a complex imaginative act: on the one hand they are to see in their own experience the typological fulfilment of the biblical narrative.... For Paul, Scripture rightly read prefigures the formation of the eschatological community of the church.[33]

B. J. Oropeza goes even further than Hays and suggests that in addition to the Corinthian Christians being encouraged to understand themselves as Israel in the first century, the two situations are being deliberately and precisely compared, with each of Israel's misdeeds having special significance.[34] For John Paul Heil, the implication that the Corinthian Church is to see itself as Israel in the present is equally clear.[35] Just as the Church may have experienced baptism as part of their Christian initiation so Paul claims that Israel was "baptised into Moses": the Corinthian community are invited to consider Israel as a prefiguration of the Church of which they are a part. Because of this identification with idolatrous Israel, the quotation from Exod 32:6 "the people sat down to eat," suggesting a formal meal beyond the simple satisfaction of hunger, would have resonated with the Corinthian's formal participation in meals of food sacrificed to idols. Wayne A. Meeks also sees a very specific relation of the wilderness generation to the Corinthian Church, despite arguing that 1 Cor 10:1–11 is based on a pre-existing midrash on Numbers 11 around the theme of idolatry, a theory also explored in some depth by C. Perrot.[36] Evidence for the midrash is largely contextual: the treatment of the wilderness generation does not fit neatly with the broader theme of ethical lenience in 1 Cor 8–10. The specific Christian interpolations to the midrash include, in Meek's estimation, the claim that the rock represents Christ and the eschatological phrase "end of the ages." The Pauline treatment of the midrash is consistent with Rom 15:4, suggests Meeks,

---

33. Hays, "Scripture and Eschatology," 400–401.
34. Oropeza, "Apostasy in the Wilderness," 69–86.
35. Heil, *Rhetorical Role*, 148.
36. Meeks, "And Rose Up," 64–78. Cf. Perrot, "Les examples du desert," 437–38 and 442–43.

noting that the idolatry of Israel's history is related to the specific issue of the Corinthian's idolatry for their learning. G. D. Collier agrees with Meeks that 1 Cor 10:1–11 is a pre-existing piece of carefully composed midrash on Num 11. However, Collier argues that the midrash is about "desire/covetousness" as the fount of all that might pervert the path of the Corinthian Christians, not idolatry.[37] Just as the wilderness generation were condemned for desiring a return to Egypt and the life they enjoyed as slaves, so the Corinthian Church are warned not to continue in their desire to share in all that pagan Corinth offers: food sacrifices to idols, factions, impressive public rhetoric, and intellectual credibility. M. M. Mitchell notes that Israel's wilderness wanderings are associated with a critique of division and factionalism in Philo *Moses* 1.161–164 and Josephus' *Ant.* 3.295. The same events Paul alludes to in 1 Cor 10:1–11 are understood here primarily as examples of disunity than they are examples of putting God to the test. Mitchell suggests that Paul was aware of this association and chose the wilderness generation appropriately for the specific conflict in the Corinthian church.[38] Finally, with an argument in the vein of Hays, Jerry Hwang argues that Paul evokes the narrative context of his quotation from Exod 32:6. He argues that the thematic context of the quotation is one of covenant disqualification: the idolatrous feast with the golden calf in Exodus signifies Israel's rejection of the covenant God is making at Sinai. The consequence of the broken covenant is seen in Moses' shattering of the stone tablets of the law in 32:19 and God's initial decision not to go further with Israel. Hwang concludes that Paul's Corinthian audience would have perceived this context and understood Paul's implication that they are in danger of violating the covenant with their participation in the idolatry of food sacrificed to idols.[39] If any of these deeper points of comparison claimed by Hays, Heil, Meeks, Oropeza, Collier, Mitchell, or Hwang are the case, "examples for *us*" might orientate Scripture, not generally to the Church, but specifically to the Church in Corinth.

The developed understanding of typological interpretation that Goppelt sees in some form in 1 Cor 10:1–11 is contingent upon a certain relationship between the past and the present. Typological interpretation depends on the assumption that past, present, and future are bound

---

37. Collier, "That We Might Not," 55–75.
38. Mitchell, *Paul and the Rhetoric of Reconciliation*, 138–40.
39. Hwang, "Turning the Tables," 573–87.

together in a determined plan for history. A type reflects the view that history has a kind of structure to it, so that an event in the past may be seen to point to a corresponding event in its future. Because of this, though a type may often only be observed after the event in its future, it has something of a predictive function. That to which a type points is essentially determined by the nature of history it shares with the type. This is certainly not the case with the use of *typoi* in 1 Cor 10:6. The present reality of the Church is in no way contingent upon the events of Israel's past described as *typoi*. These events happened and were written down, "so that we might not desire evil as they desired it." Rather than pre-figuring the necessary future, these events serve as warnings or examples to ensure that the Church of the last days might be free to choose another way than that taken by the wilderness generation.

Paul's claim in 1 Cor 10:11 suggests that his use of Scripture is far more radical than a simple extension of the horizon of historical meaning of Scripture: the events of the wilderness generation were written down for the purpose of warning the Church. For Paul, that is their true function and significance. This hermeneutic represents something far more dramatic than the subtle "re-centering" of the narrative of salvation history away from Moses, the law, and the covenant of Sinai towards Christ.[40] As Aageson writes concerning 1 Cor 10:1–11,

> The christological centering of the divine drama is finally what make Pauline Christianity and the classical Christian "story" distinctive. The "word of faith" has come near in proclamation, not the commandment of God. Christ, not the law, is the "wellspring" of divine nourishment. Christ, not Torah, is the Wisdom of God. Indeed, Christ is the agent of God in creation. The distinctly Pauline account of divine activity is arranged symbolically around the figure of Christ, even though Paul in his epistles does not feel compelled to argue on the basis of scripture for the messiahship of Jesus. In that sense, the significance of Christ is assumed. He is at the heart of the Pauline religious system.[41]

Paul appears to be saying something much simpler in 1 Cor 10:11: the history of the wilderness generation, insofar as it is written history, is entirely in the service of the Church. Aageson also ignores the ecclesial sense of Paul's interpretation. This characterization of the hermeneutics

---

40. Aageson, *Written Also for Our Sake*, 117.
41. Ibid., 127.

of 1 Cor 1:1–11 could be about John's use of Scripture as much as it is about Paul. Hays's characterization is perhaps more accurate.

> Paul reads Scripture in the conviction that its narratives and prophecies all point to his own time; the church lives in the exhilarating moment in which all of God's past dealings with Israel and the world have come to their climactic point. When Paul says that "the ends of the ages . . . have come," he is referring to the eschatological point of collision between the old age and the new. That point of collision is precisely "upon us": the church stands in the crucial moment in which a bright new light is shed upon everything past, particularly everything in Scripture. From the privileged perspective of the new eschatological situation in Christ, Paul re-reads the Old Testament stories and finds that they speak in direct and compelling ways about himself and his churches, and he concludes that God has ordered these past events "for our instruction."[42]

Paul's use of Scripture in 1 Cor 10:1–11 and the explanation that it receives in 10:6 and 11 offer an insight into how, for Paul, Scripture, as a record of Israel's past, has a single meaning and function. It exists for the Church: perhaps even in some ways for the specific context of the Church in Corinth. Through Scripture the Church sees how to be God's people in the last days as it is lead to contemplate examples and warnings from Scripture's witness to the history of Israel. While the events of Israel's past were very much the focus of God's saving work then and not necessarily eschatological in significance, as written events in Scripture they exist purely to serve the Church. As Hays suggests elsewhere, the use of Israel's history as a metaphor for Christian experience seems to deny its independent meaning as something other than something useful to the Church as a series of examples.[43] This eschatological orientation of Scripture's record of Israel's history is perhaps well-established by the time Paul writes 1 Cor 10. It is notable that Paul's conception of Scripture is not particularly explained or defended in 1 Cor 10 but seems to be taken for granted.[44] Indeed, Paul has already made passing reference to it in his manner of introducing a possible quotation from Sir 6:19 in 1 Cor 9:10, having been "written for us." This, however, is somewhat different to the claim in 10:11, since it relates Scripture specifically and possibly

---

42. Hays, *First Corinthians*, 162. Cf. Weiss, *Earliest Christianity*, 2:436–37.
43. Hays, *Echoes of Scripture*, 95.
44. Rosner, "Written for Us," 83.

prophetically to Paul's ministry and not to the Church as a whole, nor does Scripture function here as something offering an example: that function belongs properly to Scripture's historical narrative.

2 Cor 3:12–16

Something of a hermeneutic for reading the law is articulated in 2 Cor 3:12–16. Here, Paul famously uses the veil Moses puts on to cover his face in Exod 34:33–35 as a figure for explaining that without faith in Jesus Christ the true meaning of the law is veiled or covered. Paul claims that Moses veiled his face to prevent the people of Israel from seeing that the glory of his encounter with God on Sinai, and hence the glory of the law, was fading, rather than because Moses wished to protect the people from the terror of God's glory. The veil used by Moses is given a whole new figurative significance and meaning to apply to contemporary Israel as an explanation of why they have not universally received the Gospel as the fulfilment of God's scripturally attested plan for his people. Just as the glory of the law was obscured to the people of Israel in the past by the veil, so Paul argues that the same obscuring veil remains in the present. Only in Christ is that veil set aside and the law seen as it is meant to be seen. This is an assertion of the single meaning of Scripture inasmuch as without faith in Christ the meaning of the law cannot be found. Paul permits no alternative reading of the law. Such a statement about the law is similarly instructive for the Corinthian church member inasmuch as it defines the authority of the law relative to the authority of the Gospel preached by Paul. Indeed, 2 Cor 3:12–18 must be understood as part of the broader defence of Paul's ministry in the epistle. This may explain why it is that Paul apparently redefines the purpose of Moses' veil: his overwhelming purpose is to use Scripture to defend his ministry.[45]

> Since, then, we have such a hope, we act with great boldness, not like Moses, who put a veil over his face to keep the people from gazing at the end of the glory that was being set aside. But their minds were hardened. Indeed, to this very day, when they hear the reading of the old covenant, that same veil is still there, since only in Christ is it set aside. Indeed, to this very day whenever Moses is read, a veil lies over their minds, but when one turns to the Lord, the veil is removed. (2 Cor 3:12–16)

---

45. Belleville, *Reflections of Glory*, 297.

Paul appears to understand the veil itself as purely negative: it hides the disappearance of the glory of Moses face, just as it figuratively covers the end of the glory of the old covenant when read without being "in Christ." Paul's claim is that the veil was employed by Moses to ensure that the people of Israel did not rightly conclude that the authority of the law was temporary as they saw its glory fade. This appears to be quite a different explanation of the veil than that offered in Exodus itself: that Moses wished to protect the people from God's glory and that they might not be afraid.[46] Paul's argument is that the law (in the broadest sense of itself as Torah) reveals the essential problem with the law (in the legal sense): being temporary, it was never meant to govern the people of God forever.[47] However, the apparent change to the explanation of Moses veil is disputed by those who maintain that Paul uses Scripture here in a way that is more sympathetic to its literal meaning. For example, Scott Hafeman argues that Paul's interpretation of Exod 34:33–35 does not attribute such a different motivation to Moses use of the veil than that of Exodus itself. Hafeman maintains that that the infinitive *atenisai* ("to gaze") has a more of a sense of continuous looking, more than a quick glance. Paul claims then that Israel could not gaze upon God's glory constantly and directly: they could still perceive it, but to do so constantly would have meant death, which is why the law can be described as letters of death.[48] Hafeman also argues that *katargeo* does not mean "fade away," but "abolish" or "bring to an end." The veil, then, in Exodus 34, "brought to an end" the effects of God's glory if not covered: in other words, the veil protected Israel from the enduring glory of the law reflected in Moses face. Hafeman suggests, then, that Paul says simply what Exod 34:33–35 says: that Moses put on the veil to stop the glory of the law hurting the people of Israel if they were to see too much of it. Ellis and Luz argue that this is an example of antithetic typology, rather than the perhaps more common synthetic form of typology.[49] Whereas a synthetic typology regards the type as positive and sees its later referent as a continuation or development of the type, antithetic typology sees the type as essentially negative and stands in contrast to its later referent. A good Pauline example of the latter is the Adam typology of Rom 5:12–21. However, it is not at

---

46. Fitzmyer, "Glory Reflected," 630–44.
47. Hanson, *Studies in Paul's Technique and Theology*, 143.
48. Hafemann, *Paul, Moses, and the History of Israel*, 36–39.
49. Ellis, "How the New Testament Uses the Old," 59.

all clear that typological reasoning is employed in 2 Cor 3:12–16 since Paul implies that the veil is one and the same, both in the past and the present. The earlier contrast between tablets of stone and tablets of human hearts in 3:3, anticipating Paul's treatment of Exodus 34, may well be typological.[50]

When read or heard in Christ, the veil of misunderstanding is removed and the fading glory of the law is seen as it is meant to be. This is, in a sense, a hermeneutical idea, claiming a single way towards accessing meaning for the church of Corinth as those who may also wish to read Scripture. This is certainly the conclusion of Jens Schröter who sees the passage as being hermeneutical, providing a claim of how the law should be read, just as 1 Cor 10:1–11 suggests how the biblical narrative of Israel ought to be read.[51] As Peter Balla concludes regarding the hermeneutical claim of 2 Cor 3:12–18:

> The true meaning of the OT can be understood only when looking back at it from the perspective of the NT. Christ is the key to the understanding of the OT. Christians must hold on to this hermeneutical insight.[52]

At the same time, the Pauline *adjustment* of Moses's motive in veiling his face may also have hermeneutical significance. The temporary nature of the glory emanating from Moses comes from the law which itself is fading away (2 Cor 3:11). Paul's treatment of the veil is not simply a statement about how the law should be read, but also a statement of the authority of the law relative to the Gospel. It is perhaps significant that in 2 Cor 4:6, those who are exposed to the Gospel through Christ behold the glory of God as light, since light is associated with Torah in Apoc. Bar. 59.2; 77.16; and Sifre Numbers 6:25.[53] What the law should have delivered as a witness to God's glory, the Gospel provides to those for whom it also is unveiled. As S. Grindheim argues, a dualism of the law and the Gospel is the best explanation of Paul's understanding of Moses need for the veil because of its fading glory. Accordingly, this dualism best fits the abrogation statements of vv. 11–16 and claim in v. 10 that the letter now lacks the glory it once had: it has been surpassed.[54] The opposite

---

50. Balla, "2 Corinthians," 758–59.
51. Schröter, "Schriftauslegung und Hermeneutik," 231–75.
52. Balla, "2 Corinthians," 761.
53. Davies, *Paul and Rabbinic Judaism*, 148.
54. Grindheim, "Law Kills," 97–115.

view is taken by Carol Kern Stockhausen and N. T. Wright who argue that in Paul's thought here the Spirit gives access to the meaning of the law in continuity with it.[55] Similarly, Hafeman contends that the apparent letter and Spirit dualism of 2 Cor 3 is salvation-historical rather than metaphysical.[56] He suggests that the ideas alluded to from Jeremiah 31 and Ezekial 36 imply no contradiction: in the new age the law will be kept through the power of the Spirit. The difference is between them is functional. Without the Spirit the law can only be understood as letter. The Spirit, therefore, does not do away with the law. Through Paul's preaching of the cross the Spirit is received, the law obeyed and the new covenant promises fulfilled. Furthermore, the veil must be understood within the context of the broken covenant of Exodus 36, following Israel's idolatry with the golden calf. Within this setting, the veil represents mercy (in that his glory is still available and therefore dangerous to sinful Israel) and judgement (in that the glory must be veiled because the people are not worthy of access to it). Whether one concludes that the law is denigrated and contrasted with the Spirit or not, both views, in any case tend towards a claim by Paul that interpretation "in Christ" provides access to the true meaning of Scripture, without which interpretation can only be wrong. Reading the law "in Christ" provides either the insight that the law has been superannuated, or else a vision of its true glory. Without Christ, neither of these insights are possible.

In unpacking the Moses doxa material, Paul applies some scriptural texts and ideas directly to himself and the "all we" of the church, principally the new covenant language of Jer 31:31 and the promise of the Spirit of God in Ezek 11:19 and 36:26.[57] Whereas the hermeneutical value of Rom 15:4 and 1 Cor 10:1–11 is principally ecclesiological, there is a much stronger christological element in 2 Cor 3:12–16. Crucially, it is only with the veil removed in Christ that the fading glory of the old covenant can be seen. Yet even this christological approach to accessing the true meaning of the old covenant law operates within a broader ecclesiological framework. For Paul, it is within the community of the Church that the glory of the Lord is seen: "and we all with unveiled faces behold the glory of the Lord, being transformed into its image, from glory to glory (3:18)." However, Paul does more than simply relate Exod 34:33–35 to the

---

55. Stockhausen, *Moses' Veil*, 73–74; and Wright, *Climax of the Covenant*, 182.
56. Hafeman, *Paul, Moses and the History of Israel*, 39–52.
57. Balla, "2 Corinthians," 759; Dodd, *According to the Scriptures*, 45.

eschatological "we" of the Church. As noted above, this use of Scripture has specific implications for how Paul's ministerial authority is presented.

According to Hafeman, by referring to a scriptural episode in which Moses mediates God's instruction to the people of Israel, Paul implicitly evokes the theme of the call of Moses in early Jewish literature.[58] Within this tradition, God's calling of Moses makes him sufficient to his task and offers a prototype for the Old Testament prophets. Hafeman suggests that Paul sees the call of Moses as a pattern for his own calling and expects his Corinthian audience to draw the same comparison since the ultimate rhetorical purpose of 2 Cor 3:1—6:1 is a defense of Paul's authority. Or as W. C. van Unnik argues, the contrast of Moses's veil and the unhindered access to the glory of God for those in Christ, is intended to evoke Paul's "barefaced" boldness as a minister of the new covenant in opposition to his rivals in Corinth. Van Unnik assumes here that Paul's opposition is from "judaizing" false teachers akin to those in Galatia. If this is the case, Paul's relative authority is derived from his own powerful experience of Christ as opening to him the true significance of the law, in contrast to the false teachers' veiled access to it as belonging to the people of Israel but without Christ.[59]

Gal 3:19–26

Just as Paul appears to provide a hermeneutical framework within which to interpret biblical narrative in 1 Cor 10:6–11, one might regard Gal 3:19–26, alongside 2 Cor 3:12–16, as providing just such a framework within which to understand the law. Of course, the interpretation of Scripture is not the principal concern within Paul's discussion of the law, though a correct understanding of the relation of the law to the Gospel of Jesus Christ is closely related. The Galatian church needs to know what to do with the law: how to apply it to their lives, how to interpret its value for defining the identity and status of those who are in Christ. This is ultimately an issue of interpretation for which Paul supplies a hermeneutic to position the law in relation to these questions. Thus far in Galatians, Paul has suggested a dichotomy between the prospects of justification by faith and justification through the law (3:1–14). Furthermore, Paul positions the giving of the law vis-à-vis the Abrahamic promise, calling into

---

58. Hafeman, *Paul, Moses and the History of Israel*, 58.
59. van Unnik, "With Unveiled Face," 153–69.

question its relation to the issue of justification (3:15–18). This argument begs the question as to why the law exists at all in the purposes of God.

> Why then the law? It was added because of transgressions, until the offspring should come to whom the promise had been made, and it was put in place through angels by an intermediary. Now an intermediary implies more than one, but God is one. Is the law then contrary to the promises of God? Certainly not! For if a law had been given that could give life, then righteousness would indeed be by the law. But the Scripture imprisoned everything under sin, so that the promise by faith in Jesus Christ might be given to those who believe. Now before faith came, we were held captive under the law, imprisoned until the coming faith would be revealed. So then, the law was our guardian until Christ came, in order that we might be justified by faith. But now that faith has come, we are no longer under a guardian, for in Christ Jesus you are all sons of God, through faith (3:19–26).

It perhaps does not need to be noted that this part of Galatians, along with Paul's treatment of the law more generally, has attracted no small amount of discussion and disagreement. Sufficient for the present study is the observation that, at the very least, Paul seeks to assert one concept of what the law means and offers at the expense of all others. In 3:19–26, this concept of the law is advanced by a distancing of the law from God and a claim that the law had only temporary jurisdiction over the people of God, though the precise nature of both of these ideas is, of course, debated.

On one hand, Paul's hermeneutic for the law appeals to traditions about the giving of the law at Sinai which serve to diminish its status by suggesting that it was not given directly by God to Israel. Again, there has been significant discussion of what it meant by the claim about the law given by mediation in 3:20. As Terence Callan notes, natural theophanic phenomena, such as thunder and lightning on Sinai, are thought to be the work of angels in Jub. 2:2 and 1 Enoch 60:11–24 and OG Deut 33:2.[60] Psalm 68:17 suggest that God gave the law accompanied by an angelic host at Sinai. This is seen as significant in early Christian and Jewish interpretation. Indeed the angelic mediation of the law is quite well-attested from the first century (Acts 7:53; Heb 2:2, *Ant.* 15.136; and *Herm. Sim.* 8.3.3). This perhaps reflects attempts in early Judaism to place angels into all the most important events of Israel's past, while later rabbinic

---

60. Callan, "Pauline Midrash," 549–67.

interpretation tended to the opposite: to stress that God acted alone at Sinai and on the day of Passover, for example.⁶¹ Paul appears to use the former emerging tradition to distance the giving of law somehow from the personal activity of God. However, as N. T. Wright notes, this argument does not maintain that the law is a bad this: ultimately the law is still divinely intended though mediated by angels.⁶² Yet Callan also argues that it is Moses who is the divided mediator who is contrasted with the unity of God. The division refers to the narrative context of the giving of the law and Moses' divided loyalty seen in his breaking of the tablets of the law so that the law might not condemn Israel for its idolatry with the golden calf, just as he veiled his face to protect them from God's glory.

The other aspect of Paul's hermeneutic for the law is his description of the law as *paidagōgos* ("guardian," "instructor") and the related claim that its role was to provide a temporary bondage for the people of God until the coming of Christ. Paul's opponents doubtless held to the well-attested early Jewish view that the law had an eternal status (Philo *Vit. Mos.* 2:14; Wisd 18:4; Jub 1:27). While there has been significant discussion as the precise background of the term *paidagōgos* and its use by Paul, particularly associated with the origins of the New Perspective on Paul, Paul's idea of the law claims at the very least that its role and status are temporary. The majority view tends to regard *paidagōgos* as an educator of children within the context of a privileged Greco-Roman household. By its very nature, this role is temporary, terminating when the child reaches maturity.⁶³ Crucially, for many commentators, the choice of paidagōgos as a metaphor for the law is appropriate because the role of a pedagogue is both temporary but good, desirable and necessary.⁶⁴ To have a pedagogue is a sign of privilege. Indeed, Longenecker suggests that the idea of the law as *paidagōgos* relates to the argument in 4:1–7 and the subsequent treatment of the offspring of Sarah and Hagar in 4:21–31. A pedagogue would typically be employed for the legitimate sons of the household: having a pedagogue is a sign of true sonship. Christians are the true children of the promise to Abraham, descendants of Sarah and her child who was born according to the promise, as such, it is appropriate for them to have a pedagogue until such time as the promise reaches

---

61. Longenecker, *Galatians*, 140.
62. Wright, *Climax of the Covenant*, 161.
63. Young, "*Paidagōgos*," 150–76.
64. Lull, "Law was Our Pedagogue," 481–98; Gordon, "ΠΑΙΔΟΓΩΓΟΣ," 150–54.

its ultimate fulfilment.[65] The idea of the temporary role of the pedagogue is possibly influenced too by the claim about the law relative to the promise to Abraham in 3:15–18. That the law came 430 years after the promise enables Paul to claim that it was not an essential element of God's covenant with Abraham's descendants, making it possible to claim that its role must only be temporary.[66] While *paidagōgos* may be a generally positive way to describe the law, it must be noted that the law in its role as pedagogue keeps the people of God in bondage (3:22–23) contrasted with the eschatological freedom through Christ (3:24–25; 4:4–6): the law is indeed something that one should desire to be freed from. Indeed, 4:3 claims the same kind of bondage for humankind under the "elementary principles" (*ta stoicheia*), suggesting that they and the law are synonymous, or at the very least, comparable. In Col 2:20, these "elementary principles" are understood to be spiritually evil and yet also a have legalistic influence over the Church. Yet as Belleville argues, the use in Gal 4:3 is not necessarily negative, noting that in Stoic and Philonic thought that *ta stoicheia* are governing forces, creating order: a function similar to that of the law as *paidagōgos*.[67] The apparently negative aspect of the law is a feature of the essentially eschatological definition Paul gives to *paidagōgos*. Not only is the law temporary, but it is also inferior to what has been provided for God's people at the climax of history through the sending of Jesus Christ and the Spirit. Indeed, as Lull argues, the law is not seen by Paul as a moral preparation for an equivalent moral education coming with Christ.[68] Instead the law has a prophetic role, pointing as a teacher to the time when Hab 2:4 would be fulfilled and the righteous would live by faith. Moisés Silva suggests that something as formal as three salvation-historical epochs are implied by this eschatological treatment of the law in Galatians 3–4: the ages of promise, law and faith, each ultimately oriented towards the last of these epochs.[69] In terms of hermeneutical significance, the law as *paidagōgos* suggests to readers that the law should be approached is something that had a temporary authority that is now passed.

---

65. Longenecker, "Pedagogical Nature of the Law," 53–61.
66. Gordon, "ΠΑΙΔΟΓΩΓΟΣ," 150–54.
67. Belleville, "Under Law," 53–78.
68. Lull, "Law was Our Pedagogue," 481–98.
69. Silva, "Galatians," 805.

Just as the interpretation of the law in 2 Cor 3 and the scriptural narrative of Israel's past in 1 Cor 10 is defined by an eschatological relation to the Church, so is the treatment of the law in Galatians. As Moyise suggests, Paul's argument already assumes that the law should be understood as being soteriological in an eschatological sense: that the law relates to salvation from a final judgement rather than being the means for God's blessing in the land or a guide to right living.[70] The implied eschatological orientation of the law, before Paul's argument even begins, is also claimed by Gordon who does not think that the law is soteriological to Paul. Reflecting something of the New Perspective, Gordon suggests that the law offers an ecclesiological problem (to do with covenant membership) rather than a soteriological problem: the assumed problem of the law is that it offers signs of covenant status that gentile believers cannot attain to.[71] The broader argument from Scripture in Gal similarly frames Scripture eschatologically. As D. Garlington suggests, the combination of references to Scripture in 3:10–13 (Deut 27:26; Hab 2:4; Lev 18:5 and Deut 21:23) under the eschatological expectation of Paul's reading of Hab 2:4 and God's ultimate purpose "that the blessing of Abraham might come to the gentiles," means that references from the law are taken eschatologically.[72] According to Garlington, Paul uses these texts to evoke the idea that the Galatian Church has come to a moment, anticipated in Israel's history, where a choice must be made between apostasy or faithfulness, between rejecting the ultimate eschatological purpose of the law and obedience to the law. Garlington observes that Paul's quotations in 3:10–13 are taken from contexts in which apostasy is a prominent theme. The implication for those in Paul's audience who are well-versed in Scripture is that those who attempt to undermine God's eschatological purpose with his people are under the curse of the law and that true obedience to the law involves acceptance of its eschatological purpose.

Garlington's study is not alone in claiming that Paul's argument about the law assumes that the Galatian audience is aware of the scriptural context of the references he makes to Scripture. While Martyn concludes of Paul's treatment of the law vis-à-vis his view of Scripture and use of particular references to Scripture in Galatians that Paul simply receives the Scriptures as messianic prophecy and that Christ is the

---

70. Moyise, *Evoking Scripture*, 71.
71. Gordon, "ΠΑΙΔΟΓΩΓΟΣ," 150–54.
72. Garlington, "Role Reversal," 85–121.

"point of departure" for his reading of the text, many argue for a more complex interaction with Scripture here.[73] For example, Roy E. Ciampa argues Paul defines his authority in Galatians 1–2 using allusions that show depth of familiarity with Scripture in order to be able to make his claims about the value of the law in 3–4 and that, in Galatians, "Scripture is a source of apocalyptic-restorationist concepts, structures and theology."[74] For example, the phrase "it is anathema" in 1:8–9 seen by Ciampa as a deliberate an echo of the Old Greek of Deut 13:12–16 which, in its broader literary context, refers to punishment for apostasy. The implication of this echo, suggest Ciampa, is that Paul's teaching is identified as being at one with the law and his opponents are aligned with apostate Israel under the curse of the law. Furthermore, the possible allusion to Isa 49:1 in Gal 1:15, in the claim that Paul was called to the ministry of the Gospel before his birth, identifies Paul as a prophetic speaker to those in his audience who are familiar with Scripture. These possible references have a bearing upon Paul's subsequent argument concerning the law, inasmuch as they establish an idea that Paul speaks from the perspective of Scripture and the true tendency of Israel's history. Similarly T. G. Gombis claims that the literary context of the quotation from Deut 27:26 in Gal 3:10 is significant. He argues that the broader context of Deut 27:15–26 concerns sins that happen in secret, the penalty for which falls on the nation as a whole.[75] As Gombis understands it, the curse is upon those who do not conform to the law and must be cut off. The true eschatological fulfilment of the law is the Gospel, hence it is the judaizing false teachers of Galatia who are failing to remain within the law by not affirming the Gospel and who threaten the whole community with the penalty of the law through their sinfulness. Of course, the difficulty with such readings of Paul is always that they assume what can never be known: the familiarity of Paul's audience with Scripture. The tendency of such arguments in the case of Paul's use of Scripture is to affirm something of the exclusivity with Paul approaches Scripture. Paul is the one who knows the law, not his opponents: he may decide that his opponents are anathema and declare that the law itself has a temporary jurisdiction over the people of God and that to view it otherwise is quite mistaken.

---

73. Martyn, *Galatians*, 340.

74. Ciampa, *Presence and Function*, 232; Ciampa, "Deuteronomy in Galatians," 99–117.

75. Gombis, "Transgressor," 81–93.

As Callan notes, the argument of Gal 3:19–26 shares with 2 Cor 3 an exegetical reliance upon the circumstances under which the law was given. The status of the law and, consequently, its true meaning and value is seen to be contingent upon the historical situation in which it was received.[76] The style of argument is perhaps similar to the rabbinic exegetical middah in which a text is interpreted according to its context in Scripture.[77] This is worthy of note, given how Christian scriptural interpretation would develop in the centuries immediately following the New Testament period. Paul does not identify the true meaning of the law as something that supplements an apparent literal meaning, nor does he see the law as a figure signifying a higher allegorical meaning.[78] To take either of these approaches would be to permit something that Paul does not: that the meaning of the law assumed by his opponents has any legitimacy whatsoever. For Paul, the circumstances under which the law was given invalidate any other position on the law but his own. Were Paul to have employed an allegorical approach to the law, he may have had to concede that there was something in his opponents' interpretation, as inadequate as it may be as a total assessment of the significance of the law. He may then have had to admit that while it may seem that the law is eternally glorious and humankind's only hope for the righteousness of God, its true meaning is something quite different as the logic of the Gospel suggests. As it is, Paul gives no recognition at all to the plausibility of his opponents approach to the law. It is simply not possible given what Scripture itself says about how the law came to be. For Paul, the law as a whole has a single meaning, defined by its temporary status as *paidagōgos*.

As Rom 15:4 appears to makes claim about the whole of Scripture and 1 Cor 10:6–11 makes a claim about the scriptural narrative of the wilderness generation, so Gal 3:19–26, like 2 Cor 3:15–16, appears to pertain specifically to the law. Indeed, Gal 3:22 appears to distinguish between "scripture" and "law" and it does not seem likely that "law" is

---

76. Callan, "Pauline Midrash," 550. Cf. Sargent, *David being a Prophet*, 95–96 n. 254.

77. Sargent, דבר הלמד מעניינו, and Cohn-Sherbok, "Paul and Rabbinic Exegesis," 130.

78. Indeed, as Di Mattei, "Paul's Allegory," 102–22 argues, Paul's later treatment of Sarah and Hagar, which Paul himself describes as *allegoroumena* in 4:24, reflects Jewish eschatological reading of the Torah more than it does Christian figurative reading, noting that from the Antiochenes on, this argument is usually thought to be typological, not allegorical.

a synonym for the Pentateuch: it is simply the legal covenant of Sinai.[79] The issue in Galatians is a hermeneutical issue: how do those who are in Christ interpret the law? Does it compel those who are in Christ to be circumcised or not? Because of this, one cannot but understand Galatians 3 and the description of the law as *paidagōgos* mediated by angels as anything but advice on how the Galatians are to interpret Scripture, or rather the law contained in Scripture. This passage and the Pauline theology of the law are amongst the most widely discussed aspects of Pauline criticism, yet the significance of Paul's treatment of the law for an understanding of his approach to Scripture is often overlooked. As far as Paul is concerned, not only is the meaning of the law only available "in Christ" (2 Cor 3:1 5–16), it also has a single function and value: its meaning will always be contained by its pedagogical nature

1 Pet 1:10–12

A sense of the single meaning of scriptural texts is witnessed also in 1 Peter. According to 1 Pet 1:1 0–12, the prophetic utterances had no discernible meaning to the prophets themselves. Instead, they pointed to the sufferings of Christ and the glories that would follow them. Indeed, the prophets spoke or wrote as servants of the eschatological community: the Christian Church.[80]

> Concerning this salvation, the prophets who prophesied of the grace that was to be yours made careful search and inquiry, inquiring about the person or time that the Spirit of Christ within them indicated, when it testified in advance to the sufferings destined for Christ and the subsequent glory. It was revealed to them that they were serving not themselves but you, in regard to the things that have now been announced to you through those who brought you good news by the Holy Spirit sent from heaven—things into which angels long to look!

Largely thanks to the study of William L. Schutter, there is now widespread agreement that these verses form some sort of "hermeneutical statement" of significance for the way in which Scripture is used in the

---

79. Belleville, "Under Law," 53–78.

80. Osborne, "L'Utilisation de l'Ancient Testament," 74. Peter appears to understand Scripture primarily as written text, rather than prophetic utterance.

epistle.[81] At once, this "hermeneutical statement" about the prophets of Israel's past limits the potential meaning of scriptural texts. These texts do not find their meaning in anything contemporary to the prophets, nor are they written with the needs of the prophets' communities in mind. There are, of course, certain interpretive ambiguities in 1 Pet 1:10-12. The first concerns the identity of the prophets. In a commentary that gave new life to 1 Peter scholarship in the 1950s, Edward Gordon Selwyn argued that the prophets in 1 Pet 1:10-12 were Christian prophets, contemporaneous with the epistle on the basis of the language used to describe their search for meaning, language used in John 5:39 and 7:52 to refer to a searching of the Scriptures: a Christian activity.[82] If this is the case, 1 Pet 1:10-12 really has little value in understanding how Peter viewed Scripture at all.[83] However, this view has attracted very little support for various reasons. The use of the aorist tense for "made careful search and enquiry" in 1:10 places the activity of the prophets firmly in the past, to the extent that it seems most unlikely to refer to Christian prophets. At the same time, 1 Pet 1:10-12 is not unique and must be seen as comparable to Matt 13:17 and 1QpHab 7. 1-8, both of which describe the activities of the prophets of Israel's past and their desire to see the fulfilment of their words. Another difficulty is the phrase translated here as "person or time," referring to that to which the "Spirit of Christ" was directing the prophets. The question to be answered is whether *tina* ("what/which") is being used here as a pronoun, signifying a person, or an adjective, qualifying *kairon* ("time/moment in time"), both of which are possible.[84] In either case, the sense in which the prophets anticipated something somewhat unknown in the future as the true referent of their words is unaffected.

Walter C. Kaiser argues against the ignorance of the prophets in 1 Pet 1:10-12 on the basis of his view that these statements suggest an idea

---

81. Schutter, *Hermeneutic and Composition*, 35ff; Schlosser, "Ancien Testament et Christologie," 65-93; Herzer, "Alttestamentliche Prophetie," 14-22; Jobes, *1 Peter*, 51; Bénétreau, "Évangile et Prophétie," 174-91; Green, *1 Peter*, 251; Hines, "Peter and the Prophetic Word," 234; Williams, "Ancient Prophets" 223-46; Sargent, *Written to Serve*, 18-49.

82. Selwyn, *First Epistle of St. Peter*, 134-35.

83. I hold to the Silvanus amanuensis hypothesis of authorship for reasons outlined in Sargent, "Chosen through Sanctification," 117-20 and am content to call the author of the epistle "Peter."

84. On the former position see Elliott, *1 Peter*, 345 and Best, *1 Peter*, 81. On the latter see Kilpatrick, "1 Peter 1.11: TINA 'H ΠΟΙΟΝ ΚΑΙΡΟΝ," 91-92 and Goppelt, *Der Erste Petrusbrief*, 107.

of the meaning of Scripture as *sensus plenior*: that the Spirit of Christ reveals the full meaning or simply the referent of the words of the prophets.[85] Kaiser argues instead that the prophets understood the meaning of their utterances fully, but simply had no knowledge of their true referent. To substantiate this, Kaiser argues that *tina* is adjectival, providing a tautology of emphasis: the prophets knew what manner of thing to expect, but not when to expect it. In Kaiser's view, the prophetic quest for meaning was simply a quest for the true referent of their words. Of course, this view also sees 1 Pet 1:10–12 as presenting a claim that Scripture has a single meaning. Since the broader context of Kaiser's interest is in defending the idea of single meaning in Scripture, it may be that he is cautious of admitting a distinction between how the prophets received Scripture and what it truly means as a witness to Christ for the Church. A distinction of this sort might suggest that Peter held to a more polysemic variant of *sensus plenior* in which the meaning of Scripture in its earliest reception is different to its ultimate significance. Because of this, Kaiser argues that old and new meanings are one and the same. The difficulty with this view is the sort of historical and eschatological contrast Peter seeks to make in 1 Pet 1:10–12, consistent with the theological narrative substructure of the epistle which assumes a radical disjuncture between the past and the present.[86] The search that the prophets make and the need for divine revelation as to the true significance of their words imply that they did not know what their words were really about. The revelation in 1:12 that their words were intended to serve not themselves but the eschatological community of the Church does more than simply answer a question about the true referent of their words: it suggests a complete reorientation of Scripture away from the past and towards the future. The implication is that this is a change of significance which undermined the very nature of how the prophets' words were meant to be understood. Instead of relating to realities with which the prophets were familiar, Peter's claim in 1:12 is that they were written to serve the Church and the Church alone, which stands at the climax of God's redemptive plan.

> The general effect of these verses is to emphasise the importance of the scattered Christian communities. Though they may be strangers in the world, the prophets who eagerly awaited the Christ they follow are their servants. The event these Christians

---

85. Kaiser, "Single Intent of Scripture," 125. Cf. Kaiser, "Single Meaning" 57.
86. Sargent, "Narrative Substructure" 485–90 and Schelkle, *Die Petrusbriefe*, 38.

are a part of represents the climax of history. Even the angels long to hear what they have been told. Peter suggests to his readers that as they read the Scriptures of Israel, they are reading things which pertain directly to themselves. They pertain to themselves not because they speak to each generation in the same way. They do so because Scripture is *for* them in an exclusive sense. The prophets served those who would hear the good news proclaimed by the Holy Spirit sent from heaven, not previous generations and not those who have now refused to obey the Gospel of God.[87]

Because of this, it is most unlikely that 1 Peter permits even the limited polysemy needed to justify typological interpretation. There is no sense in which Peter derives meaning for the eschatological community from a prior meaning within the history of Israel. While several scholars, including Joel B. Green and Anton Prédestin Joseph, have argued that the use of Scripture in 1 Peter is typological, they do so only by imagining an additional level of meaning to that presented in 1 Peter. Green suggests that Peter sees Scripture not so much as prophecy that requires prediction, but as narrative which establishes patterns through which the life and ministry of Jesus Christ find meaning.[88] This typological understanding of Peter's use of Scripture makes the most sense as a description of his approach to narrative Scripture. For example, when Peter makes use of titles for Israel in 2:5 and 9 ("spiritual house ... holy priesthood" and "chosen people, royal priesthood, holy nation, a people set apart"), presumably alluding to Exod 19:6 and Isa 43:20–21 respectively, he applies them to the Church knowing that they first refer to God's people in the past.[89] According to Green, Peter understands Israel in the past as a pattern for the Church in the present. Of course, the observation that Exod 19:6, for example, refers to Israel in the past may seem natural to a post-Enlightenment reader concerned with literary context and the ethics of interpretation, but what is the evidence that Peter is interested in two levels of significance to Exod 19:6? For Peter, Scripture would seem to be *all* about the Church. As 1 Pet 1:10–12 appears to suggest, Peter regarded the prophets as being unable to find any other meaning to their words

---

87. Sargent, *Written to Serve*, 33.

88. Green, *1 Peter*, 251. Cf. idem, "Narrating the Gospel," 262–77 and Boring, "Narrative Dynamics," 7–40.

89. Allusion to Exod 19:6 in 1 Pet 2:5 is by no means certain, but has received near consensus since Elliott, *The Elect and the Holy*.

than their witness to the sufferings of Christ and the glories that would follow. The difficult with Green's analysis is that is assumes a degree of hermeneutical sophistication in 1 Peter for which there is no real evidence. The eschatological narrative in which Peter thinks theologically places exclusive emphasis upon the eschatological present for which the prophets longed. This exclusive claim upon the scriptural language of nation and priesthood is clarified by the comparison Andrew M. Mbuvi makes with the idea of the Temple-Community at Qumran (1QS 5.6; 8.5; CD 7.1; 20.10; and 13).[90] Just as the Qumran community saw themselves as the true embodiment of the Temple and the city of God in the last days, so Peter appears to do something similar by regarding the Church as the proper referent of scriptural language about Israel. For Peter, there is little or no sense in which Scripture was written to convey knowledge about the past: instead it was written to serve those to whom the Gospel of Jesus Christ would be proclaimed.

A similar interpretation of Peter's use of Scripture to that of Green is made by Joseph. Joseph argues, for example, that the allusion to Sarah obeying Abraham and calling him Lord as an instruction to women in the Church in 1 Pet 3:6 is typological.[91] Indeed, this would perhaps appear to be the most obvious conclusion to draw, since Sarah is presented as an example to be imitated. This is, of course, quite different from the use of Exod 19:6 in 1 Pet 2:5 where the consequence of typological interpretation would be that Scripture refers both to Israel in the past *and* to the Church in the present. By virtue of being a reference to biblical narrative rather than specific titles separated from a narrative (in the case of Exod 19:6), the story of Sarah bears a different relation to the past. For Peter to imply that the story of Sarah is about the past and offers an example to the Church in the present offers a different form of polysemic meaning than the potential claim that the titles of Exod 19:6 refer to both Israel and the Church. The typological meaning of the former is utterly contained within function of story of Sarah as a witness to the past. Whereas Exod 19:6 is specifically about Israel as it awaits the giving of the law at Sinai and Peter claims that it is also about the Church, the story of Sarah is not claimed by Peter to be a reference to the Church, but simply an example for it. However, it is not clear that Peter makes even

---

90. Mbuvi, *Temple, Exile and Identity*, 90–91.
91. Joseph, *Narratological Reading*, 146.

this distinction between Sarah in the past and the Church in the present.⁹² There is no sense of the sort of historical distanciation necessary for typological interpretation here. Past and present are combined through a narrative which enables Christian women to become the children of Sarah (1 Pet 3:6). One may also wish here to draw a distinction between the way Peter uses vague allusions to *events* of the past (and the precise text to which Peter refers in 3:6 is debated) and the way in which references to scriptural texts are used. Whereas texts are overwhelmed by the eschatological narrative of 1 Peter which can only see them as referring to the Church at the climax of history, it is not so easy to interpret events of the past in the same way. Events such as the obedience of Sarah (3:6) and the Flood (3:20–21) cannot be entirely severed from their situation in the past in the way that texts are.

2 Pet 1:19–21

This passage has assumed some importance in debates concerning early Christian scriptural interpretation, just as it has in doctrinal discussion of the authority of Scripture. Some argue that something like *sensus plenior* is implied here because an apparent distinction is made between what the prophets said and what their words meant. Because the prophets of Israel's past were "carried along" by the Holy Spirit, it is possible that they did not understand the full significance of what they said, not being in full control of their own words, with the full sense supplied at a later date.⁹³

> And we have the prophetic word more fully confirmed, to which you will do well to pay attention as to a lamp shining in a dark place, until the day dawns and the morning star rises in your hearts, knowing this first of all, that no prophecy of Scripture comes from someone›s own interpretation. For no prophecy was ever produced by the will of man, but men spoke from God as they were carried along by the Holy Spirit (2 Pet 1:19–21).

Kaiser argues against this analysis, suggesting that the term substantive form of *epilysis* ("interpretation/revelation") is otherwise unattested in the New Testament and the primary meaning of its cognate form is "to

---

92. Sargent, *Written to Serve*, 136.

93. As with 1 Pet 1:10–12, it is most unlikely that "prophets" refers to Christian prophets due to the use of the aorist tense. Cavallin, "False Teachers of 2 Pt," 265.

loose" or "to free," rather than "to interpret" which is its secondary meaning.[94] If the less likely secondary meaning were assumed, argues Kaiser, this would entail that no prophecy of Scripture had ever been understood by its prophetic human author. At the same time, Peter's claim that the prophetic witness is like "a lamp shining in a dark place" would be rendered meaningless if it failed to enlighten even the one from whose mouth it came. However, Peter's concern is for the eschatological community who will encounter the message of the prophets as enlightening, not the prophets of Israel's past. As John T. Curran argues, the phrase translated above "from someone's own interpretation" is not a genitive of origins (referring to the prophet's interpretation) but a possessive genitive ("one's own interpretation").[95] As Bauckham argues, this reading is most plausible grammatically, though he notes that *idias* ("own") is used a great deal in other contemporary literature claiming that the prophets' words are not their own (Philo *Quis Her.* 259; *Mos.* 1.281; 286; *Spec. Leg.* 4.49; *Quaest Gen.* 3.10; Hippolytus *Antichr.* 2; OG Jer 23:16 and OG Ezek 13:3).[96] However, Bauckham also draws parallels between 2 Pet 3:20 and two other texts in which "own interpretation" is that of the contemporary interpreter: *Clem. Hom.* 2.22 and Pseudo-Callisthenes *History of Alexander the Great* 2.1.5. In the latter, the interpretation of an omen is disputed, suggesting a distinction between what it actually means and what the seer takes it to mean according to her own interpretation. This suggests that a distinction is being draw between the origins of prophetic Scripture and how it is received by later "interpreters." Just as Scripture came through the direct intervention of the Holy Spirit, so to interpretation is not to be one's own. The idea here is that Scripture has a single true locus of meaning intended through the divine process of its creation. This is the meaning the author claims to proclaim against his opponents who distort the Scriptures (2 Pet 3:16).

The fulfilment of Scripture in 2 Pet 1:19-21 is wholly eschatological inasmuch as Scripture is seen to refer to events of the last days. The image of the new day and the "morning star" (*phosphoros*) evoke common apocalyptic and early Jewish images of the last days and of the messiah. As Carson notes, stars have eschatological significance

---

94. Kaiser, "Single Meaning," 57. Cf. Bauckham, *Jude, 2 Peter*, 231.
95. Curran, "Teaching of II Peter 1.20," 348-59; and Kelly, *Peter and Jude*, 321.
96. Bauckham, *Jude, 2 Peter*, 229-31.

in Levi 18.3; T. Jud. 24:1; CD A 8.1 8–20 and Rev 22:16.[97] Similarly, *hemera* ("day") is given eschatological significance in the Old Greek Scriptures.[98] Against the possibility that the phrase "in your hearts" implies some kind of psychological or idealist, rather than eschatological and historicist, fulfilment of Scripture, Terrence Callan suggests that it refers to the knowledge of the Scriptures in v. 20.[99] This idea presents the understanding of the nature and meaning of Scripture as eschatological too. It is in these last days that the prophetic witness has been confirmed. The whole sentence (1:19–21) is itself a disclosure formula, indicating how it is that the author knows what he knows, a common feature of apocalyptic literature.[100] The broader context of the defence of the author's ministry in 1:16–21 makes use of the *parousia* ("coming") of Christ. While it is most likely from the context here, with its reference to the transfiguration, that this refers to the "first coming" of Christ, the "incarnation," this still provides an eschatological framework in which the meaning of Scripture is confirmed.[101] In 2 Peter, the ministry of Jesus Christ brings the promise of glory and deliverance from the evils of the last days in which God and his people are opposed (3:1–7). This is an eschatological period, anticipated by the prophets, culminating in a final moment of justice and vindication (3:8–10).

Second Peter 1:19–21 is ambiguous in terms of its value for understanding early Christian interpretation of Scripture. Insofar as it claims an authoritative inspiration for the prophets of Israel's past it is fairly straightforward. The hermeneutical significance of the sentence hangs upon "own interpretation" as a possessive genitive. Without this, it is simply a statement about the status and origins of prophetic Scripture. As it is, 2 Pet 1:20 makes a parallel claim about how the prophetic Scriptures ought to be interpreted: not according to one's own reckoning or interpretation, just as the prophets did not write of themselves. Indeed, the prophets' lack of will or control in their utterance suggests a similar concept of prophetic ignorance to that found in 1 Pet 1:10–12 and Matt 13:17. Second Peter 1:20–21 does not go so far as to claim that the prophets knew nothing of the fulfilment of their words, their role is limited

---

97. Carson, "2 Peter," 1048.
98. Boehmer, "Tag und Morgenstern?," 228–33.
99. Callan, "A Note on 2 Peter," 265–70.
100. Porter and Pitts, "τοῦτο πρῶτον γινώσκοντες ὅτι," 165–71.
101. Neyrey, "Apologetic Use," 504–19.

to that simply of a vessel for an eschatological message. Second Peter takes away even the creative role of the prophets assumed in 1 Peter. This suggests again a single meaning for the words they were given. The prophetic word may not have been thought of by Peter as something full of meaning for the prophets themselves. Rather its meaning relates purely to the events through which it is confirmed for Peter's audience and any interpretation that suggests otherwise is a distortion of this meaning by one pursuing their own ideas.

John 5:39

Another possible example of a statement concerning the meaning of Scripture is John 5:39, "you search the Scriptures because you think you have life in them, and yet it is they that bear witness about me." Set within a discourse aimed at the Jewish religious authorities, Scripture is depicted as a witness to Jesus, alongside John the Baptist and the Father. The statement appears to deny meaning other than that which points to Jesus. The searching of the Scriptures undertaken by the religious leaders has been in vain since they have hitherto been unaware of the Scripture's true referent. Alongside this is the specifically Johannine point that they have searched the Scriptures to find life, but true life is found only in the Son of God, the Word made flesh.

Jesus' statement about the true meaning of Scripture shows some awareness of early Jewish interpretation. *Eraunan* ("search") corresponds to the Hebrew *darash* as a technical word for the study of Scripture, from the slippery characterisation "midrash" is derived.[102] Likewise, the idea that Scripture is searched because it holds out the promise of life is a claim attested in y. Aboth 2.7. Yet Jesus' claim here is that there is nothing life-giving about the Scriptures if their true referent is ignored. Of course, "life" is a significant concept within the Gospel. It is the reason Jesus, the word made flesh in whom is life (1:4), has come (10:10) and is the reason that the Gospel was written at all (20:31). John 5:39 relates the interpretation of Scripture to the exclusive offer of eternal life made by Jesus. That Scripture refers to Jesus is a johannine hermeneutical maxim (1:45; 2:22; 3:10; 5:45–46 and 20:9). In 5:39 the maxim is made exclusive: the study of Scripture does not yield the promise of eternal life unless it is understood to be about Jesus Christ, the one by whom and in whom life is found.

---

102. Barrett, *St. John*, 222. Cf. Carson, *John*, 263.

Of course, typological interpretation is a significant feature of the use of Scripture in John's Gospel and the apparent univocity of the claim in 5:39 does not characterise the Gospel as a whole. Whereas as much typological interpretation in the New Testament is implied and must be read back into what can be observed with a particular use of Scripture, John makes typological interpretation explicit. "Just as Moses lifted up the serpent in the wilderness, so the Son of Man must be lifted up" (3:14). The episode of Moses and the serpent in Num 21:9 has integrity as an event in the past and is not simply a sign of what is to come. Typological interpretation is also applied to a cited text in 6:31–33. A rendering of Exod 16:15 is introduced to give substance to the typological comparison of the manna in the wilderness with Jesus as "the bread of God . . . who comes from heaven and gives life to the world." Exodus 16:15 is then both a record of the past and a witness to Jesus Christ. This appears to be a genuinely polysemic form of typological interpretation. Unlike 1 Cor 10:6 and 11 there is no claim that scriptural events are recorded simply as a type or example from which the Church may learn. The use of Ps 78:24 in John 6:31 to refer to Jesus (as is characteristic of John's use of the psalter) shows this ambiguity.[103] One could argue that the interpretation of the psalm suggests that it is understood simply as a prophecy about Jesus feeding the five thousand, without any interest that in its own literary context the verse refers to Israel being fed in the wilderness. However, the narrative context of the quotation in John is riddled with allusions to God feeding Israel in the past. It is difficult to maintain, then, that John is interested only in the prophetic aspect of Ps 78:24. John uses the psalm quotation because it represents God feeding Israel *and* offers a prophetic witness to the ministry of Jesus. C. K. Barrett does not seem to recognise the polysemic element in John's use of typology, preferring to define the "I am" sayings as allegories with an exclusively Christological interpretation of the scriptural image, text or event they employ.

> John . . . has taken an O.T. symbol, ridded it of local associations and worked it up in a new and original Christian form; there is no use of testimonies, but the N.T. Gospel is (as it were) spoken through the O.T.[104]

It seems perhaps too simplistic to suggest that John's typological references to Scripture lack the "local associations" in their original literary

---

103. Daly-Denton, "Psalms in John's Gospel," 119–37.
104. Barrett, "Old Testament in the Fourth Gospel," 164.

contexts. In the majority of cases, John appears to deliberately build upon a prior meaning.

Much of John's typological interpretation is antithetic.[105] The leaders of God's people in the past were inadequate shepherds, but Jesus is the good shepherd who lays down his life for the sheep (10:12). Likewise, the manna eaten by God's people in the wilderness could not satisfy them completely, but Jesus is the true manna who sustains his people perfectly (6:35). Whereas Israel failed to prosper and grow as suggested in Isa 5:7, Jesus is the true vine through whom the people of God can bear fruit (15:1). An exception to this rejection or denigration of the antitype is the synthetic typology of 3:14: "just as Moses lifted up the serpent in the wilderness, so the Son of Man will be lifted up." Here the comparison does not imply that Jesus succeeds where the serpent failed, but simply that the serpent prefigures Jesus on the cross: the saving power of the serpent is not explicitly denigrated. Similarly, Moses is presented as writing about Jesus by Philip in 1:45, but his significance is much broader than a simply prophetic role. Moses performs symbolic actions which anticipate events in the ministry of Jesus (3:14) and signifies the grace given through the law, a comparable grace to that given through the ministry of Jesus (1:16–17). Indeed, the greatness of Moses is an important element in advancing Jesus authority.[106] John also offers a similar treatment of Abraham in 8:56: "our father Abraham rejoiced to see my day and he saw and was glad." This claim casts Abraham in the role of a prophet who saw in advance the coming of Jesus.[107]

John 5:39 certainly asserts a form of single meaning: Scripture is only to be understood as a witness to Jesus Christ and no other approach to its interpretation can offer eternal life. However, this statement does not appear to be characteristic of the use of Scripture generally within the Gospel. One might observe too that the orientation of Scripture in John is quite unambiguously Christological, a marked departure from the ecclesiological concern of the early Christia hermeneutical claims discussed above, perhaps anticipating a later tendency in scriptural interpretation.

---

105. Longenecker, *Biblical Exegesis*, 153–54.
106. Myers, "One of Whom Moses Wrote," 1–20.
107. Menken, "Genesis in John's Gospel," 83–98.

Single Meaning Assumed

For the most part, the New Testament writers had no concern to teach scriptural interpretation as a subject in itself. Because of this, there is very little material within the New Testament that has a bearing on the nature of early Christian interpretation and hermeneutics, and even those passages discussed have only a limited relation to the subject of hermeneutics as understood today: a distinct theoretical basis for interpretation. Enquiry into early Christian scriptural interpretation in the New Testament must, for the most part, engage with actual interpretation of particular texts, seeking to disclose the assumptions upon which interpretation works. Yet it is somewhat difficult and perhaps unwise to attempt to read hermeneutical ideas back into New Testament texts as they interpret other texts. To a certain extent, one can never really be sure what theory of scripture and its meaning has influenced the practice of interpretation as it appears in a New Testament passage. However, on the basis of the hermeneutical ideas that are witnessed in the New Testament, it is reasonable to conclude that most scriptural interpretation in the New Testament is probably guided by similar assumptions about meaning. This is especially evident in New Testament literature which employs charismatic interpretation: interpretation which depends solely on the authority of the interpreter and lacks any exegetical explanation.

It is certainly harder to explain how interpretation of this sort could arise within the context of hermeneutical ideas which admitted a degree of indeterminate meaning. A good example of this is Paul's frequent use of "as it is written" as an introductory formula to a scriptural citation. The use of this formula implies that the meaning of the citation is so clear and unambiguous that it can simply be provided to prove an assertion made by Paul, without explanation. Such a use of Scripture would not be possible without an assumption on the part of Paul or his audiences that the meaning claimed for Scripture is its exclusive single meaning. Without such an assumption, the rhetorical function of scriptural quotation in Paul would be undermined. Likewise, the interpretation of Isa 61:1–2 by Jesus in Luke 4:17–21 assumes some sort of single meaning for the scriptural excerpt. The outrage of the crowd is a result of the claim that the messianic prophecy finds its exclusive fulfilment in the person and work of Jesus.

Matt 7:24–27

The Sermon on the Mount concludes with a statement suggesting how Jesus' previous sayings should be received.

> All who hear these words of mine and do them will be like a wise man who established his house upon the rock. The rain fell, the rivers came and the wind blew and beat against that house and it did not fall because its foundation was upon the rock. But all who hear these words of mine and do not do them will be like a foolish man who established his house upon the sand. The rain fell, the rivers came and the wind blew and beat against that house and it fell. Great was its fall.

One could make the case that this also is a hermeneutical statement, since it tells readers of Matthew's Gospel how to correctly respond to the words they have just read in the Sermon on the Mount. The story must be understood as hermeneutical since it follows a collection of written teaching compiled by Matthew and is a comment on how that teaching should be received. In the simplest sense, the story Jesus tells is about the interpretation of his own words, presented as Scripture by the Sermon on the Mount. As Leon Morris notes, whether or not the pericope originated in the teaching of the historical Jesus, and whether or not it originated at the end of a speech like the Sermon on the Mount, in its setting within both Matthew and Luke it is a comment upon the writing that precedes it and suggests how that writing is to be understood.[108] However, unlike the hermeneutical statements discussed above, Matt 7:24–27 does not seek to define the nature of Scripture's meaning or its focus. Instead, it assumes that the meaning of Jesus' words are obvious: so obvious that they ought to lead directly to practice. The wise person is the one who responds to Jesus' words simply, by doing them. At the same time, given how Matthew frames the Sermon, describes the crowd's response to it and employs a certain degree of the Moses typology, it would be wrong to conclude that Matt 7:24–27 does not concern the interpretation of Scripture. As is perhaps well rehearsed now, the location of the sermon, the manner in which it starts with a list of beatitudes, the manner in which it explores the true application of the law claims a direct parallel with the giving of the law through Moses. The sermon concludes with a statement of the crowd's astonishment, claiming that Jesus' teaching has a degree of inspiration that other religious teachers lack: "when Jesus had completed

---

108. Morris, *Matthew*, 182; Knowles, "Everyone Who Hears," 287.

these sayings the crowds were amazed at his teaching for he taught them as one with authority, not as their scribes" (7:28–29). It is clear that Matthew saw Jesus words as possessing the highest status and authority as sacred Scripture.

The story of the wise and foolish builders assumes a direct course of action that will flow from listening to the instruction of Jesus. The correct interpretation of Jesus' words is action rather than inaction, or even, perhaps, action rather than reflection. According to Hans Dieter Betz, the parable denies the value of simply learning Jesus' words as well as the value of debating and theorising on his words.[109] Jesus' words exist to be done. The action his words command is straightforward and not open to interpretation: the wise person simply "does them." There is no sense in which any other act of interpretation or study is necessary. As Davies and Allison observe,

> It is perhaps noteworthy that, in 7.24–7, Matthew says nothing at all about studying the words of Jesus. For the evangelist, presumably, it is not studying that is greater but doing. Compare *m. 'Abot* 1.17, which no doubt addresses a tendency in rabbinic Judaism to exalt study at the expense of other action.[110]

The story itself is carefully crafted. The similarity of the language used to describe the builders is nearly complete, apart from the qualifying difference between them and the outcome of the storm. This, of course, serves the hermeneutical contrast: the decision not to act upon hearing (or reading) the words of Jesus Christ makes the difference between wisdom and foolishness.[111] Likewise, the few differences in the Lukan version are most likely insignificant.[112] The story is an antithetical double similitude. Gary Yamasaki, however, suggests that Matt 7:25 and 27 are not identical parallels. *Prospipto* "fell against" (7:25) and *proskopto* "beat against" (7:27) are different but often translated as though they are synonymous. Yamasaki suggests that this is a striking break in parallelism. The words make the scenarios slightly different: *prospipto*, he argues, may have had a religious meaning "to fall down before" in obeisance in the early Church. The very winds themselves know that they can only fail against the house so firmly established. *Proskopto* is not as dramatic as "beat against." A

---

109. Betz, *Sermon on the Mount*, 562.
110. Davies and Allison, *Saint Matthew*, 720.
111. Blomberg, *Interpreting the Parables*, 348.
112. Knowles, "Everyone Who Hears," 287.

good example of its use is in OG Ps 90:12 "strike your foot against a stone," made out to be a minor possible injury. The wind which destroys the foolish man's house is insignificant.[113]

There is of course a similar story attributed to Elisha ben Abuyah in *Aboth R. Nat.* 24.1–3.[114] Here, the one who does not have deeds is described first and compared to a builder who begins building his house with small bricks and completes it with large stones, while the one with deeds does the reverse. When the rains come, the house built on brick is destroyed. The emphasis here appears to be upon the foolishness of one who knows Scripture but lacks deeds, since this character is treated first.[115] The message is certainly the same: that the appropriate response to the word of God is action. The word of God is something that must be *done*. Similar statements exist are manifold in early Christianity: Luke 8:21 ("my mother and brothers are those that hear to word of God and do it") and its parallel in Matt 12:50 ("whoever does the will of my father in heaven is my brother and sister and mother"). The theme of hearing and doing the word of God is also seen in Rom 2:13 and Jas 1:25. Indeed, an emphasis upon doing would seem to be typically matthean, if one considers Matt 19:16–22; 24:26; 25:40 and 45.[116] Interestingly, the long recension of the prologue to Ignatius of Antioch's letter to the Philadelphians takes the story of Matt 7:24–27 and interprets it ecclesiologically: Jesus has built his Church upon the rock and the winds and floods have not been able to overcome it. Apoc. Pet.2 7.70.2 6–27. Another similar statement to Matt 7:24–27 can be found in Philo *Praem.* 79–84, promising victory to the one who hears and carries out God's commands. Similarly, in Sir 22:1 6–18, the one who hears and does is like a wooden beam firmly fixed against the wind of fear. The motif of the storm as a personal trial can also be seen in 1QH 14.2 2–32: by trusting in God, the speaker has his foundation upon rock, though otherwise is like a sailor in a storm.[117]

An important discussion exists regarding the question of just how much the parable is meant to convey. Does the story simply make the claim that if one hears and obeys Jesus' word they will be as wise as a man who built his house upon the rock? In other words, are the wise and

---

113. Yamasaki, "Broken Parallelism," 143–49.
114. And other parallels from Strack and Billerbeck, *Kommentar*, 469 ff.
115. Blomberg, *Interpreting the Parables*, 349.
116. Hagner, "Holiness and Ecclesiology," 178.
117. Snodgrass, *Stories with Intent*, 328.

foolish builders simply illustrations of their respective qualities? Or does the story make the claim that those who hear and obey the words of Jesus will be safe from eschatological judgement (seen in the imagery of the storm)? Even more, does the story claim that those who hear and obey Jesus' words are established on the rock that is Christ, just as wise builder builds his house upon the rock? The former view, that the builders simply provide images of wisdom and foolishness, is maintained by Klyne Snodgrass. Snodgrass suggests that the storm is more likely to be metaphorical rather than allegorical, though some of the alleged metaphorical nuances to the parable are hard to justify.

> The parable is an analogy, not an allegory. The one who hears Jesus' teachings and does them is as wise as someone who provides a strong foundation on rock. The one who hears Jesus' teachings and does not do them is as foolish as someone building a house on the sand.[118]

However, perhaps the majority of commentators consider at least the storm to be figurative, representing immanent eschatological judgement.[119] While this eschatological element appears to be lacking in the parallel story in *Aboth R. Nathan* 24, it is certainly a feature of qumranic treatment of storms.[120] Yet, whether one holds to a "minimalist" or "maximalist" view of Matt 7:24-27, the "hermeneutic" of the pericope remains the same: the wise response to hearing the word of God is doing the word of God. No act of interpretation is apparently necessary since the action demanded by Scripture is clear and incontestable. Scripture is assumed to have a single and simple meaning.

James 1:19–25

As noted above, a similar assumption of single meaning to that in the story of the wise and foolish builders is suggested in Jas 1:19–25. Here, the relationship between hearing and response is similarly simple and apparently unambiguous: the word demands action and no question of interpretive complexity is entertained.

---

118. Ibid., 335.

119. Hagner, *Matthew 1–13*, 191; Betz, *Sermon on the Mount*, 557; Nolland, *Luke 1–9*, 309–11; Jeremias, *Parables of Jesus*, 194; Caird, *Gospel of St. Luke*, 107 and Morris, *Gospel According to Matthew*, 181.

120. Albright and Mann, *Matthew*, 89.

Know this, my beloved brothers: let all people be quick to listen, slow to speak and slow to anger. For the anger of people does not produce the righteousness of God. Therefore, get rid of all filth and excessive evil. In meekness, receive the implanted word which is able to save your souls. Become doers of the word and not only hearers, deceiving yourselves. For if anyone hears the word and does not do it, they are like a person who looks at their natural face in a mirror, who looks at themself and, on going away, immediately forgets their likeness. But the one who peers into the perfect law of freedom and keeps looking, being not a hearer who forgets but a doer who acts, will be blessed in all they do. (Jas 1:19-25)

As with Matt 7:24-27, Jas 1:19-25 shares the halakhic emphasis of *Aboth R. Nat.* 24.1-3 and also *Aboth* 3.17b.[121] A similar distinction between hearing and doing is also made in Rom 2:13. The exhortation is similar also to 2 Enoch 42, in which the wicked are known through their deeds, perhaps suggesting an apocalyptic Jewish/Christian influence, alongside other features.[122] The illustration of the halakhic imperative is the character who forgets their image in the mirror: perceiving the law and acting upon it is the equivalent of looking into a mirror and remembering the image. This illustration is not without precedent and is typically associated with the reflection of divine truth.[123] Wisd. 7:26 describes wisdom as a reflection of God's light and a spotless mirror reflecting the work of God. *Odes Sol.* 13:1 describes God himself as a mirror, through which one may gain insight into the true nature of one's own person. 1 Clem 36:2 defines the significance of Christ as a glass, through which the Father is known and the glories of heaven seen. The form of Jas 1:19-25 shares a great deal with other "listen and do" exhortations. Jas 1:19-25 is a double similitude with a similar form to Matt 7:24-27; *Aboth R. Nat.* 24 (the one who listens and does is like one who builds with layers of stones followed by courses of bricks on top, whereas the one who does not do the law is like one who builds first with bricks and then stones on top) and *m. Aboth* 3.18b (the one who does what the law requires is like a tree with great roots but few branches: the one with few deeds has small roots but many branches and will not survive the wind). The similitude in

---

121. Obermüller, "Hermeneutische Themen," 234-44; Martin, *James*, 50; Carson, "James," 997 and Blomberg and Kamell, *James*, 89-91.

122. Penner, *Epistle of James and Eschatology*, 233 n. 1.

123. Jervell, *Imago Dei*, 185-89.

James may have been more of a pair like the others, with the twin of 1:23 subsumed into the application of 1:25, perhaps originally concluding, "if anyone is a doer of the word, he is like a man who looked intently into a mirror and remained and did not forget."[124]

Of course, to claim Jas 1:19-25 as "hermeneutical"—that is to say, instructing James' audience in the correct response to the Scriptures—one needs to be clear that the "implanted word" (*emphuton logon*) in v. 21 is a reference to Scripture. Ralph P. Martin suggests that the "implanted word" and the "perfect law" (v. 25) are synonymous and are distinct from the written word of the "royal law" (Jas 2:8).[125] The "implanted word," could then be the message of Jesus Christ received by James audience, leading to conversion and baptism.[126] While the stoic use of *emphuton* is with the meaning "innate" or "inborn," this does not appear to fit with the thought in James that this word needs to be received. While the need to receive the "implanted word" seems paradoxical, a similar idea is present in 1 Pet 1:22—2:2, inasmuch as those who have been born of the word should continue to crave it as pure spiritual milk.[127] While 1 Pet 1:22—2:2 is undoubtedly about the preached "word" of the Gospel, the "implanted word" and "perfect law" of Jas 1:19-25 are more likely to be references to Scripture. As Goppelt argues, the eschatological promise of Jer 31:33—the written law engraved in human hearts—is the thought in James.[128] Indeed, the description of the law as "perfect" in v. 25 is characteristic of praise of the written law in the Torah Psalms, as in OG Ps 18:8. Given the halakhic style and tradition that James appears to represent, the idea that "implanted word" refers to Scripture seems fairly certain. As with Matt 7:24-27, the interpretation of the law is straightforward: it simply must be done.

1 Cor 9:8–11

Perhaps the clearest and, to many, most troubling example of a text applied as though it has only a single meaning is the treatment of Deut 25:4 in 1 Cor 9:8–11.

---

124. Bauckham, *James*, 51–52.

125. Martin, *James*, 45–49.

126. Cf. Collins, "Coherence in James," 80–87; McCartney, *James*, 118.

127. McCartney, *James*, 117.

128. Goppelt, *Theology*, 2.203.

> Do I say these things according to human authority and does not the law say it? For in the law of Moses it is written, "you will not muzzle an ox while it treads out the grain." Is it for oxen that God is concerned or does he not speak all for our sake? It was written for our sake, because the ploughman should plough in hope and the thresher in hope of partaking. If we have sown spiritual things within you, is it too great a thing for us to reap physical things from you?

Paul applies a very specific and apparently straightforward scriptural command as though its meaning is obvious and obviously spiritual. There can be no doubt for Paul that these words have no application at all to agriculture: they are a figure for the Church and the payment of those engaged in the ministry of the Gospel. The spiritual meaning of Deut 25:4 does not supplement any other meaning: it is the only meaning that exists. Would God really be concerned about oxen? For Paul, the idea is implausible.[129] This dismissal of a quite plain meaning of a text foreshadows some of the earliest Christian uses of allegorical interpretation which proceed from perceived difficulties with the content of scriptural texts: principally that their meaning is simply too mundane to be taken seriously. However, the rejection of the apparently plain meaning of Deut 25:4 is not a result of an allegorical approach here, as Conzelmann suggests, claiming that Paul adopts a Hellenistic metaphysic of meaning.[130] The use of Scripture here seems to reflect instead the eschatological principle of Rom 15:4; 1 Cor 10:6 and 11, inasmuch as Scripture is interpreted as though it really is for the Church as the community standing at the climax of salvation history.

William F. Orr and James Arthur Walther argue that 1 Cor 9:8–11 is an example of the exegetical principle *e minori ad maius*: if it is not appropriate to stop an ox eating grain while it works, how much more should ministers of the Gospel be supported during their labours.[131] But Paul appears to deny that Deut 25:4 is about an ox at all. *E minori ad maius* is evidenced by a more explicit interest in some initial meaning to the text before its meaning is extended to a new situation. There is no evidence that this is taking place in 1 Cor 9:8–11. Similarly Brian S. Rosner

---

129. Weiss, *Der Erste Korintherbrief*, 236; Robertson and Plummer, *First Epistle to the Corinthians*, 183–84; Barrett, *First Epistle to the Corinthians*, 205 and Longenecker, *Biblical Exegesis*, 126–27.

130. Conzelmann, *1 Corinthians*, 154–55.

131. Orr and Walther, *1 Corinthians*, 241.

sees 1 Cor 9:9 as an example of the rabbinic equivalent *qal wahomer*.[132] In Deuteronomy itself, 25:4 appears to be disconnected from its immediate context inasmuch as it concerns livestock, whereas the other commands of Deuteronomy 24–25 concern marriage, work, justice for the marginalized and gleaning. Rosner argues that the common theme of the context from which Deut 25:4 is taken is the good treatment of the poor and marginalized and that 25:4 reflects this theme. This is how Philo treats Deut 25:4 in *Virt* 125–47. Similarly, in *Ant.* 4.233 Josephus interprets the command as though it is about the right to glean, as in Deut 24:21–22 immediately before: oxen, as fellow labourers, must be allowed to glean as they work. Because Deut 25:4 is a command to care for the lowliest beast of burden, how much more should ministers of the Gospel of Jesus Christ be cared for? Rosner suggests that within the history of the interpretation of Deut 25:4, Paul's use does not seem so surprising. The command is consistently related to the need to care for other people, in part because of its context. But again, what is the evidence that *qal wahomer* is being used? Isn't it just as likely that the oxen interpretation is rejected on the grounds of it being "written for us"? As David Lincicum suggests, Paul's interpretation of Deut 25:4 is wholly absorbed by his own contemporary interest, drawing a comparison with the halakhic interest of the Temple Scroll.[133] Again, this is a text in which the need for contemporary interpretation is associated with an eschatological understanding of the significance of the contemporary community.

The use of Deut 25:4 in 1 Cor 9:8–11 is, of course, a difficult example of the interpretation of Scripture in the New Testament for those who seek to argue that a commitment to determinate meaning requires the original meaning of the scriptural quotation and the meaning given to it in the New Testament to be one and the same. The same is true for those who seek to argue that the interpretation of Scripture in the New Testament should make sense to modern readers. For Walter C. Kaiser, one of the issues is the meaning of *pantōs* ("all") in 9:10, variously translated "altogether" or "entirely," as in the NRSV, "does he not speak entirely for our sake?" Kaiser argues that the term could equally mean "especially" in this context: "does he not speak especially for our sake?"[134] This does not imply a rejection of the plain sense of Deut 25:4 in

---

132. Rosner, "Deuteronomy in 1 and 2 Corinthians," 128. Cf. Ciampa and Rosner, "1 Corinthians," 718–22.

133. Lincicum, "Paul and the Temple Scroll," 51–69.

134. Kaiser, "Current Crisis in Exegesis," 14.

quite the same way. Moses wrote for his own generation and yet for the Church especially. This reading, which is quite plausible but not taken by the majority of commentators, also enables Kaiser to argue that Moses' agricultural guidance is one and the same meaning as that claimed by Paul. He then argues, as does Garland, that the wider context of Deut 25:4 is concern for the just treatment of others and that Paul's interpretation reads the command within this context and is justified in applying it to the treatment of gospel workers.[135] Similarly, David Instone-Brewer argues that 1 Cor 9:9c should be understood as meaning "not said for the ox's sake": that the command was given for *people* to obey, not for oxen, and that its intention is human flourishing through ethical treatment of livestock.[136] Instone-Brewer argues that Paul's interpretation of Deut 25:4 is consistent with some rabbinic interpretation which emphasises the human benefit of keeping this law. However, this does not dissolve the difficulty that Deut 25:4 is about oxen yet Paul writes that it is not about oxen but Gospel ministers. Paul apparently assumes that the command has a single meaning, and that meaning is to do with the material support of ministry. Given the Pauline claim that Scripture is "written for our learning," there is no need to speculate that Paul perceives an ethical theme within the literary context of Deut 25:4, nor consciously builds upon a tradition of interpretation, in order to explain why he interprets Scripture in a way that post-Enlightenment readers would not interpret it.

Heb 3:7—4:11

Single meaning as an assumed hermeneutical principle behind the interpretation of Scripture can also be seen where a New Testament author engages in interpretation which consciously attempts to deny other possible interpretations of the same text. In such cases, the interpreter suggests that no alternative to their interpretation can seriously be entertained. Interpretation, here, proceeds from an assumption of single meaning. Yet such interpretation is unusual. Interpretations of Scripture in the New Testament are most often simply asserted, without explanation or reference to an exegetical process. Therefore, alternative interpretations are rarely mentioned explicitly, even if they are being challenged by the interpretation being given.

---

135. Garland, *1 Corinthians*, 410.
136. Instone-Brewer, "1 Corinthians 9:9–11," 554–65.

The use of Ps 95:7–11 in Heb 3–4 is one example of an interpretation of Scripture in the New Testament that assumes a single meaning. At no point does the author of Hebrews offer anything that could be regarded as a hermeneutical statement, though the use of multiple exegetical arguments to claim one particular meaning for the idea of "rest" in Ps 95:11 is revealing. Scholars like Graham Hughes, R. T. France, Ken Schenk, and Susan E. Docherty who have made substantial contributions to the understanding of the interpretation of Scripture in Hebrews, have done so on the basis of what the author actually does with Scripture, including the manner in which scriptural excerpts are introduced with citation formulae, without explicit statements about the meaning of Scripture in Hebrews with which to engage.[137] Even if one takes 4:12–13 to be about Scripture, its interest is far more to do with what the word of God does, than what it is about. In Heb 3:7—4:13, the author of Hebrews attempts to deny the interpretation of Ps 95 that views the threat of v. 11 as referring simply to the past: a threat to the wilderness generation—they would not enter into the Promised Land.

> For we who have believed enter into that rest, as he said "so I swore in my wrath that they will not enter into my rest," though his works were finished since the foundation of the world. For he said somewhere concerning the seventh day, "and God rested on the seventh day from all his works" and this again, "that they will not enter into my rest." Since, therefore, it remains for some to enter into it, whilst those who first had the good news proclaimed to them did not enter through unbelief, God again appointed a certain day, "today," saying through David after this time, as has been said already, "today if you hear my voice, do not harden your hearts." For if Joshua had given them rest, he would not have spoken of another day after this time. Therefore, there remains a Sabbath rest for the people of God, for the one who enters into his rest has rested from his works, as God rested from his own. (Heb 4:3–10)

The author employs a variety of arguments to persuade his audience to reject this interpretation. Firstly, he appears to assume that the "today" of the psalm must make the psalm relevant for the "today" of his hearers

---

137. Hughes, *Hebrews and Hermeneutics*; Schenk, "God has Spoken," 321–26; France, "Writer of Hebrews," 245–76; Willi-Plein, "Some Remarks," 25–35; and Docherty, *Use of the Old Testament*. A possible exception to this is the reflection upon the relation of the prophets to the ministry of the son in Heb 1:1–2 in Smillie, "Contrast or Continuity," 543–51.

(3:12–13). Secondly, he uses the rabbinic exegetical principle of *gezerah shewah* to explain the meaning of "my rest" in the psalm through comparison with "God rested" in Gen 2:2. His contention here is that "rest" does not mean "land" but must be understood in relation to God's rest as the climax of his act of creation. Through this comparison, "rest" is defined as something heavenly and, perhaps, eschatological. Finally, the author of Hebrews argues that because the psalm is by David, "rest" cannot refer to the land. The psalm came into being some time after Joshua led Israel into the land, so that when the Holy Spirit says through David that those who fail to hear God's voice in the correct manner will not enter his rest, that rest must be something other than the Promised Land.[138] The author of Hebrews attempts to deny a certain interpretation of Ps 95:7–11 as, in effect, promising possession of the land to those who long for just that, whether before or after the destruction of the Temple. Clear in the author's mind is an understanding that the psalm does not mean what others think it means, because it means what he argues that it means. This is an assumption of single meaning. Whereas single meaning is derived from sectarian eschatology in 1 Peter and perhaps Romans and 1 Corinthians, single meaning is understood in this part of Hebrews to be derived from particular ideas about the author of Ps 95. This identification of meaning with the supposed Davidic origin of the psalm is also likely to be a result of a salvation-historical narrative. Such recourse to the identity of an author in interpretation as witnessed in Heb 3–4 is almost without precedent in the early Jewish and Hellenistic milieu of the New Testament period. Some have argued that this type of interpretation is an expression of the seventh exegetical rule attributed to Hillel in *b. Sanh.* 7.11, *a word discerned by its context*.[139] However, this is most unlikely, since the context Hillel might have been interested in was literary context rather than historical context: how a text can be explained by its context within its own narrative or other passages near it, rather than the historical situation or person from which the text came to be.[140] The Davidic geographical setting of Ps 95 is not obviously a feature of the psalm's literary context, though it might be implied by a superscription if such was available to the author of Hebrews. The most probable inspiration behind this unusual approach to single meaning is unlikely to be contemporary exegetical technique, but rather the particular

---

138. Sargent, *David Being a Prophet*, 14–17.

139. E.g., Longenecker, *Biblical Exegesis*, 182. Cf. Longenecker, "Early Church Interpretation," 87.

140. Sargent, "דבר הלמד מעניינו."

theology of the past in Hebrews. Rather than assuming a theological narrative substructure which emphasises a discontinuity between Israel's past and the Church's present, Hebrews depicts Israel's history as occupied by a succession of witnesses of which Jesus Christ is the last and greatest.[141] David is mentioned as one of these witnesses from the past in Heb 11:32 and it is likely that the author of Hebrews identified Ps 95 as a voice of witness from the past because of the integrity given to people of the past by the Hebrews' view of history. Whereas, the prophets are depicted as ignorant of the meaning of their words in 1 Pet 1:10-12, for Hebrews it matters immensely that David spoke Psalm 95 as a conscious witness to Jesus Christ and the eschatological "rest" he would provide for the people of God.

Mark 12:35-37 and parallels

The single meaning of Scripture is also an apparent assumption in the interpretation of Ps 110:1 in Mark 12:35-37 and its synoptic parallels, a pericope traditionally referred to for convenience as the *Davidssohnfrage*. Here, Jesus interprets the scriptural excerpt with reference to its origins on the lips of David. "If David calls [the Messiah] Lord [in the psalm], how can he be his son?" While there is a degree of ambiguity regarding what this pericope is intended to convey in terms of the exact identity of the Messiah, the use of Ps 110:1 is meant to undermine a simple understanding of the Messiah as the son of David. It is unclear whether the use of the psalm provides a straightforward denial of the Messiah as the son of David: this would be problematic in view of the identification of Jesus' Davidic identity and descent in the Synoptic Gospels.[142] Of course, the pericope may also never have been intended to sit side-by-side with material claiming Davidic sonship for Jesus. Whose son is the Messiah then? The Son of God?[143] The Son of Man?[144] What is beyond doubt is that the exegetical argument of Mark 12:35-37 is intended to limit the meaning of the psalm by denying the possibility of its interpretation in support of

---

141. Löhr, "Geschichtliches Denken," 446-47. As Smillie, "Contrast or Continuity," 543-51 has shown, Heb 1:1-2 does not imply a stark qualitative contrast between the prophets of Israel's past and the revelation in the last days through a son. See also the "cloud of witnesses," culminating in Jesus the author of faith in Heb 11:4-12:2.

142. The position taken by Wrede, *Vorträge und Studien*, 166; and Burger, *Jesus als Davidssohn*, 52-59. Against which, see Fitzmyer, "Son of David Tradition," 44.

143. Kingsbury, "Son of David," 596 and Levin, "Son of God," 415-42.

144. Neugebauer, "Die Davidssohnfrage," 91-96.

the Davidic sonship of the Messiah. Its meaning is assumed to be simple and single: it is assumed that it offers unambiguous proof of the theory of the Messiah as somewhat more than a son of David. What is more, the exegetical argument assumes that the meaning of the psalm can only be disclosed once its authorship is taken into account: that its meaning is totally contingent upon David as its author or speaker.[145]

While the practice of providing scriptural proof texts is widespread in the New Testament and betrays assumptions that scriptural texts have an unambiguous single meaning, the *Davidssohnfrage* is important inasmuch as it exposes the hermeneutical basis for the belief in single meaning: the limitation imposed upon interpretation by the identity of a supposed author. This explanation for single meaning is, of course, uncharacteristic when considering other New Testament and early Christian scriptural interpretation. While some have argued to the contrary, it is most unlikely that Paul shares such an interest of how the identity of an author guides interpretation, particularly as seen in the famous example from 1 Cor 9:8–11. While the single meaning of Scripture appears to be a common assumption of New Testament writers, it is an assumption held for a variety of reasons, understood within a variety of hermeneutical frameworks.

Mark 10:2–9 and Matt 19:3–9

Another example of interpretation which clearly assumes single meaning might be the interpretation of the Deuteronomic institution of divorce in Mark 10:2–9 and the parallel in Matt 19:3–9.

> But Jesus said to them, "because of your hardness of heart Moses wrote you this command, but from the beginning of creation "God made them male and female [Gen 1:27]. For this reason, a man shall leave his father and mother and be joined to his wife and the two will be one flesh [Gen 2:24]." So they are no longer two, but one flesh. Therefore, what God has joined together let no-one separate." (Mark 10: 5–9)

While the religious authorities consider the passage from Deuteronomy to establish divorce as a legitimate and justifiable conclusion to a

---

145. Sargent, *David Being a Prophet*, 100–4; Gould, *Gospel According to St. Mark*, 236; Loader, "Christ at the Right Hand," 200; Cullmann, *Christology of the New Testament*, 131 and Bateman, "Psalm 110:1," 445.

marriage, Jesus interprets it in the light of Gen 1:27/2:24 to undermine that interpretation and claim quite the opposite. According to Jesus, Deuteronomy simply introduces divorce as a possibility for sinful Israel. This is achieved because of a hermeneutic for reading the law: that the law was given because of the hardness of heart of God's people and must be interpreted in the light of this historical purpose. While this is not explicit, Carroll D. Osburn notes the probability that the exegetical argument rests upon a chronological distinction between Genesis and Deuteronomy, which claims the former as more authoritative through precedence or antiquity.[146] Since Gen 1:27/2:24 is older that Deut 24:1-4, it represents something far more permanent than the institution of divorce, which is by contrast claimed to be temporary and its authority relativized.[147] This argument is similar in nature to that in Gal 3:17, where the law is contrasted negatively with the Abrahamic promises, because it was apparently instituted 430 years after the Abraham's covenant with God. The opposite view of scriptural antiquity and authority is assumed in Heb 7:11. Here, Ps 110:4 has value because it is later, or more recent, than the law instituting the levitical priesthood: if the old priesthood was sufficient, why was there the need for Ps 110:4 to introduce another form of priesthood after the order of Melchizedek? asks Hebrews. Perhaps the most significant difference between these arguments and that of Mark 10:5-9 is that chronological distinction only represents part of the argument about the interpretation of Deut 24:1-4. Perhaps more significant is the giving of a reason for introduction of divorce that claims that Deut 24:1-4 is contingent upon a particular situation in Israel's history which limits the authority and scope of the scriptural text. This situation is far more specific than any Pauline claim about the law vis-à-vis the temporary nature of its jurisdiction. As Fitzmyer argues, the exegetical argument about divorce here is indeed very unusual, especially inasmuch as it seeks to move a well-established debate away from its principal text through a claim that appears to denigrate that text.[148] Of course, Deut 24:1-4 is not entirely condemned. As the question of the Pharisees admits (Mark 10:4), Moses "permits" divorce in Deuteronomy, which by no means implies a view of divorce as good or compulsory in certain cases. Similarly, as R. J. Banks observes, Jesus' argument doesn't seek to claim that Moses

---

146. Osburn, "Present Indicative," 199.

147. Blomberg, "Matthew," 61.

148. Fitzmyer, "Matthean Divorce Texts," 197-226. Cf. Laney, "Deuteronomy 24:1-4," 14.

words in Deuteronomy are his own, whereas the references to Genesis are God's own words.[149] What is clear, however, is that Jesus' exegetical approach to Gen 1:27/2:24 and Deut 24:1–4 witnesses to yet another understanding of single meaning in the New Testament, in this case, an assumption about the reason for the giving of the law. This assumption limits the potential meaning of Deut 24:1–4 and is the basis for the claim that the vision of marriage offered in Genesis still remains.

Acts 2:14–39

The Pentecost Speech of Acts 2:14–39 provides multiple examples of scriptural interpretation that assume single meaning. Firstly, Joel 2:2 8–32 is interpreted on the basis of straightforward correspondence between the apparent referent of the prophecy and the situation on that day of Pentecost. There is no doubt for Peter that "this is what was spoken about through the prophet Joel (Acts 2:16)." This interpretation of Joel as a having a single referent in history, now fulfilled, is partly a feature of the prophecy itself which envisages a certain period called the "last days" in which the events it describes will take place and partly a result of the Lukan conviction that the whole of Scripture "from Moses and all the prophets" (Luke 20:27) finds its fulfilment in the ministry of Jesus Christ, which in Acts is still underway as Christ begins his heavenly session.

Of greater complexity, but from the same assumption about the single referent of prophecy, is the subsequent interpretation of Ps 16:8–11.

> Men, brothers, I can say to you with confidence about the patriarch David that he died and was buried and that his tomb is with us to this day. But being therefore a prophet, and seeing that God has sworn an oath to place one of his descendants upon his throne, he foresaw and said concerning the resurrection of Christ that "he was not abandoned to Hades, nor did his flesh see decay." (Acts 2:29–31)

Here, Peter interprets the psalmist's claim that he will not see the decay of death as a reference to the resurrection of Jesus Christ. This is achieved through a definition of the psalm's assumed author, David, as a prophet (Acts 2:30). The psalm cannot refer to David because it is well-known that David died, yet the psalm appears to promise immortality to its speaker. As with other early Christian and Jewish scriptural interpretation, the

149. Banks, *Jesus and the Law*, 146–51.

psalm must have an identifiable referent: the word of God return without accomplishing its purpose.[150] But because David is understood to be a prophet, the psalm is understood as a prophecy of the Christ, not a description of David's own future.[151] Through this interpretation, it is likely that a number of other possible interpretations are consciously denied. Peter denies that the psalm can refer to David because David is dead and his tomb is well-known to be in Jerusalem (2:29). *Ps Midr* 16 witnesses to an early interpretation of the psalm as referring to the state of David's entombed corpse: that it has not decayed or seen corruption. Peter appears to deny this interpretation by establishing the nature of the psalm as messianic prophecy.[152] As Gregory V. Trull concludes, Luke/Peter does not argue for a theologically defined, Christological *sensus plenior*, but rather aims for a single interpretation on the basis of an assumption about the identity of David as the author of Ps 16.[153]

A similar argument to that concerning David's grave is used to explicitly deny an interpretation of Ps 110:1 as referring to David in Acts 2:34.

> For David did not ascend to the heavens, but he said, "the Lord said to my Lord, 'sit at my right hand, until I place your enemies as a footstool for your feet.'"

Here, popular knowledge that David did not ascend to heaven is drawn upon to show that the one to be seated at the right hand of God could not possibly be David. The denial of rival interpretations of a passage is evident in the Pentecost Speech, doubtless a reflection of earliest Christian preaching, rather than a record of an impromptu sermon.[154] This denial of alternative interpretation is a significant indicator of an assumption of single meaning. Again, as in Hebrews 3–4, the exegetical interest in David as the author of the psalm is likely to be dependent upon the specific salvation-historical narrative of Luke-Acts and the Lukan approach to Scripture as "proof from prophecy." Because Luke engages in a conscious attempt to demonstrate that the events he records are fundamentally fulfilment of Scripture, the idea of David as a prophet, itself unusual, is of immense value in claiming Ps 16 as a prophetic text. As in Hebrews

---

150. Strauss, *Davidic Messiah*, 138.

151. Sargent, *David Being a Prophet*, 62–63; Jervell, *Die Apostelgeschichte*, 147; and Fitzmyer, "'Being Therefore a Prophet,'" 332.

152. Juel, "Social Dimensions," 547–48; and Sargent, *David Being a Prophet*, 81–82.

153. Trull, "Views on Peter's Use," 205.

154. Bowker, "Speeches in Acts," 96–111; and Soards, *Speeches in Acts*.

and 1 Peter, the assumption of single meaning is not a coincidence: it is a feature of the essential theological nature of writing.

1 Peter

The exclusively Christological and ecclesiological orientation of Scripture defined in the "hermeneutical statement" of 1 Pet 1:10–12 appears to be demonstrated in the use Scripture in the epistle. A particularly clear example of the hermeneutic of 1:10–12 in practice is in the use of a collection of three "stone" texts in 1 Pet 2:6–10—Isa 28:16; Ps 118:22; and Isa 8:14.[155] While each of these texts are employed elsewhere in the New Testament, there is insufficient evidence that Peter had access to them as part of a testimonia collection and, indeed, Peter's use of these texts appears to be distinctive.[156] Romans 9:32–33, for example, uses the same form of the Greek text of Isa 28:16 as 1 Pet 2:6 (and uses Isa 8:14 too) to establish Jesus as Israel's "stumbling stone." In Eph 2:20, Isa 28:16 is alluded to in order to establish the Church as a "living temple," built on Christ as the "cornerstone." First Peter appears to combine both the christological and ecclesiological emphases of these uses as he attempts to present the community to which he writes as the elect "Temple Community," similar to the qumranic conception.[157]

It seems most unlikely that the use of these stone texts is typological: that Peter conceives of them as referring to Israel before they refer to the Church.[158] Indeed, as M. Black contends, the use of this stone material is anti-Jewish and supercessionist.[159] Peter appears to be claiming that these texts refer simply to the Church, without any sense that they have a prior meaning.[160] Likewise, the Qumranic interpretations of these texts assume that the Qumran community is their single referent. In 1QS 8:7

---

155. Hines, "Peter and the Prophetic Word," 235; and Schutter, *Hermeneutic and Composition*, 123.

156. Other use of these texts is detailed in Hillyer, "Rock-Stone," 58–60. Best, "1 Peter II: 4–10," 270–93, argues that the "Catena" is not traditional but that the texts were chosen by Peter.

157. Mbuvi, *Temple, Exile, and Identity*, 98; Elliott, *Elect and the Holy*, 38 and 219; Schlosser, "Ancien Testament," 65; and Goppelt, *Typos*, 153.

158. Though Green, *1 Peter*, 63 and Goppelt, *Typos*, 153 argue that the use of these texts is typological.

159. Black, "Christological Use," 11–12.

160. Sargent, *Written to Serve*, 68 and Best, "Spiritual Sacrifice," 280–90.

these "stones" are the heads of the twelve tribes of restored Israel, understood as derived from the Qumran community; in 1QHod 6:26 they are the Sons of Truth and in 4QIsa 54:12 they are the current leaders of the Qumran community. This orientation of Scripture towards the eschatological community is mirrored in 1 Peter, for whom the prophets of Israel's past wrote to serve the community who would one day have the Gospel proclaimed to them (1 Pet 1:10–12).

As I have argued elsewhere, an exclusive application of scriptural texts to the eschatological situation of the Christian community is a consistent feature of 1 Peter, suggestive of a theory of single meaning established in 1 Pet 1:10–12.[161] While this is not the place to detail each use of Scripture which adheres to this theory of single meaning in the epistle, it is worth noting two other uses of Scripture, one immediately before and one immediately after the use of the "stone" texts. At the end of chapter 1, Peter provides a quotation from Isa 40:6 and 8 concluding with the phrase "but the word of the Lord remains forever." Peter's interpretation claims that the referent of this phrase is the particular message preached to the communities to which he writes: "and this is the word which was proclaimed as good news to you." The general statement of Isa 40:8 is made specific by Peter in relation to the Church. Rather than Isa 40:8 offering a description of the word of God through all time, of which the message preached to the Church is but one example, Peter reads Isa 40:8 as a simple prophecy of that message alone. This is, of course, consistent with Peter's view that the prophets of Israel's past, Isaiah included, wrote to serve those who have now had the message of the Gospel proclaimed to them (1 Pet 1:12). Similarly, in 1 Pet 2:10, at the conclusion of the argument about belong to the people of God that employed the three stone texts, Peter alludes to the opening chapters of Hosea to describe the specific situation of the communities to which he writes. The names of Hosea's symbolic children, intended to convey Israel's condemnation and restoration, are applied directly to the Church: "once you were *not a people*, but now you are the people of God: then you had *not received mercy* but now you have received mercy." Of course, whether an allusion to Hosea was meant to be heard here is open to question (though it is assumed by most scholars),[162] there is no evidence that Peter uses this text as though its meaning is for both Israel in the past and the Church in the

---

161. Sargent, *Written to Serve*, 50–146. Cf. Sargent, "Narrative Substructure," 489.

162. Sargent, *Written to Serve*, 122–23; and Jobes, "Minor Prophets," 135–54.

present: there is no evidence to suggest that for Peter, Hosea's meaning is typological or that in applying the text to the Church he is providing its *sensus plenior*. These ideas belong to a different way of thinking about Scripture than Peter's eschatological view within which Scripture has a single meaning.

Jude 9

Another possible example of scriptural interpretation in which single meaning is assumed is the interpretation of the Archangel Michael's words in Jude 9. Wherever this quotation is taken from, it is likely that the actions of Michael in "reviling" the devil in his dispute over the body of Moses have significance for Jude's opponents.[163] The opponents assume this event is an example of "reviling" that might be imitated. The evidence for this underlying issue is the incongruence of Jude himself introducing a problematic scriptural allusion and accompanying quotation. Jude has no need otherwise to introduce Michael contending with the devil: it is a potential obstacle to his argument that needs to be addressed. Jude wishes to make plain that the interpretation of his opponents is not warranted by the direct speech associated with this event, which claims "reviling" as something only to be done by God himself. Again, in a very simple sense, the denial of one false interpretation and the assertion of another held to be true rests upon an assumption of the text's single meaning. Jude is not suggesting that his opponents have failed to see the full significance of the scriptural text: they are simply wrong and do not understand the meaning of the text.

Revelation

The book of Revelation does not appear to have what one might regard as a hermeneutical statement reflecting the author's understanding of how or why Scripture refers to the images and events he takes Scripture to refer to. However, it cannot be doubted that Revelation employs allusions to Scripture as though it is straightforwardly prophetic, finding its true fulfilment in the eschatological divine drama. As Richard Bauckham suggests,

---

163. Schäfer, "Nachbiblische Traditionen," 147–74.

> John was writing what he understood to be a work of prophetic scripture, the climax of prophetic revelation, which gathered up the prophetic meaning of the Old Testament scriptures and disclosed the way in which it was being and was to be fulfilled in the last days. His work therefore presupposes and conveys an extensive interpretation of large parts of the Old Testament.[164]

For the most part, Scripture is interpreted in Revelation following a principle that G. K. Beale and Sean M. McDonough term "eschatological enhancement."[165] Rather than making the fulfilment of Scripture explicit through the use of citation formulae, scriptural images and events are re-used and elaborated as though they have always truly referred to the events that concern Revelation. For example, the scroll of Ezek 2:9–10 is picked up in Rev 5:1. Whereas God opens Ezekiel's scroll, only the lamb can open the scroll in Revelation; whereas the scroll in Ezekiel is full of lamentation and woe, the scroll in Revelation tastes bitter. Rather than offering another similar vision to that of Ezek 2:9–10, Rev 5:1 re-tells and applies Ezekiel's vision to give it its true significance.[166] As John Sweet observes, Revelation clarifies and expands the vision of Ezekiel, since it is concerned to provide a "Christian re-reading of the whole Jewish scriptural heritage."[167] Similarly, as D. Matthewson observes, scriptural prophecy provides the basis for the vision of a new creation in Rev 21:1—22:5.[168] For example, the distinction between new heavens and a new earth in Isa 65:17 provides an organising principle for Rev 21:1—22:5, which both alludes to Isa 65 and elaborates on its meaning. Likewise, the promise of a new exodus in Isa 43:18–19 is expanded in Rev 21:5 and applied to the situation it truly refers to: the future exodus of God's people from Babylon to the new Jerusalem.

The reason for this application of Scripture to John's immediate future, rather than Israel's past, has to do with an understanding of that future as part of age of fulfilment. This is seen in Rev 22:10, in which the words of the scroll cannot be sealed up because the time of fulfilment is near. As Bauckham notes, Revelation adopts the scroll of the vision from Dan 8:26 and 12:4.[169] Whereas in Daniel the scrolls are sealed because

---

164. Bauckham, *Climax of Prophecy*, xi.
165. Beale and McDonough, "Revelation," 1085.
166. Bauckham, *Climax of Prophecy*, 246.
167. Sweet, *Revelation*, 39–40.
168. Matthewson, *New Heaven and a New Earth*, 217–18.
169. Bauckham, *Climax of Prophecy*, 251.

they relate to the future, in Revelation the seals are broken because the age of fulfilment has now arrived. In a manner similar to 1 Pet 1:10–12, the prophetic witness of Israel's past is something of a mystery, meant to have meaning only in relation to the future. This can be seen in Rev 10:5–7, in which an angel announces that the moment in which the "mystery of God," spoken by the prophets in the past, is to be fulfilled without delay. This notion that the meaning of Scripture is somehow obscured until the moment of fulfilment is common to apocalyptic Jewish literature and bears particular comparison with 1QpHab 7. 1–8. As Elizabeth Schüssler Fiorenza contends, the closest parallel to the use of Scripture in Revelation is the exegetical literature of Qumran.[170] In a manner similar to many exegetical documents from Qumran, the exegetical interest of Revelation is not towards understanding the Scriptures, but using Scripture to understand the revelation that is occurring in the author's historical and theological situation, which is also the fulfilment of those prophetic Scriptures. This interpretation assumes that the meaning of scriptural prophecy is singular, on account of the nature of salvation history which reaches its climax in the revelation of Jesus Christ: the moment in which the mystery of God finds its fulfilment.

Evangelical Treatment of Hermeneutical Issues Raised by the Use of Scripture in the New Testament

While many have undertaken the study of the use of Scripture in the New Testament as a purely historical enquiry, without seeing any theological or hermeneutical significance to the subject apart from what it reveals about earliest Christianity, for many evangelical scholars the use of Scripture in the New Testament is naturally part of a broader theological and hermeneutical discussion. In many ways, evangelical scholarship on the use of Scripture in the New Testament has pursued its own, often very detailed, areas of study from the conviction that the earliest Christian interpretation of Scripture is important for the theological interpretation of the Old Testament and, in some cases, needs to be justified. Several of these "in-house" discussions have a bearing upon the analysis of the use of Scripture offered in this chapter, vis-à-vis the assumption of its single meaning in the New Testament. Of particular interest is the debate between Steve Moyise and G. K. Beale on the use of Scripture in Revelation,

---

170. Schüssler Fiorenza, *Book of Revelation*, 136.

which extends to discussions of the nature of textual meaning and authorial intent, subjects many scholars schooled in historical criticism would consider as being outside of their interests and expertise. The other "in-house" evangelical debate discussed below relates to the issue of whether or not the New Testament provides something like a *sensus plenior* for the Scripture it interprets and, if so, how that "full sense" relates to authorial or historic meaning. These two debates are important because they revolve around the subject of whether New Testament authors understood themselves to be supplementing another prior meaning of Scripture as they interpreted it, or whether they saw themselves as supplying what they thought of as the true, single meaning of texts, as has been argued above is most often the case.

The Debate between Moyise and Beale

The debate between Moyise and Beale over the issue of whether the use of Scripture in the book of Revelation features the misreading of biblical texts, explored early Christian interpretation of Scripture within the context of hermeneutical questions, such as the limitation on meaning posed by authorial intention.[171] At the heart of this debate is the question of the singularity of scriptural meaning, with Beale maintaining that Revelation uses Scripture in accordance with its original meaning. Steve Moyise's monograph on the use of Scripture in Revelation appeared in 1995, closely followed by G. K. Beale's in 1998.[172] Beale took issue with Moyise's claim that YHWH's promise to Eliakim in Isa 22:22 is taken out of context in Rev 3:7. Beale argued that John would have taken Isa 22:22 to be an historical statement about Eliakim, not a prophecy and so read it typologically as something that could apply to Christ.[173] Beale claimed that Moyise rejected the idea the Revelation interprets Scripture

---

171. While one might dispute whether this is an "in-house" evangelical debate, rather than an evangelical (Beale) versus liberal (Moyise) debate, it is worth noting where this debate started. Steve Moyise's reflections on the questions involved in the debate began with an article in the evangelical Anglican journal *Anvil* (Moyise, "Does the NT Quote," 133–43). This article was itself an engagement with another article from an evangelical journal (Longenecker, "Who is the Prophet Talking About," 4–8).

172. Moyise, *Old Testament in the Book of Revelation* and Beale, *John's Use of the Old Testament in Revelation*. Much of this debate is detailed in Paulien, "Dreading the Whirlwind," 5–22 to which the discussion here is indebted.

173. Beale, *Old Testament in Revelation*, 117–18.

in continuity with authorial intent, arguing that rather than creating new meaning, Revelation simply places scriptural texts in new contexts which provide new significance. Beale used the analogy of a basket of fruit: an apple, even when removed from its context in the fruit bowl, still remains an apple. Just so, the meaning of a scriptural text is essentially retained when placed in a new context in the book of Revelation.[174]

The next year, Moyise responded by arguing that Beale was obscuring the difference between what Revelation does with Scripture and the historical/authorial meaning of Scripture.[175] He claimed Beale was drawing a false distinction between meaning and significance, based on an apparent fixity in the idea of meaning. Moyise outlined three areas of perceived difference between his view and Beale's: whether Revelation gives new meanings; whether texts are taken out of context; whether meaning is derived purely from authorial intention or through reader response also. Moyise's view, drawing upon the idea of *intertextuality*, defined in the work of Julia Kristeva, places emphasis upon the varying relations of text to contexts, raising the question of whether a text can ever have the sort of essential meaning that Beale assumes. Each act of interpretation within and for a new context, such as that of Revelation, necessarily entails the creation of new meaning, not simply the extension of original meaning. In response, Beale reiterated that it is new significance, not new meaning, that is created by John.[176] Drawing upon the work of Hirsch and Vanhoozer on authorial intent, Beale argued for a surplus of meaning, that the meaning intended by the human authors of Scripture could exceed their intentions and yet be in complete sympathy with them. In applying Scripture to a newly-conceived eschatological context, John was aware of what scriptural texts "meant" and simply saw a new significance in that meaning. He argued that the prophets themselves would have understood this new significance as the true meaning of their sayings had they been alive to see the interpretive context in which their words were now to be understood.

At this point in the debate, J. Paulien published an analysis of some of the issues involved. Paulien suggested that in *John's Use of the Old Testament in Revelation*, Beale sees Moyise as a radical reader-response

---

174. Ibid., 51–52.

175. Moyise, "Reply to Greg Beale," 54–58. Cf. Moyise, "Language of the Old Testament," 97–113; Moyise, "Intertextuality," 14–41 and Moyise, "Models for Intertextual Interpretation," 31–45.

176. Beale, "Questions of Authorial Intent," 152–80.

critic, making the text mean whatever he wants it to mean.[177] This analysis seems to imply that the issue for Beale is Moyise's own approach to the interpretation of Scripture, not his understanding of what John does with Scripture, necessarily. However, Paulien argued that Moyise and Beale are really not that different: indeed both are trying to claim a sense of appropriateness about the use of Scripture in Revelation. Paulien suggested that the fruits of their exegesis of Revelation would probably be similar if Moyise were to write a commentary. However, Paulien criticised Beale's identification with Hirsch, noting that Hirsch's account of authorial intention, as something identified through objective historical awareness, is not something the author of Revelation is interested in.[178] Furthermore, Paulien claimed that many of the answers are somewhere between Moyise and Beale. The author of Revelation reads Scripture in the light of Scripture and the bigger salvation-historical narrative of which both Scripture and the Church of Jesus Christ are a part. This is "responsible" exegesis in that John would certainly have thought that the prophets would agree with the interpretation he gives to their words, but it is also interpretation that seeks to meet the needs and understanding of the communities for which Revelation was written. Beale went on to respond to Paulien himself, claiming that Paulien had misrepresented his view of authorial intention.[179] Authorial intention, Beale argued, should be understood as a broad concept, involving the authors own awareness that his/her work stands within a narrative within which it will legitimately be read to suit a variety of contexts. Yet each of these new readings should maintain a governing relation to the limited meaning of the texts original and authorial context.

However, for Moyise, this blurring of the lines of authorial intention as traditionally understood within historical critical biblical scholarship fails to account for the disjuncture between what scriptural texts seem to have meant in their earliest contexts and the use Revelation makes of them.[180] Again, Moyise disputed the claim of Beale that Ezekiel has new significance not new meaning in Revelation. A restored temple is what Ezekiel meant but Revelation speaks of an absent temple. It is quite different, Moyise argued, and not in obvious continuity with what Ezekiel en-

177. Paulien, "Dreading the Whirlwind," 15–19.

178. See discussion in Sargent, *David Being a Prophet*, qualifying the identification of NT authors with exegetical interest in authorship.

179. Beale, "Response to John Paulien," 23–34.

180. Moyise, "Misappropriate the Scriptures," 3–21.

visages. However, Moyise contended that the meaning given to Scripture in Revelation is not arbitrary. Drawing upon the work of Thomas Greene, Moyise sought to define what Revelation does with Scripture as "dialectical imitation," seeking a trajectory of interpretation from original meaning to contemporary context. Revelation does not transform Scripture into something new and utterly unrecognizable: Ezekiel is still plainly Ezekiel in its imitation in Revelation. However, neither is the new interpretive context provided by Revelation overwhelmed by the limitations of the single authorial meaning of Ezekiel. Instead, this new interpretive context permits certain elements of Ezekiel to be changed to provide a meaning that makes sense within the next context.

> John is serious about the original context of his allusions, in so far as the trajectories have a starting point. But his focus is not on that starting point. It is on what has happened since, as a clue to what is still to come. John is a seer not a scholar.[181]

The apparent motivation for the debate between Moyise and Beale appears to be the need to demonstrate that the use of Scripture in the Revelation is acceptable in some sense. For Beale, it can only be acceptable if it can be demonstrated that Revelation does not distort the single, authorial meaning of Scripture. For Moyise, the use of Scripture in Revelation can only be seen as acceptable if one abandons the need to judge early Christian interpretation by the standards of Modernity. The argument of this chapter has been that, regardless of whether one agrees with the interpretation of Scripture in Revelation, John's own view appears to be that Scripture has a single meaning, though this meaning is governed not by authorial context but by his own eschatological context.

Sensus Plenior

For the most part, scholars working on the use of Scripture in the New Testament have shown little interest in issues relating to multiplicity of meaning. However, the single meaning of Scripture in the New Testament has been of significant interest to some evangelical scholars working in this area. The place where this issue receives some of the most concentrated attention is the introductory but rigorously detailed book *Three Views on the New Testament use of the Old Testament*, with substantial

181. Ibid., 21.

contributions from three prominent scholars: Walter C. Kaiser, Darrell L. Bock, and Peter Enns.

Kaiser argues for the single meaning of Scripture as received in the New Testament.[182] He argues that the interpretation of scriptural texts in the New Testament agrees substantially with what those texts were intended to mean when originally conceived. Because of this, Kaiser suggests that the New Testament writers were aware of and respected the original contexts of the scriptural material they interpret. The authors of Old Testament texts consequently were fully aware of the meaning of their words: indeed, the only thing they lack was a knowledge of the single referent of their words. A slightly different position is taken by Darrell L. Bock who argues that New Testament authors understood the single meaning of Scripture to relate to a variety of referents. As an example, Bock discusses the use of Ps 2:1–2 in Acts 4:25–26.[183] The psalm, with claims about the unique status of the Davidic king, is likely to be a general psalm like Ps 1, rather than one relating to a specific context. Bock notes that the psalm is alluded to in the different historical contexts of Pss Sol 17:21–25 and 4QFlor 1:18—2:2. Despite application of the text to different scenarios, the meaning of the text stays the same: that the nations must bow before God's chosen king. This meaning is applied to a new context in Acts 4:25–26 without any suggestion that it refers only to the situation of the early Church. Ps 2 is understood to have a single meaning but many referents as it witnesses to a broader principle. However, While Acts 4:25–26 by no means denies early claims about the referent of the text, nor does it consciously affirm them. Indeed, it may be somewhat anachronistic to infer that Luke knows the original setting of Ps 2 and its reception history. It must not be forgotten that much of the access New Testament authors had to Scripture was via the medium of testimonia collections. Here, excerpted texts would contain no information concerning their original literary or historical contexts.

The same historical factors are problematic for the view put forward by Peter Enns: that Scripture is understood in the New Testament as having a single Christological *telos*, but by no means lacks meaning without this.[184] Scripture has multiple meanings but a single goal: the ministry of Jesus Christ. An example Enns gives is the interpretation

---

182. Kaiser, "Single Meaning," 45–89
183. Bock, "Single Meaning," 125–29.
184. Enns, "Fuller Meaning," 167–217.

of Gen 13:14–16 in Gal 3:15–29, where Paul famously argues that the "seed" which bears the weight of God's promises to Abraham is singular, referring to Jesus Christ. Enns argues that Paul would have known that "seed" was a collective noun in Hebrew and does not necessarily refer to a single person. Likewise, Paul would have understood that the term refers too to the people of Israel as the plural seed of Abraham. Knowing that Gen 13:14–16 is a promise relating to Abraham's descendants, Paul seizes upon an aspect of the text which has Christological potential: the ambiguity of the collective noun "seed." This enables Paul to provide the promise made to Abraham with its fuller Christ-oriented meaning. The difficulty here is that Paul's interest in the prior meaning of these promises for Israel is assumed and by no means evident. An equally plausible analysis is that Paul wants to say that God's promise to Abraham to bless the world is realized exclusively through his one seed, Jesus Christ, rather than the circumcised people of Israel as once thought. This is certainly more consistent with Pauline "hermeneutical statements" which seem to imply an exclusively eschatological orientation for much of Scripture.

The difficulty with these and other evangelical assessments of singularity or multiplicity of scriptural meaning in the use of Scripture in the New Testament is that analysis is often clouded by the question of whether the use of Scripture in the New Testament is justified. Because of the influence of historical criticism upon evangelical scholarship, we wonder whether the use of Scripture in the New Testament is intellectually credible or whether it is fundamentally at odds with the hermeneutics of modern biblical scholarship. Because of this, it is possible to see scholars go to great lengths to demonstrate that the authorial intent of Old Testament writers is respected in the New Testament. Consequently, any account of scriptural hermeneutics in the New Testament proceeds from the assumption that New Testament authors are doing something with the original meaning of the texts they refer to, whether they extend it typologically or give it its full redemptive-historical meaning. This is even seen in the approach taken by Peter Enns, which permits for a significant disjuncture between the original meaning of Israel's Scriptures and that given in the New Testament. Even for Enns, the historically contingent meaning of texts is something New Testament authors are understood to be aware of, even if they treat it in theologically innovative ways. The difficulty here is that, not only is too much knowledge of authorial intent and original context on the part of New Testament authors assumed, but a hermeneutical interest in authorial intent and the meaning of texts to ancient audiences is assumed. With the exception of a small number of cases within the New Testament which I have documented elsewhere, there is simply too little evidence for these assumptions.[185] Doubtless the use of Scripture in the New Testament was intellectually robust enough to be persuasive to early Christians as rhetorical devices, but not on the basis of terms necessarily recognizable to a reader schooled in the hermeneutics of modernity. Once a need to see the original, author-intended meaning feature in the use of a certain scriptural text in the New Testament is placed to one side, it is somewhat easier to understand issues relating to singularity or multiplicity of meaning in the New Testament. Once a desire to justify what the New Testament does with Scripture is laid to rest, the distinctive hermeneutics of New Testament writers becomes more apparent. This problem ought to be seen as more closely related to the discussion of the inspiration and authority of Scripture. For some evangelicals, Scripture is understood to be true in every type of truth claim made within it, in statements about the natural world as much as upon the character of God. For others, perhaps the majority in the British evangelical context, the Bible's truthfulness does not extend to all of its claims which sit outside its dominant purpose in revealing the redeeming work of God. From this perspective, it is recognized that, for example, the opening chapters of Genesis are not to be read as though they were written to be heard as an exhaustive scientific account of the world's creation. The assumption is made that the authors of Genesis wanted to tell audiences about the Creator and the innate goodness, order and dignity of creation, not the exact process through which it came to be. This view of inspiration might extend to another assumption that the New Testament authors did not write to teach us hermeneutics or exegetical method. The New Testament authors ought to be permitted to fall short of modern interpretive values, since the modelling of exegesis was not the mission they saw themselves as having. Certainly, the charismatic element of Paul's interpretation of Scripture implies that his manner of interpreting Scripture is connected to his apostolic authority. To think that it exists to be mimicked would be to make a significant error.

Typology, in particular, is resorted too readily as a description of what a New Testament author is doing with a particular scriptural text. But unless there is evidence that the meaning of that text is both something historical *and* something present or future, such descriptions need

---

185. Sargent, *David Being a Prophet*, 163.

to be treated with caution. The dominant conception of Scripture in the New Testament is of text that awaited fulfilment until the coming of Jesus Christ. This does not necessarily imply that Scripture had another fulfilment or referent before the coming of Christ which itself relates to Christ typologically. To assume this is to go beyond the evidence and to deny something of the eschatological orientation of early Christianity.

Conclusion

The use of Scripture in the New Testament is utterly dominated by hermeneutical frameworks and salvation historical narratives, whether implicit or explicit, which demand that interpretation asserts a single meaning of texts. This hermeneutical assumption is so widespread that it has not been thought worthy of comment until now. It would possibly be anachronistic or, at least, misleading to label this treatment of Scripture as guided by a theory of determinate meaning given the complexities of this concept. Indeed, it would certainly be difficult to provide evidence of a dominant base interpretation which governs a series of other derived interpretations. Instead, one sees a simple assumption of single meaning. Insofar as it is ever substantiated, single meaning is a feature of interpretation derived from early Christian eschatology and salvation history. History has a single meaning because it is seen in 1 Peter as orientated towards a single eschatological reality: the ministry of Jesus Christ and his people. Peter and Paul both understand the prophets of Israel's past, or at the very least their inspiration in the past, as ultimately concerned with the people of God in the last days: Scripture is written for their learning, Scripture was written to serve them and their people. While the single meaning of Scripture is related to the Church of Jesus Christ as eschatologically distinct, it also relates to Church as spiritually or soteriologically distinct. According to Paul, those who are "in Christ" and who hear the old covenant, do so with the Mosaic veil lifted while those who hear it without Christ will never behold its glory, fading though it is.

Of course, so much of the use of Scripture in the New Testament occurs with little or no evidence with which to articulate possible hermeneutical perspective. Yet, even without an explicit hermeneutical statement about Scripture, it is possible to see a widespread assumption of single meaning: that the interpretation of Scripture is simple because meaning is unambiguous, done with authority and without fear that the meaning of a passage could be contested. The evidence appears to suggest that, for the most part, single meaning is a feature of eschatology, whether related to the central importance of Jesus Christ as the fulfilment of Scripture, or the Church itself as the eschatological community on whom the end of the ages has come. As Richard N. Longenecker concludes,

> As Christians, convinced by the resurrection of their Lord from the dead, they were prepared to stake their lives on the fact that in Jesus of Nazareth the focal point of God's redemption had been reached. From such a perspective, therefore, and employing concepts of corporate solidarity and correspondences in history, all the Old Testament became part-and-parcel of God's preparation for the Messiah. The Old Testament contained certain specific messianic predictions, but more than that it was "messianic prophecy" and "messianic doctrine" throughout when viewed from its intended and culminating focal point.[186]

Donald Juel tends to miss the significance of statements made about Scripture in the New Testament, focusing on the use of particular passages, yet also concludes appropriately:

> Overall, NT scriptural interpretation is more like the "sectarian" exegesis at Qumran than the "scholastic" exegesis in rabbinic literature. Eschatological convictions pervade everything: the prophetic dimensions of the Scriptures are central; the present is understood as the last days and as a time of fulfilled promises (1 Corinthians 10:11; Acts 2; Matthew 1–2; Luke 1–2; etc.) . . . In Luke and John it is explicitly stated that inspiration is required for a proper understanding of the Scriptures (2 Corinthians 3; John 6).[187]

---

186. Longenecker, *Biblical Exegesis*, 208.
187. Juel, *Messianic Exegesis*, 57.

2

Written for Christ
Single Meaning in the Fathers

It is something of a Church-historical commonplace to regard the earliest centuries of Christianity as representing a move away from thought influenced by Jewish apocalypticism towards the influence of Platonism and its Hellenistic successors. In the case of the theological frameworks that have made possible the reading of Scripture as though its meaning is determinate, this common assumption bears true. While, as the previous chapter attempted to demonstrate, single meaning in the New Testament period was a feature of eschatology and an understanding of the priority of the interpretive context in relation to time, single meaning in the Patristic period began to depend upon the metaphysical assumptions of allegorical interpretation. While eschatological or, at least, salvation-historical approaches to interpretation appear to dominate the reading of Scripture in some of the Apostolic Fathers, by the late Second Century some were beginning to claim a single allegorical meaning for scriptural texts. In the case of Origen, this single meaning is related to the perceived implausibility of the "literal" meaning of some texts. During the period explored in this chapter, the orientation of Scripture towards a single end becomes less eschatological and more theological. Whereas, one could argue that single meaning is the dominant assumption in earliest Christianity as evidenced in the New Testament, in this period single meaning becomes more of a minority position. However, at no point does single meaning disappear from Christian interpretation of Scripture in the period.

The Apostolic Fathers

There is much in the interpretation of Scripture in the Apostolic Fathers that differs little from the variety of approaches seen in the New Testament. With regard to the single meaning of Scripture, the ecclesiological and Christological hermeneutical frameworks which facilitate single meaning in the New Testament can also be witnessed in the Apostolic Fathers. The use of Scripture by Clement of Rome is case in point.

Clement of Rome

In 1 Clem 22:1-8, Ps 34:11-17, 20 (OG Ps 33:12-8, 20; Cf. 1 Pet 3:10-12) is quoted as the voice of Jesus Christ, spoken directly to "us," being Clement and the Corinthian Church. Yet more striking is the use of Scripture in 29:1-3. Here, Clement speaks of the election of the Church, citing in support Deut 32:8-9, which relates to the election of Israel. For Clement, Scripture is about the Church. While the eschatological element common in the New Testament is perhaps lacking, the centrality of the Church in the purposes of God is assumed. Therefore Scripture is seen to relate directly to the Church. The principal means of relating Scripture to the Church in 1 Clement is by citing scriptural characters, events and texts as examples to the Church in Corinth. Donald A. Hagner identifies examples of supposed literal, typological and allegorical interpretation in 1 Clement, suggesting that Clement's clear preference is for the former, often employed to provide such exemplars to serve the letter's paranetic purpose.[1] For example, in 1 Clem 12:7, Rahab is offered as an example of faithfulness. What is interesting here is that Rahab is seen not only as an exemplar of faith, but also as a prophet of salvation, since her red cord is understood as representing the saving blood of Christ (Cf. Justin, *Dial.* 111). This could be understood as typological or allegorical, depending on how one views those terms. What is interesting is that this additional prophetic meaning is not seen as a separate observation by Clement providing the *sensus plenior* of Rahab's action, but an inherent meaning stemming from Rahab's role as a prophet. While Clement does not offer an explicit "hermeneutical statement" as such, the single ecclesiological and Christological orientation of Scripture in 1 Clement appears to differ little from the thought of 1 Cor 10:11, albeit without an

---

1. Hagner, *Clement*, 126; Cf. Simonetti, *Biblical Interpretation*, 12.

obvious eschatological understanding of the significance of the Church. As Hagner concludes,

> For Clement the OT is a thoroughly Christian book which is directly pertinent to the contemporary Church in Corinth. Indeed, so timeless is the OT revelation for Christ that the adjective "Old" would doubtless have seemed singularly inappropriate to him.[2]

Pseudo Barnabas

Quite a different approach to the single meaning of Scripture is seen in the pseudonymous Epistle of Barnabas. Here, the true meaning of Scripture is discerned through "perfect knowledge" (1.5). While this "knowledge" is not explicitly linked to the correct interpretation of Scripture, its delivery to the Church is stated as the purpose of the letter and the letter is dominated by the interpretation of Scripture.[3] It is possible that the concept is expanded in 2.7: "for the master (*despotēs*) has made known to us, through the prophets, that which has taken place, that which present and has given us a foretaste of that which is still to come." Assuming that "prophets" refers to the prophets of Israel's past, rather than early Christian prophets, the substance of the knowledge with which true interpretation can be effected is salvation-historical. Of course, the Epistle of Barnabas is notorious for its supercessionist interpretation of Scripture: this "knowledge" pertains to the understanding that the Church has now assumed the place of Israel as the true focus of Scripture. Indeed, *Ep. Barn.* 4:6–8 makes the claim that God's covenant was broken on the day that Moses shattered the stone tablets of the covenant. As a feature of this hermeneutic, the letter rejects a seemingly literal interpretation of the law, arguing instead that its meaning is entirely symbolic. In 2:3—3:6, this is construed on the basis of scriptural texts which themselves undermine such a literal interpretation of the law, such as those which question the nature of sacrifice and fasting (Isa 1:11–13; Ps 51:19; and 58:4–10).[4] So, for example, the Sabbath is interpreted as an eschatological concept in *Ep. Barn.* 15:1–5. Likewise, the scapegoat of Lev 16:7–9 is interpreted as a type of Christ in 7:6–11 and in 10:4, the injunction not to eat birds

---

2. Hagner, *Clement of Rome*, 120–21 and Trigg, "Apostolic Fathers," 309.
3. Trigg, "Apostolic Fathers," 313.
4. Ibid., 314.

of prey in Lev 11:13–15 is interpreted as instruction not to associate with people who do not work for a living but who seize what belongs to others. Similarly, Isa 66:1 is used in *Ep. Barn.* 16:2 as a critique of the Jerusalem Temple (cf. Acts 7:49). As Yaron Z. Eliav contends, Pseudo-Barnabas emphasises the Temple Mount ("my holy mountain") instead of the Temple itself in its choice of scriptural texts and its possible redaction of them (Isa 16:1–2 and 45:2–3). This, he argues, is unusual since the Temple Mount itself has little significance in Second Temple Judaism until AD 70 and the destruction of the Temple, after which it becomes a way of speaking about the temple itself. In *Ep. Barn.* 11.2 the Temple Mound is seen as a wasteland or "death pit" as a consequence of Jewish rejection of Christian baptism, for which they have "built a substitute for themselves" (11:1): another allusion to the Temple.[5] The exclusivity of Pseudo-Barnabas's scriptural hermeneutic is emphasized in the "two ways" of 18:1—20:2, in which the notion of interpretive "knowledge" is associated with the "way of light," while the "way of darkness" is that of Jewish faith and practice.[6] Whereas Clement of Rome assumes a single relation of Scripture to the Church, Pseudo-Barnabas has the single meaning of Scripture depend upon an exegetical insight that anticipates something both of gnostic belief and a Catholic "rule of faith."

Ignatius of Antioch

Considering the significance attributed to Ignatius of Antioch for understanding and dating the "parting(s) of the ways" between Christianity and Judaism, Ignatius's use of Scripture is remarkable consistent with that of some New Testament literature.[7] Here, again, the single meaning is assumed, in Ignatius's case, through a theory of prophecy and history as orientated towards the Gospel. Ignatius refers to Scripture a possible three to seven times within the seven genuine epistles, an infrequency that is not as significant as often thought for the divergence of Christianity from Judaism: of course, the deutero-pauline letters also contain few if any explicit references to Scripture. These possible references in

---

5. Eliav, "Interpretive Citation," 359. Cf. Paget, *Epistle of Barnabas*, 156.

6. Hvalvik, *Scripture and Covenant*, 65.

7. More recent scholarship in this area tends towards asserting the complexity of the divergence. Dunn, *Partings of the Ways*, xi–xiv. Cf. Reed and Becker, "Introduction," 1–33.

Ignatius are not evenly spaced: *Magnesians* contains three possible references, while *Romans* and the letter to Polycarp contain none at all. All three of the "quotations" in *Magnesians* are introduced with a citation formula ("as it is written" and "for") and are certainly intended to be heard as references to Scripture. The remaining references could simply be "biblicisms": Scripture inspired language, rather than a reference to a particular text. According to Simonetti, Ignatius's lack of reference to Scripture is related to his and his audiences' pagan background and the accompanying suspicion of the Scriptures of Israel.[8] However, the truth is that Ignatius's use of Scripture bears many points of comparison with the New Testament. The lack of explicit reference to scriptural texts need not be seen as a reflection of Hellenism: the deutero-Pauline epistles are similarly void of such references and yet are filled with scriptural imagery and salvation-historical narrative based on the story of Israel. The Ignatian citation formulae used to introduce three references to Scripture (Eph. 5:3; Magn. 12; and Tral. 8:2) are the same as those frequently used by New Testament writers who also employ texts in the same manner as in these instances: as simple proofs in support of an assertion. A more detailed indication of Ignatius's scriptural hermeneutic might be glimpsed in the possible reference to Isa 66:18 ("I am . . . to come and gather all peoples and tongues and they will see my glory") in *Magn.* 10:3.

> It is monstrous to talk of Jesus Christ and to practice Judaism. For Christianity did not believe in Judaism, but Judaism in Christianity, wherein *every tongue* believed and *was gathered together* unto God.

This statement scarcely makes sense without the underlying assumption that Judaism, through Isa 66:18, affirms Christianity as its Scripture heralds the work of Christ in reconciling the nations to God. Scripture is regarded as straightforwardly prophetic and the prophets of Israel's past are understood as "Christians-in-waiting."[9] The idea that Israel's prophets witnessed to Christ is a prominent aspect of Ignatius's understanding of Scripture, one which bears comparison with 1 Pet 1:10–12 and other New Testament expressions of Scripture's eschatological orientation. Ignatius appears to have understood Scripture as focused exclusively upon Jesus Christ and the Church, and Jewish interpretation of Scripture to be false.

---

8. Simonetti, *Biblical Interpretation*, 97–106. Cf. Trigg, "Apostolic Fathers," 306.
9. Robinson, *Ignatius of Antioch*, 210 n. 26.

Like 1 Pet 1:10–12 and 1QpHab 7:11, discussion focuses on the prophets as those responsible for Scripture. For example,

> Some people ignorantly deny him, but more that they have been denied by him, being advocates of death more than the truth. Neither the prophets nor the law of Moses have convinced them, nor, until now, the Gospel nor the portion of each person's suffering. (Smyrn. 5:1)

Here, the prophets, along with Moses, are seen as witnesses to Jesus Christ. The manner in which they bear witness is in some way similar to the way the Gospel bears witness, the difference being that the prophets anticipate the Gospel. Indeed, the prophets *continue* to be able to convince the disobedient about the one God manifest in his Word, Jesus Christ. It is possible that this claim about the prophets is a Christological version of Wis 18:4, "through whom the imperishable light of the law was given to the aeons."[10]

> But pay attention to the prophets and especially to the Gospel in which the passion has been made plain to us and the resurrection completed. (Smyrn. 7:2)

Here the witness of the prophets testifies with the same voice at the Gospel. Both speak of the death and resurrection of Christ (cf. 1 Pet 1:11 and 1 Cor 15:3–4). It is as though the passion and resurrection are witnessed by the prophets, assuming a pattern of prophecy and fulfilment that is wholly fixated upon the events of the Gospel.

> And we love the prophets because they proclaimed the Gospel beforehand: they hoped in it and waited for it. Because they believed they were saved, being one in Jesus Christ, holy ones worthy of love and worthy of wonder, borne witness to by Jesus Christ and included in the Gospel of common hope. (Philad. 5:2)

In view of the accusation against Ignatius that he seeks to address in the epistle to the Philadelphians (see below), this statement is significant. Ignatius attempts to claim a delight in Scripture by giving a detailed image of the prophets as pre-emptively trusting in Jesus Christ who testified directly to them (cf. "spirit of Christ" in 1 Pet 1:11). Philad. 5:2 claims that the prophets proclaimed with the Gospel in view. According to W. R. Schoedel, Ignatius's principal aim here is to show the incompleteness

---

10. Saebo, *Hebrew Bible, Old Testament*, 378–80. Cf. Cabaniss, "Early Christmas Text," 97–102.

of the prophetic witness: that it only make sense when the Gospel comes, anticipating his main argument.[11]

> But I exhort you to do nothing with contentiousness, but according to the learning of Christ. For I heard some saying, "if I do not find it in the archives, I do not believe it in the Gospel." I said to them, "it is written . . ." and they answered, "that is the issue!" But to me the archives are Jesus Christ: the unchangeable archives are his cross and death and his resurrection and the faith which comes through him. (Philad 8:2)

The exchange recorded here has been seen to have great significance for Ignatius's use of Scripture, suggesting that it reveals Ignatius's relative ignorance of Scripture and explaining the paucity of scriptural reference in the extant epistles. Ignatius's response to the demand to prove the authority of his message with reference to the Scriptures seems to call into question the need to do so at all, claiming that the authoritative "archives" (*archeia*) are the events of Jesus' ministry themselves. While unusual, "archives" is also used in Josephus' *Contra Appion* 1.29 to refer to the Scriptures. However, too much is often made of this apparent denigration of the Scriptures.[12] Ignatius's response to his opponents in Philad. 8:2 does nothing to undermine his insistence that the Scriptures are an essential witness to Christ, able to persuade unbelievers, though he may have been a little unclear of how specific scriptural texts witness to the Gospel. Ignatius is more interesting in talking about Scripture than he is in using Scripture. Indeed, the dispute seems to have arisen because he readily used the expression "as it is written," suggesting an appeal to Scripture, but without sufficient substance. Indeed, the letter goes on to reiterate the authority of the prophets in Philad. 9:2, suggesting that Scripture is not replaced by Christ in Philad. 8:2, but that he is principal content of Scripture.

> But the Gospel contains something special: the coming of the saviour, our Lord Jesus Christ, his suffering and the resurrection. For the beloved prophets preached towards this and the Gospel is imperishable and finished. All of this together is good if you believe in love. (Philad. 9:2)

In Magn. 8:2 and 9:2, Ignatius develops his claims about the exact relation of the prophets to the Gospel. Whereas Philad. 5:2 claims that the

---

11. Schoedel, "Ignatius and the Archives," 202.
12. Ibid., 207–9.

prophets hoped in the Gospel, waited for it and were saved by it, Magnesians enhances this to claim that the prophets were disciples of Christ, that their lives were shaped in some way by him and they even suffered for his sake (cf. Heb 11:26). Schoedel argues that this emphasis upon the prophets *living* according to the way of Christ aims to combat a judaising interpretation of Scripture and, in particular, observance of Jewish religious ritual.[13] In addressing this judaising interpretation in Magn. 8:1, Ignatius uses language borrowed from the pastoral epistles, antiquated "fables" (*mytheumasin tois palaiois*) which are "useless" (*anophelesin*): 1 Tim 1:4, 4:7, and Tit 1:14. Both appear to share the assumption that Judaism and the Scriptures are not necessarily related.

> For the godliest prophets lived according to Christ Jesus. Because of this they were persecuted, having been inspired by his grace for the conviction of the disobedient that there is one God who has revealed himself through Jesus Christ his son, who is the word which came from silence, who in everything pleased the one who sent him. (Magn. 8:2)

> How are we able to live apart from him whom the prophets, being his disciples in the Spirit, were expecting as their teacher? And because of this, the one for whom they were justified in waiting raised them from the dead when he came. (Magn 9:2)

Ignatius's actual use of Scripture is predominantly orientated towards paraenesis, because of which, discerning a hermeneutical framework for interpretation is difficult.[14] The use of Scripture in this manner can be in itself indicative of a view of single meaning, that a scriptural text applies unambiguously to the situation it is used to address. However, as has been noted above, Ignatius is more interested in talking about Scripture than talking with Scripture and the claims he makes indicate a strong conviction that Scripture has a single meaning. Ignatius's understanding of the prophets of Israel's past is an important part of this. The prophets hoped in Christ, spoke of Christ and even followed Christ. By them, the nations ought to know of Christ. The ministry of Israel's prophets, the authors of Scripture, was wholly orientated towards the events of the Gospel. Ignatius does not go so far as to claim the prophets' words did not relate to their own time or circumstances (as in 1 Pet 1:10–12), but he is at pains to show that the prophets tell the same story that he now

---

13. Ibid., 118.
14. Saebo, *Hebrew Bible*, 378–80.

tells. Any opposition to this by means of alternative interpretation of the prophets is to go against the grain of salvation history. Indeed, the events of the Gospel provide something of an essential hermeneutical principle for the interpretation of Scripture, without which Ignatius has little interest in what his opponents conclude from Scripture (Philad. 8:2).[15]

Allegory, the Rule of Faith, and Single Meaning

It may seem surprising to consider patristic allegorical interpretation as an example of scriptural interpretation that assumes single meaning. It is easy to understand early Christian use of allegory as hermeneutically comparable to the use of allegory in the biblical interpretation of the Middle Ages, as part of a four-fold understanding of meaning. Of course, points of comparison can be made. For instance, it is clear that the fruits of allegorical interpretation in the patristic period are reflected in the interpretation of Jean Gersom and Hugh of St. Victor, among others. However, the allegorical meaning of a text in the patristic period is not always defined as one meaning among many: it is not always presented as needing to sit alongside other levels of meaning, such as literal or anagogical meaning. Indeed, an allegorical meaning of a text is often presented as the true meaning of that text (as it is in *Ep. Barn.*) when the plain sense of the words themselves is either nonsensical or incompatible with the truth of the Christian faith.

Origen

For Origen, the meaning given to a text by allegorical interpretation can, at times, be the only plausible reading of that text. This is not to say that Origen bypasses literal meaning entirely, nor is it to argue that Origen rejects polysemy. Origen's three-fold view of meaning is well known. In *De Principiis* 4.3.4–5, Origen describes forms of meaning analogous to parts of the human person: body (literal), soul (a "non-mystical level of allegory") and spirit (allegorical).[16] These are probably to be understood as *levels* of meaning with an obvious hierarchy of value, rather than *senses* in the later medieval understanding.[17] Already, in *De Principiis* 4.1.7 Ori-

15. Hoffman, "Authority of Scripture," 75.
16. Trigg, *Origen*, 126.
17. Daniélou, "Les divers sens de l'Ecriture," 119–26.

gen had made the distinction that it is the doctrines, not the words of Scripture that are inspired: that it is the ideas behind the text, referred to figuratively, that are significant. This appears to draw a bipartite theory of meaning, rather less polysemic than that of 4.3.4–5. Similarly in 4.2.1, Origen argues that the false interpretation of Scripture undertaken by Jews and heretics is due to them not seeing through the literal meaning of Scripture to its spiritual meaning. Instead of a polysemic notion of meaning as multi-leveled, body, soul and spirit, much of *De Principiis* hints at two levels of meaning, one of which is to be ignored in favour of the other. As K. J. Torjeson observes,

> There are two levels to Scripture: the level of the words, characterized by Origen variously as the level of the history, the level of the sensible, the level of the letter; then there is the level of *dogmata*, or the *noêmata*. This is the level of the spiritual teachings, the divine teachings that have such power to persuade and to transform. But when Origen comes to discuss his exegetical method, it appears that he ignores the hermeneutical structure he has erected in *PA* IV.3. 1–7. Instead of speaking of the two levels—the level of the sensible word and the level of the spiritual teachings—he introduces a tripartite division of body, soul, and spirit.[18]

The claim made in the following pages is that single meaning, while clearly not a principle Origen articulates when describing the nature of biblical interpretation, is an important element within Origen's use of texts: a principle resorted to on many occasions where a particular allegorical interpretation seems the only solution to the problems posed by the text. When interpreting texts such as the creation accounts of Gen 1–2 or the Song of Songs, Origen reads as though only one meaning is really possible because of the nature of the text's apparent "literal" meaning. Origen often associates literal reading with Judaism, or a lack of education and dismisses it completely. At other times, literal meaning is rendered subordinate to the allegorical meaning derived from it.[19] In such circumstances, scriptural meaning is probably only polysemic to the extent that *sensus plenior* is, the literal meaning simply providing basic ideas and terms for a subsequent "truer" meaning. For Justin Martyr, allegorical interpretation is necessary to demonstrate the true referent of the Scriptures of Israel. For both of these well-known patristic interpret-

---

18. Torjesen, "Origen's Theory of Exegesis," 19.
19. Hanson, *Allegory and Event*, 237.

ers of Scripture, allegorical meaning is not necessarily a supplement to literal or grammatical meaning: it can be the only meaning of a text.

Returning to *De Principiis*, when Origen interprets the opening chapters of Genesis in 3.1 he suggests that the meaning of the text cannot be entertained as a "literal" account of the creation of the world.

> Now what man of intelligence will believe that the first and the second and the third day, and the evening and the morning existed without the sun and moon and stars? And the first day, if we may so call it, was even without a heaven? And who is so silly as to believe that God, after the manner of a farmer, "planted a paradise eastward of Eden" and set within it a visible and palpable "tree of life," of such a sort that whoever tasted its fruit with his bodily teeth would gain life; and again that one could partake of "good and evil" by masticating the fruit taken from the tree of that name? And when God is said to "walk in the paradise in the cool of the day" and Adam to hide himself behind a tree, I do not think that anyone will doubt that these are figurative expressions which indicate certain mysteries through a semblance of history and not through actual events.[20]

The words of Genesis simply cannot mean what they might appear to mean, according to Origen. The apparently literal meaning of the text is nonsensical as far as he is concerned. The only legitimate conclusion to draw, asserts Origen, is that the events described here are not meant to be understood as referring to events which took place as described. The divine intention behind the text is entirely related to the figurative and allegorical significance of what is described. There is no other meaning besides this. The apparently literal meaning is ludicrous and cannot be what God wishes interpreters of Genesis to focus their attention on. Related to this is a Platonist denigration of the material world. This is why Origen resists the anthropomorphic language of Genesis: it is simply not an appropriate way in which to speak of God. As Trigg argues, the claim that allegory is needed here has much in common with the use of allegory to provide a moral defence of Homer by Heraclitus: the apparent meaning of the text is so embarrassing for those who hold it in high regard that another meaning must be claimed.[21] This is an example of Origen claiming that the literal meaning of the text must be replaced, rather than simply supplemented. This is not a polysemic use of allegory, but one in which

20. Origen, *On First Principles*, 4.3.1.
21. Trigg, *Origen*, 121–25.

allegorical meaning is exclusively true. Perhaps ironically, Origen's sense of what constitutes the literal meaning that he rejects often demonstrates little understanding of figurative language. As M. F. Wiles notes, Origen often fails to take style into account, such as when he takes the literal meaning of the phrase "truth reaches to the skies" in Ps 57:10 as suggesting that God's truth really does touch the sky.[22] This apparently simplistic and materialist claim is rejected by Origen who argues that, because of its implausibility, the true meaning of the phrase must be spiritual. The idea of allegory as something made necessary by the apparent failure of literal meaning is one of several ways in which Origen had a direct influence upon Jerome.[23]

A similar emphasis upon a perceived allegorical meaning as the true interpretation of a text can be seen in Origen's use of John 8:37 in his dispute with Heracleon in his commentary on John.[24] Heracleon followed the Valentinian distinction between the material, soul-like and spiritual natures of humankind as fixed natures, incapable of change. A proof-text for Heracleon's position was John 8:23—"you are from below, I am from above"—suggesting to him that the Jews were incapable of moving beyond the materiality of their natures. Origen argues for the free will of the Jews in John's Gospel: that they can change and become children of God. Origen, describes Heracleon's reading as his own interpretation, not the true meaning of the passage, claiming for himself an apostolic status through which he can correctly interpret the passage (*Jo.* 2.14.102). To further his argument, Origen observes that in John 8:37, Jesus calls the Jews "seed of Abraham," not "children of Abraham" (*Jo.* 20.2–3). This, Origen maintains, indicates that the passage is meant to be taken spiritually, since the Jews really are descended from Abraham. Read allegorically, the "seed" needs to be cultivated since a seed is full of potential to change, hence the Jews have potential spiritual status. What is particularly interesting here is that Origen takes his perceived cue from the text itself as to whether it should be interpreted literally or spiritually. It is assumed that the literal interpretation of "seed of Abraham" is impossible because it is contrary to fact. Therefore, only the spiritual interpretation is possible. Again, spiritual meaning for Origen is exclusively true where it applies. It does not sit comfortably alongside another meaning. As is

---

22. Wiles, "Origen as Biblical Scholar," 454–88.
23. Sparks, "Jerome as Biblical Scholar," 538.
24. Trumblower, "Origen's Exegesis," 138–54.

often the case, polysemic understanding of meaning is set aside when Scriptural interpretation is performed for polemical reasons.

A similar disinterest in the apparent literal meaning of a text can also be seen in Origen's treatment of Songs of Songs. Origen's interpretation of the Song of Songs is particularly interesting because there are two extant texts in which Origen treats this book in some detail: a commentary and a homily written sometime later. In Origen's commentary on the Song of Songs a very small amount of attention is given to the "simple" meaning of the text before "inner" and allegorical meaning is explored in great detail. Origen's homily approaches the text without this complexity. Here, the Song explores the relationship between Christ and the Church on the basis of the bride and bridegroom metaphor employed within the John's Gospel. It is perhaps no coincidence that between the likely dates for the composition of the commentary and the homily, Origen produced his commentary on John. It is well know that Origen saw the Gospel of John as being of great significance through its clear expression of the deity of Christ the incarnation of the divine Word. The Johannine metaphor overwhelms the Song in Origen's Homily, to the point where the allegorical interpretation it inspires appears to be the true meaning of the Song. In the commentary, though Origen recognizes Song of Songs as an *epithalamion* ("marriage hymn"), he rejects the sexual meaning of the text entirely as likely to produce lust. Only those who approach the text spiritually will be able to discern its true meaning and encounter the Word that it both speaks of and conveys.

> But it behoves us primarily to understand that, just as in childhood we are not affected by the passion of love, so also to those who are at the stage of infancy and childhood in their interior life—to those, that is to say, who are being nourished with milk in Christ, not with strong meat and are beginning *to desire the rational milk without guile*—it is not given to grasp the meaning of these sayings. For in the words of the Song of Songs there is that food, of which the Apostle says that *strong meat is for the perfect*; and that food calls for hearers *who by ability have their senses exercised to the discerning of good and evil*... But if any man who lives only after the flesh should approach it, to such a one the reading of this Scripture will be the occasion of no small hazard and danger. For he, not knowing how to hear love's language in purity and with chaste ears, will twist the whole manner of his hearing of it away from the inner spiritual man and on to the outward and carnal... and it will seem to be

the Divine Scriptures that are thus urging and egging him on to fleshly lust!²⁵

Origen says that Song of Songs can only be understood in relation to the other Songs of Scripture of which it is the best. This means that, by virtue of its title, the Song relates to Scripture and is about the "Word." To understand why this approach to Song of Songs is so appropriate, as far as Origen is concerned, one needs to understand the nature of language in Origen's thought. Language, for Origen, can be non-referential, empty of semantic sense, but may still have meaning in a given context.[26] Language is divine and refers to the deepest meanings of things, it does not merely represent or imitate reality. Words, then, have an inherent value and power that goes beyond their use by a speaker or writer—especially so with Hebrew, the original language. Hebrew words have a power which does not translate. Hence Origen's transliteration of Hebrew terms in the *Hexapla*. The Word is a medium of divine speaking and its meaning in a text like Song of Songs need not have much to do with their apparent literal sense. Indeed, the reader and his or her comprehension of the Song as an erotic *epthalamion* is lost in the singing of the song, because the word takes over. "Let him kiss me with the kisses of his mouth" in Song 1:1, becomes not a request for a kiss, but for the transference of the Word. The Word is seen to have a kind of agency upon readers of the Song that in itself banished the possibility of a multiplicity of meaning as the reader is lost to the power of the Word. P. C. Miller goes to far as to draw parallels with Roland Barthes' understanding of the text as "text of pleasure": the text that is wounding and almost erotic in its agency upon the reader.[27]

While Origen affirms the polysemic nature of the meaning of Scripture in *De Principiis* 4.3.4–5, in practice he often interprets Scripture as though only one meaning is true, despite the formal possibility of other meanings. This is perhaps surprising since the one on whom Origen's allegorical interpretation is largely dependent, Philo of Alexandria, does not go quite so far as this.[28] Certainly, Philo favours allegorical interpretation on the basis of a neo-platonist cosmology, but he understands allegory as offering a deeper insight into the meaning of texts, not the

---

25. Origen, *Song of Songs*, 22 (*Cant.* 1.1).
26. Martin, "Origen's Theory of Language," 99–106.
27. Miller, "Pleasure of the Text," 241–53.
28. Daniélou, *Origène*, 164.

only means of access its true meaning in some cases.[29] For example, in *Leg. All.* 3.79, Philo interprets the figure of Melchizedek according to the "literal" narrative of Gen 14 by calling him the king of peace (the meaning of "Salem") before drawing attention to the etymological meaning of the name "Melchizedek." Both of these elements to the interpretation of Melchizedek are mirrored in Heb 7:2. Finally, Philo contemplates what one might label the allegorical significance of Melchizedek as the embodiment of true kingship, in opposition to tyrannical rule. These three elements are all worthy insights into the text of Scripture, though it is the last which receives the most attention from Philo. Yet the literal sense of Scripture remains worthy of attention for Philo. This is particularly clear in Philo's works which purport to have an historical interest: *Vita Moses*, *de Plant.* or *Migr. Abr.*, for example. For Origen, the allegorical reading of Scripture can be its *literal* meaning, in the sense of it being that text's most obvious and intended meaning, because the words themselves tell of something not worthy of consideration: a nonsensical account of the creation of the world, or an embarrassingly explicit account of sexual intercourse.

Justin

As noted above, single meaning is often a feature of polemical biblical interpretation. This is certainly the case with much of Justin's extant works. Of course, the obvious place in which to encounter this polemical interpretation is Justin's *Dialogue with Trypho*, in which the correct interpretation of Scripture is a central theme. Here, Justin distinguishes between natural and legal morality in the Mosaic law: the natural he affirms while the legal he denies. Matthew 19:8, with Jesus' claim that the law was given because of the people of Israel's hardness of heart, forms the basis of a hermeneutic with which to approach this part of Scripture.[30] In addition to this, Justin asserts that Scripture makes sense when understood as a witness to Christ. Without this hermeneutical key there can be no true understanding of Scripture. In addition to this, Justin appears to denigrate the apparently plain sense interests of rabbinic exegesis, insofar as he is aware of it.

---

29. Trigg, *Origen*, 122.
30. Keith, "Justin Martyr," 64.

> But you, expounding these things in a low [and earthly] manner, impute much weakness to God, if you thus listen to thus merely, and do not investigate the force of the words spoken ... But if your teachers only expound to you why female camels are spoken of in this passage, and are not in that; or why so many measures of oil [are used] in the offerings; and do so in a low and sordid manner, while they never venture to speak of or to expound the points which are great and worthy of investigation, or command you to give no audience to us while we expound them, and not to come into conversation with us; will they not deserve to hear what our Lord Jesus Christ said to them: 'Whited sepulchres, which appear beautiful outward, and within are full of dead men's bones; which pay tithe of mint and swallow a camel: ye blind guides!' (*Dial.* 112.)

For Justin, Scripture refers to Christ both by providing "types" as well as providing "words," or prophecies.

> For the Holy Spirit sometimes brought about that something, which was the type of the future, should be done clearly; sometimes he uttered words about what was to take place, as if was then taking place, or had taken place. And unless those who read perceive this art, they will not be able to follow the words of the prophets as they ought.... But you do not comprehend me when I speak these things; for you have not understood what has been prophesied that Christ would do, and you do not believe us who draw your attention to what has been written. For Jeremiah thus cries: "Woe unto you! Because you have forsaken the living fountain, and have dug for yourselves broken cisterns that can hold no water." (*Dial.* 114)

While Justin limits the potential meaning of Scripture by dismissing the apparently literal interpretation of the law and by claiming Christ as the only means through which to understand the true meaning of Scripture, he is able to articulate more than one figurative or prophetic meaning for a single text of Scripture. For example, in *Dial.* 138, Justin contends that the eight righteous persons saved from the Flood correspond to the eighth day as the day of Christ's resurrection, being the first day of the new week. At the same time, the saving wood of the ark is seen as a type of the saving wood of the cross and the Flood itself is a prophetic warning of judgement. Likewise, in 2 *Apol.* 7, the Flood is a means of understanding the future eschatological judgement. As a single event, the Flood is seen to have a multiplicity of meaning, though it could be seen that each aspect of the Flood, as received by Justin, has a single referent.

However, as Thomas F. Torrance argues, Justin's use of allegory is somewhat different than Origen's.[31] Justin knows no philonic metaphysical division between the sensible and intelligible. Justin doesn't develop a theology of language as Origen does, the active "Word" is the divine mind acting upon us through the text, through the prophetic spirit (1 Apol 1.3–39; Dial. 102.1). One needs God's grace to understand the Word (Dial. 58.1). This understanding comes not through esoteric knowledge, as with Pseudo Barnabas and the Valentinians, but through faith in the Christian Gospel, in some ways anticipating the role of the Rule of Faith in Tertullian and Irenaeus.[32] Perhaps the most important distinction between Justin's allegory and Origen's is in the type of truth to which the "symbol" of the apparent literal meaning of the text refers. "Symbol" is not a figure pointing to an eternal reality but a sign of events in history. The story of salvation history is the theological truth to which Scripture always refers, in the light of which obscure passages are to be understood. Torrence concludes that in Justin, one must be implicated in the story (by belonging to the Church) to grasp its significance.

Justin's use of typology and allegory aims to show that the Jewish reading of Scripture cannot be right: Scripture can only refer to what Justin thinks it refers to. This is, of course, a similar assumption to that of the New Testament writers. Naturally, it is not simply Jewish interpretation of Scripture which is false, pagan claims about the fulfilment of prophecy are seen by Justin as demonic, such as the claim that Isa 7:14 refers to the birth of Perseus (1 Apol. 54, Dial. 69).[33] Yet there is very little that is exegetically novel in Justin's interpretation of Scripture. Justin's interpretation of Scripture follows particular uses of Scripture in the New Testament, 1 Clement, and the Epistle of Barnabas.[34] Similarly, as Willis Allen Shotwell notes, Justin uses many of the same exegetical rules as Trypho, which may indeed reflect post-Christian Judaism, rather than simply Justin's own imagination, including the seven *middoth* attributed to Hillel.[35] What is significant is the manner in which Justin's

---

31. Torrance, *Divine Meaning*, 94–101.
32. Aune, "Justin Martyr's Use of the Old Testament," 180.
33. Keith, "Justin Martyr and Religious Exclusivism," 70.
34. Aune, "Use of the Old Testament," 81.
35. Shotwell, *Biblical Exegesis of Justin Martyr*, 89–93. Cf. Hirschman, *Rivalry of Genius*, 130.

use of allegory as a means of asserting the single meaning of a scriptural text differs from Origen. Single meaning, projected through allegorical interpretation, proceeds from a variety of philosophical and theological convictions in early Christianity.

Tertullian

Tertullian's use of Scripture is, more often than not, born of controversy and in many places assumes or asserts the single meaning of Scripture. Tertullian's allegorical interpretation of the land as referring to Christ, in *De Resurrectione Carnis* 26.11, follows *Ep. Barn.* 6.8 and explicitly denies any other meaning. Similarly, the interpretation of parts of the Lord's Prayer in *de Oriatione* 4.1–2 is exclusively figurative (*interpretatione figurata*). For example, the phrase "thy kingdom come on earth as it is heaven" is understood to represent the earthly and heavenly aspects of the human person, the flesh and the spirit. In *Ad. Praxeam* 13, Tertullian argues that his proof texts say what he says they mean about the plurality of persons in the Godhead by claiming that any other reading would be illegitimate.

> Either deny that these things are Scripture, or let me ask what sort of person are you who does not expect to understand words in the sense that they are written, even when they are not written in allegories and parables, but which are declarations of certain and simple meaning? (*haec aut nega scripta, aut quis es ut non putes accipienda quemadmodum scripta sunt, maxime quae non in allegoriis et parabolis sed in definitionibus certis et simplicibus habent sensum?*)

This is certainly a claim of single meaning. Tertullian contends that to read his proof texts as though they say something other than how he takes them is to go against "the sense [in which] they are written," seemingly an appeal to something like authorial intent. This certainly fits with the way R. P. C. Hanson attempts to characterise Tertullian as a biblical interpreter, claiming that Tertullian's interpretation is characterized by restraint and "common sense," and not too dissimilar to historical criticism.[36] This is almost certainly taking Tertullian's assumption of Scripture's single meaning too far. Tertullian's belief in the single meaning of Scripture is more likely contingent upon his legal understanding of Scrip-

---

36. Hanson, "Notes on Tertullian's Interpretation," 275.

ture and scriptural argumentation. As J. H. Waszink argues, as a result of his possible legal background, Tertullian viewed the scriptural text as though it were a witness to the truth against heresy in a courtroom.

> ... it is from this [legal] training, conferring as it did familiarity with a number of basic notions of Roman Law, that we may explain a leading principle of Tertullian's exegesis of Holy Scripture—namely, the continuous endeavour to exclude by all means arbitrariness from interpretation. His conscious aim was to attain a certitude that the opponent cannot undermine by any form of argument.[37]

There is certainly an emphasis upon the simplicity and singularity of truth in Tertullian's writing. Since Jesus promises "seek and you shall find" (Matt 7:7), Tertullian regards faith as something sure and settled, not open to endless variety and questioning (*De praescriptione haereticorum* 14.10). Without this settled and simple faith, there can be no real understanding of Scripture. Tertullian maintains that heretics are those who claim to seek the truth and yet have not found it. Since this failure to find the truth is at odds with Jesus' promise, Tertullian concludes that heretics have false motives and are unworthy interpreters of Scripture. The Rule of Faith is the essential qualification for biblical interpretation and is intended to identify false interpretation and false interpreters. An idea of single meaning is fundamental to Tertullian's use of the Rule of Faith, as it is for Irenaeus (*Demonstration* 3). Tertullian also considers brevity as a sign of correct understanding and an agent of certainty in faith (*De Anima* 2). Consequently, he is able to accuse his opponents of obscuring the simple meaning of a scriptural text with their own false interpretation, as in *De Anima* 35.

> To this effect does he tamper with the whole of that allegory of the Lord which is extremely clear and simple in its meaning, and ought to be from the first understood in its plain and natural sense (*simplex intellectus*).[38]

De Anima 35 concerns the correct interpretation of Matt 5:25–6, Jesus' exhortation in the Sermon on the Mount to settle legal disputes so as to avoid imprisonment. What is interesting here is that Tertullian reads the passage allegorically and claims this meaning as "clear and simple" and "its plain and natural sense." The single (and, one might even say,

---

37. Waszink, "Tertullian's Principles," 18–19.
38. Tertullian, *Treatise on the Soul*, § 35.

literal) meaning Tertullian sees in Matt 5:25–6 is allegorical, as is the case in some of Origen and Pseudo Barnabas. Tertullian does not, however, cite the same reasons for employing allegorical interpretation as Origen. Whereas Origen sees allegorical interpretation as a solution to the difficulties of a possible literal meaning (as with Gen 1 and Song of Songs), Tertullian rejects this use of allegory. In *Ad Marcionem* 5.5.10, Tertullian contends that embarrassing parts of the Bible should not be allegorized away because God chose the foolish to shame the wise, referring to 1 Cor 1:27.

Hilary of Poitiers

At times, Hilary of Poitiers also employs allegorical interpretation as though it is the exclusive means of access to the true meaning of a scriptural text. Perhaps unsurprisingly, this is particularly evident in Hilary's works of a more polemical nature, such as *De Trinitate*. The use of allegory in Hilary's *Commentary on Matthew* is somewhat nuanced. Hilary does not use the word "allegory" at all in the commentary but employs a variety of terms including *interior significantia* ("inner sense") and *intelligentia caelestis* ("heavenly instruction"). When commenting on narrative, this figurative meaning exists in addition to the plain descriptive meaning of the text, as is the case in 1.5.

> Just as the Magi were prohibited from retracing their route and returning to Herod in Judea, so we ought never to look to Judea for our knowledge and learning. Instead, we are admonished to refrain from following the "route" of our former life by all our salvation and hope in Christ.[39]

It cannot be doubted that Hilary understands Matt 2:12 as a description of the way in which the Magi returned home. In addition to this meaning, the text also offers a spiritual admonition and perhaps even an anti-Jewish warning. Yet when Hilary interprets the teaching of Jesus, only one meaning is entertained: he often introduces interpretation by inviting his readers beyond the perceived meaning of a text to discover its true figurative meaning. Indeed, Hilary seems to understand spiritual or figurative meaning as the plain meaning of the text, as suggested in *De Trinitate* (1.18):

---

39. Hilary of Poitiers, *Commentary on Matthew*, 46.

> For he is the best student who does not read his thoughts into the book, but lets it reveal its own; who draws from it its sense, and does not import his own into it, nor force upon its words a meaning which he had determined was the right one before he opened its pages. Since then we are to discourse of the things of God, let us assume that God has full knowledge of himself, and bow with humble reverence to his words. For he whom we can only know through his own utterances is the fitting witness concerning himself.[40]

As in Origen, the scriptural text has a kind of agency with which it engages the reader and makes its true meaning known. Interpretation is a spiritual task, since it is God who makes himself known through the words of Scripture. The divine voice of God in Scripture limits the potential polysemy of the words themselves. As Hilary maintains in *Tracticus Super Psalmos* 2.2, concerning the origins of the Septuagint:

> Accordingly, the elders, when translating these books, had acquired the higher knowledge of these hidden teachings in conformity with the Mosaic tradition, and were able to translate words and expressions which in Hebrew are ambiguous and in themselves indicate different realities with an unambiguous and non-metaphorical use of words, so as to indicate the [true] properties of the things signified. They were able to "control" the polysemous aspect of the [Hebrew] words by their knowledge of the [oral] teaching. And thus it comes about that those who translated later, who [also] translated according to diverse methods, have given many a misleading translation to the Gentiles. For being ignorant of that secret tradition which originated from Moses, they rendered with uncertainty, relying only on their own notions, that which had been expressed in a polysemous fashion in Hebrew.[41]

Hilary's claim here is that the Septuagint was translated with the aid of "higher knowledge," which enabled its translators to employ words with more definite meanings than the Hebrew terms they sought to translate. As noted above, Hilary regards the spiritual meaning as in some ways the plain and natural meaning of the text, rather than a secret contained within it. This is particularly evident in *De Trinitate*, 4.14, which attempts

---

40. Hilary of Poitiers, "On the Trinity," 1.18
41. Kamesar, "Hilary of Poitiers," 271.

to establish a scriptural hermeneutic for answering the use of Scripture by Hilary's opponents.

> Therefore let private judgment cease; let human reason refrain from passing barriers divinely set. In this spirit we eschew all blasphemous and reckless assertion concerning God, and cleave to the very letter of revelation. Each point in our enquiry shall be considered in the light of His instruction, Who is our theme; there shall be no stringing together of isolated phrases whose context is suppressed, to trick and misinform the unpractised listener. The meaning of words shall be ascertained by considering the circumstances under which they were spoken; words must be explained by circumstances not circumstances forced into conformity with words.[42]

Here, Hilary comes close to claiming the exegetical practice of Jerome, the School of Antioch and the rabbinic tradition upon which they both draw. Some comparison could be made with the seventh of Hillel's exegetical middoth, *dabar halamed mianynu* ("a word discerned from its context"). The true meaning of Scripture is both spiritual, given through the guidance of God, and yet literal in its dependence upon the letter of the text and its function within a specific scriptural context. A similar hermeneutical claim is made in the Pseudo-Clementine *Recognitions* 10.42.

> Ingenious men, as I perceive, take many verisimilitudes from the things which they read; and therefore great care is to be taken, that when the law of God is read, it be not read according to the understanding of our own mind. For there are many sayings in the divine Scriptures which can be drawn to that sense which everyone has preconceived for himself; and this ought not to be done. For you ought not to seek a foreign and extraneous sense, which you have brought from without, which you may confirm from the authority of the Scriptures, but to take the sense of truth from the Scriptures themselves; and therefore it behoves you to learn the meaning of the Scriptures from him who keeps it according to the truth handed down to him from his fathers, so that he can authoritatively declare what he has rightly received.

Here, the true meaning of Scripture is associated too with theological tradition as with plain meaning. As with Hilary, the implication is that

---

42. Ibid.

false interpretation is purely a human creation and cannot be entertained at all.

Single Meaning and the School of Antioch

In one sense, it is perhaps obvious that Antiochene exegesis should be claimed as example of Christian interpretation of Scripture that is both theological in inspiration and interest and yet assumes the single meaning of texts, with its dismissal of allegorical interpretation and interest in approaching Scripture in a manner which bears some resemblance to the critical approaches of modernity. Yet, to argue that the representatives of the School of Antioch broadly assume the single meaning of Scripture is to make a judgement as to whether typological interpretation depends on a polysemic understanding of meaning.

As with later interpreters associated with the School of Antioch, Diodore of Tarsus viewed the meaning of Scripture as primarily historical with tropological significance. In the preface of his Commentary on the Psalms, Diodore makes it clear that his understanding of what Scripture is for comes from a reading of 2 Tim 3:16—Scripture is *useful* for teaching, rebuking and training in righteousness: its purpose is moral. Any other spiritual significance a text might flows naturally from the literal and historical sense, as though the text has its own agency upon the reader.

> Nevertheless, as far as possible we shall with God's grace give a commentary also on the erroneous parts without avoiding the actual reality; instead, we shall treat of it historically and literally and not stand in the way of a spiritual or more elevated insight. The historical sense, in fact, is not in opposition to the more elevated sense; on the contrary, it proves to be the basis and foundation of the more elevated meanings. One thing alone is to be guarded against, however, never to let the discernment process be seen as an overthrow of the underlying sense, since this would no longer be discernment but allegory: what is arrived at in defiance of the content is not discernment but allegory.[43]

What was clear to Diodore was that spiritual meaning is not an additional level of meaning to the literal meaning, but is itself a feature or product of that literal meaning: the basis for spiritual meaning is history. Allegorical

---

43. Diodore of Tarsus, *Commentary on the Psalms 1–51*, 4.

meaning bears no relation to historical meaning and may be in defiance of it. Seemingly anticipating the historicism of Theodore, Diodore was reluctant to claim Christological meaning for all of the psalms. While the Psalms were prophetic in Diodore's view, they often refer to events in David's life or Hezekiah's: not necessarily to Christ. Diodore even went so far as the question whether Psalm 22 refers to Christ.

Theodore of Mopsuestia's interest in history in scriptural interpretation stemmed from an understanding of history as the place in which God has acted. The Bible itself is theological, not as the basis for allegorical meaning, but as a witness to God in history.[44] As with Tertullian, Theodore thought that true interpretation was likely to be simple and concise. Indeed, the general tendency in Antiochene commentary on Scripture is to simply paraphrase the apparent literal meaning of the text under discussion. Theodore went to great lengths to dismiss the need for allegorical interpretation. Famously, Theodore argued that despite seeming to use allegorical interpretation and even using the term itself, Paul does not interpret Scripture allegorically in Gal 4:24. Theodore's earliest work on the Psalter went to extremes in severing the historical and literary meaning of the psalms from their later messianic interpretation, something he was to regret. In time, Theodore developed a distinctive view of typology which is helpful here, not because it is based on a theological assumption about salvation history, but because it is grounded in the detail of texts. As Frances Young notes, Theodore looked for correspondence between texts in which an Old Testament pattern is met, perhaps deliberately, by a New Testament author.[45] Yet this does not undermine Theodore's essential belief in determinate, univocal meaning. Typology is *Theoria*, a supplementary insight built upon the detail of the text. Theodore understood this as an extension of the literal meaning of the text, rather than a separate meaning in itself or another level of meaning. *Theoria* enables a vision of the significance of the text through time as God continues his work in history and the meaning of the text unfolds.

This view of *theoria* as expressing the larger significance of the literal and historical meaning of Scripture is also witness in the work of Theodoret of Cyrrhus.[46] Theodoret recognized that there are different types of meaning, but that these types of meaning didn't operate concurrently

---

44. Wiles, "Theodore of Mopsuestia," 507.
45. Frances, "Alexandrian and Antiochene Exegesis," 342.
46. Guinot, "Theodoret of Cyrus," 176

upon the same text: *theoria* is the ability to distinguish between types of meaning as appropriate for the passage in question. Some passages are intended to be understood figuratively. To that extend, figurative or metaphorical interpretation is in fact literal interpretation.[47] Theodoret followed the typically Antiochene practice of glossing passages of Scripture as though their meaning was unambiguous, again looking for simply and brief explanation. This can be seen in his straightforward reading of Ps 1:6, simply repeating and expanding on the words of the text itself.[48]

The exegetical basis of determinate meaning in Antiochene biblical interpretation is not without precedent. The interests of Theodore and others can be seen both in elements of rabbinic interpretation as well as in the Homeric scholarship of some of the Alexandrian Grammarians, such as Aristarchus of Samothrace (c. 220—c. 143 BC). The exegetical *middoth* or rules given by Hillel in *b. Sanh.* 7.11 attest the importance of literary and grammatical features in interpretation. For example, the rule *gezerah shewah* seeks verbal analogy or comparison of one word with another to clarify its use in a particular context. Similarly, the rule *dabar halamed mianynu* encourages a reflection upon the specific literary context of a word or passage.[49] Aristarchus's approach to interpreting Homer with a view to creating an authentic edition of the *Iliad* bears a number of important points of comparison with Antiochene biblical exegesis. Aristarchus approach to interpreting the *Iliad* begins with a conception of Homer as the perfect poetic craftsman, situated within a particular historical and geographical context.[50] This conception enables Aristarchus to make decisions about elements within the text that fail to meet the standards of true Homeric styles, or elements which cannot be reconciled with apparent facts relating to Homer's own context. Aristarchus' approach to Homer is both literary and grammatical, willing to define both correct and deviant readings of the *Iliad* and able to criticise the apparent meaning of the received text. Certainly, like Origen before them, the Antiochenes had real text critical interests, interests which to many seem quite modern.

---

47. Weaver, *Theodoret of Cyrus on Romans 11:26*, 42.
48. Theodoret of Cyrus, *Commentary on the Psalms, 1–72*, 51 (1.11).
49. Sargent, דבר הלמד מענינו.
50. Sargent, "Interpreting Homer," 125–39.

Conclusion

While by no means a universal aspect of the use of Scripture in early Christianity, the assumption of single meaning is well-attested in the period covered in this chapter. A variety of theological and philosophical frameworks enable such views of meaning. First Clement mirrors the ecclesiological reading of Scripture in the New Testament. Pseudo-Barnabas understands the single meaning of Scripture to be the figurative explication of an eschatological mystery now unveiled to true believers. Origen's practice of interpreting Scripture as though it has a single allegorical meaning is motivated both by apologetic and metaphysical concerns. Tertullian's approach to single meaning is governed by his understanding of the simplicity of true faith in the Gospel of Christ. The single meaning assumed by the School of Antioch is motivated by an interest in God's action through history, as well as interest in language itself. What is clear is that Christians throughout the period, from the first century to the fourth century, from France to Africa, employ Scripture as though it has a single meaning.

3

Written for Correction
Single Meaning in Medieval Theology

The interpretation of Scripture in the Middle Ages has been the victim of a caricature. Liberal accounts of history have tended to portray medieval exegesis as wholly preoccupied with the four senses of Scripture. The priority of the literal or plain meaning of Scripture in the Renaissance and Reformations come then as a bolt from the blue, a seemingly divine miracle of progress towards modernity. What is lost in this account is the real sense of continuity in biblical interpretation, through which one sees not only that the new emphases of the sixteenth century reformers are not that new, but also that much of the scriptural interpretation of the Middle Ages resembles various strands of Patristic interpretation. Of course, the commitment of Catholic thought to polysemic meaning in this period cannot be denied, yet the two principal elements of the argument for single meaning in this chapter show a degree of continuity with the Patristic period. Firstly, the School of St. Victor employed seemingly Antiochene exegetical practices and principles. Secondly, as had been the case from the New Testament period onward, medieval polemical writings, such as those of William of Ockham, tend to use Scripture as though its meaning is unambiguous and incontestable.

Littera gesta docet, quid credas allegoria, Moralis quid agas, quid speres anagogia (the literal meaning speaks about deeds, the allegorical about belief, the moral about actions, the anagogical about the end). This anonymous medieval rhyme represents the *Quadriga*, the fourfold meaning of Scripture likened to the four wheels of a chariot. The rhyme appears to consider the four senses of Scripture as having the same authority but different functions. The literal meaning speaks of the past, the allegorical of faith, the moral of day to day life, and the anagogical of the future. Yet, despite this popular expression, it is somewhat unusual to find all four senses employed in relation to the same text in medieval biblical interpretation.[1] As with much Patristic exegesis, attention is typically focused upon the literal and allegorical senses of a text. Again, there is significant debate about how the senses relate to one another and whether all senses have equal value. The range of views expressed during the period is very broad, from an outright rejection of the literal or grammatical sense, to the outright rejection of any figurative interpretation, and everything in between. The popular caricature of biblical interpretation in the Middle Ages as dominated by the polysemy of the *Quadriga* does not do justice to its real complexity.

As in some patristic biblical hermeneutics, a multiplicity of scriptural senses was often derived from and dependent upon a governing literal meaning. This is evident in the exegetical rules of the Dominican John of Ragusa, given to the Council of Basel in 1433 which he opened as papal representative. Speaking against the Hussites, John asserted that Scripture has many senses of which the literal is one. The literal sense in John's view was the meaning the author intended. It is infallible and contains everything necessary for salvation.

> Scripture has many senses, of which the literal sense is the principal one and contains within it the figurative sense. The literal sense is the sense that the author intended. It is infallible. It contains everything necessary to salvation. When he is trying to understand a passage, the reader should look at what becomes before it and after it. He should ask what kind of material the text contains. . . . Heretics have interpreted Scripture falsely. The aim of all interpretation is to arrive at the truth.[2]

The notion of the primacy of literal meaning, and that it contains all the information one needs to be saved, while debated in the period, is well attested.[3] Indeed, the popular glosses on Scripture, such as those of Fulbert

---

1. A good example of this is found in the anonymous Harley Ms. 2276, which expounds four senses of the wedding at Cana in Galilee. Bowers, "Middle English Treatise," 590–600.

2. Evans, *Language and Logic of the Bible*, 39.

3. Ginther, "Robert Grosseteste," 237 who also argues against the traditional view that Grosseteste was only interested in spiritual meaning, noting that his commentary

of Chartres, Berengar of Tours and the *Glossa Ordinaria*, dwell primarily upon the literal meaning alone and could be taking to constitute evidence of assumed single meaning. But the compiling of literal meanings in a text such as the *Glossa Ordinaria* suggests an idea that literal meaning itself may be complex and even "multivoiced."[4] Thomas Aquinas's use of Scripture suggests as much. As Stephen E. Fowl argues, in *Summa Theologiae* 1a.1.10 Isa 7:14 is interpreted as though its author intended a reference to contemporary events as well as to future events, i.e., the birth of Christ.[5] Fowl argues that one cannot maintain that the literal sense in medieval exegesis is determinate to the extent that it governs other levels of the text's meaning. Even in Thomas Aquinas, the "literal" sense of a text is manifold since Aquinas understands this sense as that which is divinely intended. Indeed, Fowl notes that Aquinas understands the literal sense as bearing a possible plurality of meaning in order to ensure that Scripture speaks to a variety of people with differing degrees of learning.[6]

Biblical interpretation of an Antiochene flavor appears to have survived throughout the Middle Ages. In earlier parts of the period, Carolingian and Anglo-Saxon biblical interpretation was influenced to some extent by the methods and emphases of the School of Antioch.[7] For example, Theodore of Tarus, also known as Theodore of Canterbury, the eighth Archbishop of Canterbury seems to have had a great deal of sympathy with the values of Antiochene interpretation. It is likely that Theodore founded a school in Canterbury for the study of Greek and Latin and interpreted the levitical food laws literally, which may have had some impact upon Alfred the Great's food laws.[8] Theodore's disciple, Aldhelm of Malmesbury also seems to have favored Antiochene exegesis and the literal sense of Scripture. Aldhelm's, *Epistola ad Acircium* demonstrates detailed knowledge of poetic metre and elaborates a complex biblical theology of the number seven. G. T. Dempsey suggests that the *Epistola* may have been a "graduation piece" demonstrating knowledge acquired as a disciple of Theodore.[9] Similarly, the Paris Psalter contains

---

on Ecclesiastes is entirely literal.
4. Smith, "Bible in the Twelfth and Thirteenth Centuries," 5.
5. Fowl, "Multivoiced Literal Sense," 53–60.
6. Fowl, *Engaging Scripture*, 37–39.
7. Ramsey, "Theodore of Mopsuestia," 452–97.
8. Firey, "Letter of the Law," 204–24.
9. Dempsey, "Aldhelm of Malmesbury," 381–82.

Antiochene ideas in the short introductions to Pss 2 and 50, ideas seen in Theodore of Mopsuestia and probably mediated through *Liber Bedae de Titulis Psalmorum*, supposedly by Bede.[10]

Single Meaning and the School of St. Victor

The Abbey of St. Victor in Paris was founded in 1107 by William of Champeaux and, particularly under the leadership of Hugh of St. Victor, was a prominent place for the learning of the liberal arts at the University of Paris until Walter of St. Victor became prior in the mid-1170s. A common assessment of the Victorines is that they stand out as an exception to the dominant polysemy and allegorical obsession of the period: exegetes who anticipate Wycliffe and the Reformation. Yet this does not do justice to the great variety of approaches to Scripture that exists, for example, between Andrew of St. Victor and Godfrey of St. Victor. Making the Victorines simply an antitype of later biblical interpretation also ignores the substantial disagreement in the scholarly assessment of their biblical hermeneutics. For example, Henri de Lubac's view of the Victorines is that they tried to balance the literal and spiritual, that asserted the value of literal meaning but did not elevate to the point of making it of greater significance than spiritual meaning.[11] Beryl Smalley, on the other hand, views the Victorines as prioritising the literal or historical meaning, in a marked contrast to the biblical interpretation of the majority of their contemporaries.[12] Franklin T. Harkins offers a *via media* between these two positions, particularly in relation to Hugh of St. Victor and his understanding of the multiple purposes of reading. Hugh's *Didascalicon* 1 discusses the nature of all reading as redemptive reordering of the self. The aim of reading is to get to know and to love divine Wisdom, the source of both secular and sacred learning. Reading Scripture has two goals: knowledge through history and allegory, and morality through tropological interpretation (*Didascalicon* 5.6).[13]

> Although, as Beryl Smalley and many subsequent scholars have duly noted, Hugh "enormously increased the dignity of the historical sense" in the schools of the twelfth century, it must not be

---

10. Ibid., 378.
11. de Lubac, *Exégèse médiévale*, 287–436.
12. Smalley, *Bible in the Middle Ages*, 87.
13. Harkins, "General Introduction," 33.

forgotten that the Victorine master's emphasis on *historia* is the foundation, rather than the *telos*, of his exegetical theory. That is, Hugh intended that the reader's attention to the scriptural narrative and the primary significance of its words would facilitate his allegorical and tropological understanding of the sacred text, which would, in turn aid his progress toward perfection.[14]

Through reading Scripture as a witness to what God has done in history, it is possible to discern Scripture's theology (allegorical meaning) and the implications for Christian morality (tropological meaning). It is easy to see, at least, that for Hugh the allegorical and tropological senses of Scripture are the created through a correct discernment of the historical meaning. Rather than claiming these senses of Scripture as separate or distinct, as is the case with Origen's use of allegory when the literal meaning cannot be entertained, Hugh sees them as expressing the significance of the literal/historical meaning. This understanding that an awareness of the full significance of a text develops from a grasp of the literal meaning of the text can be seen in Hugh's description of the process of reading itself in *Didascalicon* 3.8.

> The exposition of a text takes place at three levels: the letter (*literam*), the sense (*sensum*), and the meaning (*sententiam*). The letter is the suitable arrangement of words, which we also call grammatical construction. The sense is the simple and clear signification that the letter displays on the surface. The meaning is the deeper understanding that is discovered only through exposition and interpretation. The proper order of inquiry among these is first the letter, then the sense and finally the meaning.[15]

It would be incorrect to define this as an articulation of three separate senses. Instead, Hugh claims that there are three steps to the fullest understanding of Scripture, each dependent upon the step before. The first step, as defined by Hugh, is not a sense at all until it is made to mean something in the step of interpretation. The final step, the full meaning of the text, is only grasped when the sense is discerned on the basis of the text's words. Hugh's statement here is not polysemic, but a claim that reading is a process beginning with and never departing from the possibilities of words and history. Meaning, as the goal of interpretation, which may be indeed figurative or tropological (*De Scripturis* 5), is simply the

---

14. Ibid., 36. Cf. Smalley, *Study of the Bible*, 89.
15. Harkins and van Liere, *Interpretation of Scripture*, 124–25.

correct understanding of the significance of the plain sense of the words of the text. As Jeremy Worthen argues, Hugh provides a solution to the distinction between historical sense and contemporary significance, so separated by historical criticism and movements like liberation theology. Allegory is bound up in history and rests upon a knowledge of what God has done, witnessed in Scripture.[16]

A more limited view of literal meaning is taken by Andrew of St. Victor. If a cautious comparison is made of the Victorine and Antiochene Schools, Andrew might be seen in a similar light to Diodore of Tarsus. Both tended towards commentary exclusively on the literal sense of Scripture, both employed rabbinic literature in their exegetical work, both were willing to question the established Christological reading of some psalms, neither offer a detailed explanation of their hermeneutical position. Andrew used rabbinic exegesis because he considered it to represent the approach of the early Church better than contemporary methods.[17] At the same time, Andrew criticized Jewish exegesis when it employed allegorical interpretation. Compared to Hugh, Andrew went further in his interest in the literal meaning of Scripture. As Michael A. Signer argues,

> Andrew of St. Victor concentrated exclusively on the historical aspects of the biblical texts. His commentaries are devoid of allegorizations and focus consistently on narrative. Obscure passages are clarified first by a careful definition of each term, then by setting the words in proper order, and finally, by setting the passage into its sequence with earlier and later parts of the book.... Prophetic metaphors, such as the valley of dry bones in Ezekiel 37, are explained within the context of the entire chapter, i.e. the restoration of the people of Israel. No further explanation relating the vision to the tradition of resurrection was necessary for Andrew.[18]

Andrew's influence is seen very clearly in the work of one his students, Herbert of Bosham. Herbert appears to have known Hebrew and have been familiar with rabbinic exegesis. Like Andrew, he also doubted that some texts taken by the New Testament as Christological were in fact so in their historically intended sense.[19]

16. Worthen, "Interpreting Scripture," 54–70.
17. Harkins, "General Introduction," 42.
18. Signer, "Peshat, Sensus Litteralis," 203–16.
19. Loewe, "Herbert of Bosham's Commentary," 44–77.

A broader interest in the fullness of meaning that stems from the literal sense of Scripture, similar to that of Hugh, is seen in the work of Richard of Saint Victor. Richard thought that Andrew was too radical in following rabbinic reading of the Old Testament without reference to Christ. Yet Richard's approach to Scripture was similarly characterized by a fixation upon history and literal meaning with, like Hugh, a concern for tropological meaning. Richard had a nuanced view of literal meaning as embracing figurative meaning in the interpretation of images and symbols in his commentary on Revelation. Richard's commentary on Ezekiel begins with a statement of intent to find truth, not simply to repeat the teaching of the fathers. While Richard defends the Gregory the Great's allegorical interpretation of Ezekiel's visions in the prologue to his Ezekiel commentary, his reading is largely an engagement with the primary text of Scripture, rather than secondary literature. Like other Victorines, Richard was interested in the identity of biblical authors and the exegetical insights that might be gained from understanding who they were. *Liber exceptionem* gives an historical account with which to understand biblical authors and their background, placing authors within an historical context. Certainly, within the context of medieval biblical interpretation, Richard represents an attempt to limit meaning around the concept of the literal sense of Scripture.

Of course, it must not be thought that the School of St. Victor represents a single and distinctive approach to Scripture. While Hugh, Andrew and Richard were primarily interested in literal meaning, Walter and Godfrey of St. Victor affirm polysemic meaning and the four senses of Scripture as separate exegetical possibilities, rather than aspects of literal meaning.[20] Yet the School, as represented by Hugh, had a wide influence upon biblical interpretation in this period, especially upon the work of Peter Comestor, Peter the Chanter, Stephen Langton, Robert Grosseteste and, to some extent, Bonaventure.

Single Meaning in the Political Writings of William of Ockham

William of Ockham is, of course, best known for his philosophical works in which the interpretation of Scripture is not particularly prominent. Ockham's most famous idea is his principle of parsimony, by which

---

20. Syman, "Four 'Senses' and Four Exegetes," 225–27.

nothing should be postulated without necessity. This principle applies quite well as a characterisation of Ockham's interest in the single meaning of Scripture. This interest is most evident in Ockham's polemical writings.

Ockham's problems with the papal authorities began in 1328 with the belief that John XXII was a heretic who attacked the poverty of the Franciscan order, of which Ockham was a member.[21] Pope John's bull *Ad conditorem* asserted that the papacy would no longer own property given to the Franciscan order, but that the order itself would own it. This was a direct challenge to many in the order who were devoted to the apostolic poverty of St. Francis. The idea of franciscan poverty was itself derived from an apparently plain and unambiguous reading of the Gospels. In response to *Ad conditorem*, Ockham began to write on the status of papal power, particularly calling to question the papal claim to temporal power.

In *Octo quaestiones de potestate papae* (Eight Questions on Papal Power) II.7, Ockham employs Scripture to provide an historical account to undermine Pope Nicholas's argument for the supremacy of the Roman Church, noting that other churches existed before the Roman Church was able to invest them with authority. Whereas proponents of the temporal power of the papacy tended to construct arguments on the basis of figurative interpretations of texts or sought to demonstrate that their arguments follow the logical implications of the literal meaning of texts, Takashi Shogimen shows that Ockham sought interpretations of Scripture that were as specific as possible.[22] For example, Ockham argued for a limited understanding of Matt 16:19 ("whatever you bind on earth will be bound in heaven . . .") as specific to Peter, not the basis of a legal reading to establish the Pope's temporal power.

> Ockham denies the pope's regular power over temporal matters and, when demonstrating this, he attempts to understand the verse in a limited sense by maintaining that Christ's word "whatever" allowed for some exceptions. To show this, Ockham applies his own exegetical method, which he elaborated in the *Opus nonaginta dierum*, manifesting his opposition to the pope's juristic understanding of Scripture. According to this method, the meaning of scriptural testimonies must be determined as specifically as possible by regarding the Bible as an aggregate of cross-references. An implicit or general statement in Scripture

---

21. Kilcullen, "Political Writings," 302–25.
22. Shogimen, *Ockham and Political Discourse*, 215.

ought to be understood by reference to other testimonies found elsewhere therein.²³

As part of this scriptural cross-referencing, Ockham made note of 2 Tim 2:4 ("no one serving as a soldier gets entangled in secular affairs"), suggesting that this text drew a distinction between the sacred ministry of the clergy and secular interests, limiting the potential meaning of Matt 16:19 as a proof for papal dominance over both realms. In *Breviloquium* 5, Ockham discusses the "two swords" argument for the temporal power of the papacy, based on Luke 22:38 ("look, Lord, there are two swords"). The argument, as reflected by Ockham, was based on a figurative reading of the verse, with the two swords representing temporal and spiritual power. Ockham thought that figurative reading was acceptable when done in Scripture itself, as in the treatment of Sarah and Hagar in Gal 4 or of Melchizedek in Heb 7.

> For although a mystical sense of Scripture that is not contrary to the truth can be adduced for edification and exhortation, nevertheless, if it is not in divine Scripture explicitly in itself or in something which implies, it should not and cannot be adduced to prove and confirm disputable and doubtful things about which Christians disagree. For the mystical sense of the statement in Genesis that Abraham had two sons, one by a maidservant and one by a free woman, which is explicit in Galatians, chapter 4, can be adduced to prove contentious points; similarly the mystical sense of the things written in Genesis about king Melchisedech, which is explicit in Hebrews, chapter 7, can be adduced to prove doubtful points. But a mystical sense not explicit in sacred Scripture can never be adduced in this way, except in so far as it rests on another Scripture or on evident reason.²⁴

Ockham develops the traditional idea that the literal sense of Scripture is the foundation of allegorical meaning, and that nothing is essential to salvation that can be found in an allegorical interpretation alone, by seemingly denigrating allegorical meaning entirely.²⁵ Allegorical interpretation, Ockham argues, provides the possibility for an interpreter to claim anything they please (*Brev.* 5.3).

23. Ibid., 167.
24. Ockham, *Short Discourse*, 133–34.
25. Minnis, "Material Swords and Literal Lights," 295.

> However, since some try to prove whatever they please by mystical senses which they invent, and want such proof accepted as beyond doubt, it will be proved by authority and reason that such a mystical sense need not be accepted. Blessed Augustine says to Vincentius: "Who would dare, without the greatest impudence, to interpret in his own favor something expressed in allegory, unless he had manifest testimonies whose light would illumine the obscurities?" From these words we gather that one disputing with another should not adduce an allegorical sense unless it is explicit in Scripture, because if it cannot be proved explicitly by Scripture his opponent will say that it can be as easily despised as approved.[26]

According to Ockham, the exegetical writings of the fathers, with their allegorical interpretations of Scripture, must be distinguished from the text of Scripture itself and rejected if necessary. Only the literal sense of Scripture was reliable enough to be the basis of Christian doctrine. Ockham argued that popes should never try to prove anything through mystical interpretation, expect insofar as they follow Scripture's own mystical interpretation. If a pope maintains a view through mystical interpretation that cannot be proven and which seems to contradict the literal sense of the text, it must be judged that they have erred. It is not that Ockham denied the possibility of additional meaning, but maintained that there are too many problems with the nature of allegorical meaning for it to be really worthwhile.

Ockham's view of allegorical meaning seems to have been that it is not often justified or warranted. While this is never made explicit, perhaps the singularity of scriptural meaning in Ockham's polemic is a result of his philosophy, not wanting to posit anything unnecessary. Ockham's rejection of the universals makes his theological epistemology much more dependent upon the need for divine revelation and, indeed, Ockham is clear that Catholic theology is entirely a matter of scriptural interpretation. Catholic truth, says Ockham, must be based on the Bible alone, to which nothing can be added, alongside universally received doctrine and new revelation attested by a miracle. (*Dialogus* 1.II.6–7). Since human thoughts and words do not adequately correspond to eternal reality, theology can only rely on literal meaning since allegory strays into uncertain void created by the nominalist disjuncture between the sensible and the noumenal. This association of Ockham's metaphysics

---

26. Ockham, *Short Discourse*, 134.

and hermeneutics seems to be suggested by Gerald Bray.[27] Certainly, the the nominalist disjuncture between God and the created world, subject to its own laws of cause and effect is responsible for an eventual hermeneutic turn in many post-liberal accounts of the history of Christian doctrine and biblical interpretation.[28] If this account of Ockham's hermeneutical theory is correct, this is yet another theological framework in which the single meaning of Scripture has been realized within Christian theology.

Single Meaning in the Work of Nicholas of Lyra

Nicholas of Lyra offered an approach to Scripture comparable to Hugh of St. Victor. Nicholas's governing interest was in the literal meaning of texts, understood in a broad sense to embrace mystical and tropological meaning. Like the Victorines, Nicholas was interested in the biblical languages and rabbinic exegesis, having the linguistic advantage of being Jewish in his youth. Nicholas tried to establish the most plausible literal meanings of the texts he discussed, like the Victorines, preferring comment on a whole book of the Bible. Attentive to detail, Nicholas examined the differences between the Vulgate and Hebrew scriptures in *De Differentia Nostrae Translationis ab Hebraica Littera*, attempting to discern the correct reading of the text. In *Postilla Litteralis super Totum Bibliam*, Nicholas defined the nature of literal meaning as being the plain sense of the text, the meaning which requires no explanation before the reader can perceive it and argued that the literal sense is the true voice of Scripture and the basis proper basis for Christian theology. Yet Nicholas also saw the literal sense as multi-faceted. In the prologue to *Postilla Litteralis*, Nicholas argues that the four senses of Scripture can be seen in the four biblical senses of the word "Jerusalem." Jerusalem, he notes, is an historical place, the capitol city of Judea. It has moral significance as a metaphor for faithful Israel, as in Isa 52:2. Furthermore, "Jerusalem" has allegorical meaning as a reference to the Church in Rev 21:2 and anagogical meaning in Gal 4:26. Like Ockham, these multiple senses are all seen to be derived from Scripture's own treatment of "Jerusalem." Scripture itself takes the lead in suggesting the possibility of another sense or level of meaning. Similarly, in Nicholas's interpretation of the Song of Songs, the literal meaning is seen to have two distinct aspects.[29] In one sense, the

27. Bray, *Biblical Interpretation*, 154.
28. And, though not "post-liberal," Webster, *Holy Scripture*, 19 and 54.
29. Dove, "Literal Senses," 129–46.

Song describes a romantic relationship. In another literal sense, the Song is a parable. The parabolic sense is understood to be literal on the basis of the rest of Scripture in which marriage is a source of parabolic imagery. To Nicholas's mind, the Song of Songs must be intended to convey this as well, the obvious extension of its other literal meaning.

At other times, Nicholas seems to suggest that the senses of Scripture are mutually exclusive: that they do not always operate at the same time. In the prologue to the *Postillae Moralis seu Mysticae* Nicholas argues,

> But it should be noted that although sacred Scripture has the fourfold sense previously mentioned, not all are to be found in each place.... For sometimes there is only a literal meaning, as at Exodus 20 [:], *Hear Israel, the Lord your God is one Lord*; and at Deuteronomy 6:5: *You shall love the Lord your God with your whole heart*. In these passages, and in others like them, no mystical meaning is necessary. But some passages have no literal sense, strictly speaking. For example, at Judges 9:8: *The trees went forth to anoint a king to rule over them*, and so on. And at Matthew 5:30: *and if your hand causes you to sin, cut it off and throw it away*. The literal sense is that which is signified by the words, as it has been said: and there is no such sense in these passages, nor in others like them.[30]

As Nicholas viewed a range of scriptural texts, he saw that the meaning readers should perceive in them might be allegorical or it might be literal, both of which could be united in a conception of the plain meaning of the text as that which makes itself obvious to the reader. While the literal sense of Scripture was a broad concept for Nicholas, it remained the sole focus of his work. It is perhaps not surprising that Nicholas was much-loved as a biblical commentator by Martin Luther.

Conclusion

Few biblical interpreters of the Middle Ages were so radical as to exclude the possibility of multiple senses. For some, the multiple senses of Scripture were unified within a generous conception of literal meaning. Even Ockham, who makes the strongest case for the single meaning of Scripture, does not dismiss the possibility of multiple senses but considers them unnecessary in one sense and problematic in another. Interest

---

30. Turner, *Eros and Allegory*, 391.

in single meaning is less exclusive in this period than in early Christianity, it would seem, but is nonetheless important in understanding the concentration of some interpreters on a single type of meaning which must be extended to embrace others. Single meaning is seen through the way in which some interpreters focus their energies upon one way of accessing meaning, most notably in the acquisition of biblical languages, in textual analysis and literary interest. In the centuries that follow, the dominant orientation of interpretation for Hugh and Andrew of St. Victor and Nicholas of Lyra would become more exclusive and other levels of meaning or senses ruled out entirely.

4

Written for You

Single Meaning in Renaissance and Reformation

The European Renaissance and Reformations can be understood as part of a hermeneutical revolution. This should not be understood as a complete reinvention of biblical hermeneutics, rather it represents a series of attempts to bring voices from the margins of biblical interpretation into the most prominent position. There is little that is completely new in the biblical hermeneutics of the renaissance and the reformation movements. While Nicholas of Lyra, Hugh of St. Victor, and others had argued for a prominent role for the literal meaning of texts during the middle ages, this revolution saw literal, or plain sense meaning become dominant: in many cases becoming the single meaning of Scripture. At the same time, the sufficiency of Scripture as containing all things necessary for salvation, as expressed by William of Ockham, John of Ragusa and many others in the Middle Ages, received a new prominence. Accompanying these concepts was a radical, but again not new, emphasis upon the clarity or perspicuity of Scripture: Scripture readily yields its fruit to the faithful reader.

The other issue this period brings to discussion of single meaning is not so much whether there is any evidence that Christian thinkers made this kind of assumption about Scripture, but whether Christians of the sixteenth century did so for theological reasons. As has been noted, within our own time as we struggle to come to terms with the apparent end of modernity and the loss of a dominant hermeneutical framework within which to interpret Scripture (namely, historical criticism and its associated disciplines), single meaning has been understood as a product of modernity's rejection of theology. To some, modernity's *untheological* approach to Scripture began in the period discussed in this chapter, to others it began even earlier as Scotus made modernity philosophically possible. A more plausible case for the origins of the secular neutrality and exclusive historicism of historical criticism identifies Hobbes and Spinoza, but as will be seen in the next chapter, even Spinoza saw biblical interpretation as a predominantly theological activity. Part of the discussion in this chapter, examining scriptural interpretation at the possible dawn of the modern period, is whether single meaning is understood as a theological concept. Certainly the eschatological, allegorical, grammatical, and other approaches to single meaning in earlier periods proceeded from theological assumptions about language, Scripture, salvation-history and the Church.

This chapter explores the argument for and assumption of single meaning in renaissance humanism, focussing particularly upon Erasmus and works of French renaissance satire, before examining the discussions concerning biblical interpretation in the Zurich Reformation and the English Reformation(s). It is noted that much of the argument for and assumption of single meaning proceeds from theological ideas about Scripture.

Single Meaning in Erasmus and Renaissance Satire

Desiderius Erasmus is a figure of profound importance in the history of biblical interpretation. As the humanist scholar par excellence and the creator of a critical edition of the Greek text of the New Testament, it may seem obvious to include a discussion of Erasmus here. But, as those who know Erasmus's work well will realize, his commitment to the grammatical and literary interests of renaissance humanism does not equate to a simple hermeneutical position.

Erasmus's early works relating to biblical interpretation are Origenist in their hermeneutical stance.[1] Perhaps surprisingly, considering his eventual position and subsequent reputation, Erasmus emphasized the weakness of literal meaning and the necessity for allegorical interpretation. This is particularly evident in his popular 1505 *Enchiridion militis*

---

1. Godin, "Fonction d'Origène," 17–44.

Christiani (Handbook for a Christian Soldier). In the second chapter of the Enchiridion, Erasmus exhorts his readers to read commentators who look for spiritual meaning beyond the literal sense of a text.

> From the interpreters of Holy Scripture choose those especially who depart as much as possible from the literal sense. Of this sort, after Paul, among the first are Origen, Ambrose, Jerome, Augustine. For I see the modern theologians too freely and with a certain captious subtlety drinking in the letter, rather than plucking out the mysteries and giving their attention (as if Paul had not spoken the truth) to the fact that our law is spiritual. I have heard some who are to such an extent pleased with these little human comments that they contemn the interpretations of the ancients almost as if they were dreams.[2]

What is particularly notable here is Erasmus's supposedly Pauline distinction between the law and the spirit, which was a characteristic feature of renaissance humanism and a significant influence upon Martin Luther's biblical hermeneutics. As Alister E. McGrath notes, Erasmus moved from emphasis of spiritual meaning in the *Enchiridion* to literal meaning in *Ratio Verae Theologiae*.[3] He eventually argued that the spirit was *bound to* the letter and that the best way to discern the spirit was to study the letter using literary and linguistic tools. By the time Erasmus published his satirical *Morae Encomium* ("In Praise of Folly/Praise of More"), he had moved to a position from which he could offer a critique of allegorical interpretation, and perhaps indeed, polysemic interpretation too.

> And besides him I met with another, some eighty years of age, and such a divine that you'd have sworn Scotus himself was revived in him. He, being upon the point of unfolding the mystery of the name Jesus, did with wonderful subtlety demonstrate that there lay hidden in those letters whatever could be said of him; for that it was only declined with three cases, he said, it was a manifest token of the Divine Trinity; and then, that the first ended in *S*, the second in *M*, the third in *U*, there was in it an ineffable mystery, to wit, those three letters declaring to us that he was the beginning, middle, and end (*summum, medium, et ultimum*) of all. Nay, the mystery was yet more abstruse; for he so mathematically split the word Jesus into two equal parts that

---

2. Erasmus, "Enchiridion," 305.
3. McGrath, *Origins of the European Reformation*, 150.

he left the middle letter by itself, and then told us that that letter in Hebrew was *schin* or *sin*, and that *sin* in the Scotch tongue, as he remembered, signified as much as sin; from whence he gathered that it was Jesus that took away the sins of the world. . . . In the third place, they bring in instead of narration some texts of Scripture, but handle them cursorily, and as it were by the bye, when yet it is the only thing they should have insisted on. And fourthly, as it were changing a part in the play, they bolt out with some question in divinity, and many times relating neither to earth nor heaven, and this they look upon as a piece of art. Here they erect their theological crests and beat into the people's ears those magnificent titles of illustrious doctors, subtle doctors, most subtle doctors, seraphic doctors, cherubin doctors, holy doctors, unquestionable doctors, and the like; and then throw abroad among the ignorant people syllogisms, majors, minors, conclusions, corollaries, suppositions, and those so weak and foolish that they are below pedantry. There remains yet the fifth act in which one would think they should show their mastery. And here they bring in some foolish insipid fable out of *Speculum Historiale* or *Gesta Romanorum* and expound it allegorically, tropologically, and anagogically. And after this manner do they and their chimera, and such as Horace despaired of compassing when he wrote "Humano capiti," etc.[4]

In Erasmus's later writings, the emphasis is exclusively upon the literal meaning of Scripture, understood as primarily tropological in orientation. For example, Erasmus's treatment of *Iustitia Dei* (the righteousness of God) appears to be tropological.[5] Indeed, the need for moral improvement is at the heart of Erasmus's thought from the *Enchiridion* onwards and is central to his concept of the *Philosophia Christi*. As Lisa Jardine argues, salvation for Erasmus was more about being learned and exposed to the power of the Scriptures than being holy and removed from the temptations of the world.[6] Mary Jane Bennet suggests that Erasmus came to reject the *quadriga* and emphasise tropological interpretation as expressing the goal of biblical language, though he never went so far as to claim that language has a pure and adequate relation to its referents.[7] Being and word are never totally united in Erasmus's thought: there is

---

4. Erasmus, *Praise of Folly*, 51–52. Cf. Weimann, *Authority and Representation*, 138.

5. Vogelsang, *Die Anfänge von Luthers Christologie*, 16–30.

6. Jardine, *Erasmus*, 55–82.

7. Bennett, "Erasmus and the Hermeneutics," 542–72.

always the potential for words to mean more since they refer to realities that cannot be contained by them. This is made clear in Erasmus's 1528 *De recta Latini Graecique sermonis Pronuntiatione*, a dialogue on the nature of language between a bear and a lion. The bear argues that words are determined by the reality they seek to convey, as in onomatopoeic terms. The lion, being the voice of wisdom, rejects this position. And yet Erasmus became increasingly interested in language as the sole conveyor of biblical meaning from after the publication of the *Enchiridion*. Language, for Erasmus, is something that must be done: it must performed to have an effect, as in rhetoric, and what biblical language seeks to effect is personal transformation. It is this tropological understanding of biblical meaning that motivates Erasmus's desire to discern the true text of the Greek New Testament: this approach to the text is what Erasmus assumes will transform individual Christians and indeed Christendom itself. Ultimately, it is the tropological emphasis upon what Scripture does that breaks down the distinction between literal and spiritual meaning, the law and the Spirit. This is not quite as clear as the idea of the single meaning of Scripture expressed by Erasmus's fellow Catholic humanist, Jacques Lefèvre d'Étaples. In the preface to his *Quincuplex Psalterium*, Lefèvre proposes that there are two literal senses: one false, historic, carnal and Jewish, the other prophetic and Christological, the latter of which is intended by the Holy Spirit. It is only the true and prophetic literal sense that exposes Christological meaning.[8]

Regardless of the hermeneutical complexity of Erasmus's contrasting views on the interpretation of Scripture and his journey from exclusive Origenist spiritual interpretation to a very detailed attentiveness to "literal" meaning, it is Erasmus's hermeneutics embodied in his *Novum Testamentum* that appears to have had the most significant influence, particularly upon the scriptural interpretation of John Calvin. There is, of course, an indirect relation between Erasmus and Calvin through Johannes Oecolampadius.[9] Oecolampadius helped Erasmus with the Hebrew *vörlagen* of the scriptural references in the New Testament. Oecolampadius and Calvin came into contact with each other in Basel where Calvin wrote his *Institutes of the Christian Religion*. Calvin did not discuss biblical interpretation as a separate issue, even in the *Institutes*: he was a practitioner of interpretation, rather than a theorist, whose ex-

---

8. McGrath, *Intellectual Origins*, 152.
9. Brashler, "From Erasmus to Calvin," 161–66.

egetical output was vast.¹⁰ Yet Calvin assumed the necessity of reading Scripture according to its grammatical meaning which he assumes is its spiritual meaning also. As Hans Frei suggests, Calvin did not distinguish between literal and spiritual senses, not even to say that they were one and the same.¹¹ The position Calvin assumes reflects Erasmus's later views of meaning: that the single meaning of Scripture is associated with the power of Scripture to do something to its readers and is best accessed through the grammatical and literary techniques of humanist scholarship, applied to the earliest possible version of the text of Scripture. Neither Erasmus nor Calvin perceive the means of accessing meaning, or indeed the nature of true meaning itself to be anything other than derived from a theological conception of the text as possessing divine agency.

Within the broad range of thinkers and literature that might be considered humanist in this period, the single meaning of Scripture is assumed particularly in certain works of French satire. As with much polemical use of Scripture, as seen in previous chapters, single meaning is often assumed within the context of an argument in which an opponent is presented as unambiguously opposed by texts of Scripture or is claimed to have misinterpreted Scripture. This is certainly an assumption made by Pierre de Ronsard. Ronsard was certainly as familiar with Scripture as he was with the classical texts favoured in renaissance satire.¹² Ronsard made frequent appeals to the authority of Scripture, agreeing with much evangelical critique of the church but also using Scripture to criticise evangelical doctrine. For example, in his elegy for Guillaume des Autels, written in a biblical style, Ronsard redefines the significance of Jacob's rivalry with Esau, used to justify predestination by Calvinists (based on Gen 25:23, "two peoples are in [Rebekah's] womb ... and the elder shall serve the younger"), giving the text its correct meaning. Similarly, in his *Remonstrance au people de France*, Ronsard uses Pss 105 and 106 as though they directly justify violence against evangelicals.¹³ Perhaps more sympathetic to the evangelical cause (though this is debated) is the François Rabelais' *Gargantua et Pantagruel*. Following Gargantua's visit to the Abbey of Thelema, *Gargantua* 58 contains a prophecy written in a biblical style based in part on 1 Tim 4:1–4 and 2 Tim 3:1–11, warnings

---

10. Jensen, "Figuring Calvin," 45.
11. Frei, *Eclipse of Biblical Narrative*, 23.
12. Franchet, *Le Poète et son oeuvre d'après Ronsard*, 244.
13. Hanks, *Ronsard and Biblical Tradition*, 91 and Ford, "Biblical Imagery," 15.

about false teaching and impiety in later times. These are both texts employed by Erasmus and are common to much anti-monastic critique in the period.[14] The prophecy seemingly relates to things that are to come, described in terms similar to the Pastoral Epistles: people living solely in accord with their desires, disputes, godless people in positions of power, widespread public apostasy and violence. On hearing the prophecy, Gargantua sighs and concludes,

> This is not the first time that men called to the Gospel faith are persecuted. But happy indeed is he who is not offended and shall always aim at the mark or target that God, by His dear Son, has set up for us, and shall not be distracted or lured aside by his carnal affections.[15]

But the monk, Gargantua's travelling companion, expresses surprise at his interpretation of the prophecy, accusing Gargantua of interpreting it allegorically, while he sees it as a "description of a game of tennis wrapped up in strange language." The reader is perhaps meant to see the irony that it is the churchman who has got the meaning wrong by himself seeing an allegorical meaning at odds with the language of the prophecy itself. Assuming that the prophecy is meant to be understood as a specific reference to the persecution of evangelicals, Rabelais takes his texts from the Pastoral Epistles to refer directly and unambiguously to this persecution. The monk's comment serves only to enforce the idea that such events predicted in Scripture cannot be interpreted any other way, though corrupt elements within the church are determined to try to do so.

Single Meaning in the Zurich Reformation

As well as making an impression upon Calvin, Erasmus's style of biblical interpretation also influenced some aspects of the magisterial reformation in Zurich. For example, John B. Payne argues that the use of "Come unto me . . ." at the beginning of many of Zwingli's and Bullinger's works is derived from Erasmus's use of that text, as is their simple identification of the "burden" in the same verse (Matt 11:28) with medieval religious law.[16] The single meaning of Scripture is an important feature in under-

---

14. Telle, "Thélème et le Paulinisme," 104–19. Cf. Screech, "Rabelais's Enigme en Prophétie," 395.

15. Rabelais, *Gargantua and Pantagruel*, 163.

16. Payne, "Erasmus's influence on Zwingli," 63–80.

standing the Zurich Reformation. From the moment Huldrich Zwingli stepped into the pulpit of the Grossmünster, having been appointed Leutpriestertum ("people's priest"), he exhorted the faithful of Zurich to read the Bible for themselves, confident that they could easily discern its true meaning for themselves.[17] Zwingli held to a radical view of the perspicuity of Scripture, believing that the plain meaning intended by the Holy Spirit could be discerned by any reader or hearer. As suggested, this approach to perspicuity was initially wholly theological: readers could find the true meaning of a text, not because they possess the correct linguistic tools, nor because of the nature of language as naturally or normally perspicacious, but because the Holy Spirit alone makes true understanding possible. One of Zwingli's earliest works on biblical interpretation is the 1522 treatise *Die Klarheit und Gewissheit des Wortes Gottes* (On the Clarity and Certainty of the Word of God). Here, scriptural perspicuity is asserted on the basis of the power of the Holy Spirit to speak through the text, in spite of the frailty of human intelligence to grasp the true meaning of Scripture of itself. At this time, Zwingli operated with a dualism of reason and revelation that is echoed in the opening statement of the First Zurich Disputation.

> Pious brothers in Christ, Almighty God has always shown His divine grace, will and favour to man from the beginning of the world, has been as kind as a true and almighty father, as we read and know from all the Scriptures, so that everlasting, merciful God has communicated His divine word and His will to man as a consolation. And although at some times He has kept away this same word, the light of truth, from the sinful and godless struggling against the truth, and although He has allowed to fall into error those men who followed their own will and the leadings of their wicked nature, as we are truly informed in all Bible histories, still He has always in turn consoled His own people with the light of his everlasting word. . . . This I say to you, dear brethren for this purpose: You know that now in our time, as also many years heretofore, the pure, clear and bright light, the word of God, has been so dimmed and confused and paled with human ambitions and teachings that the majority who by word of mouth call themselves Christians know nothing less than the divine will.[18]

17. For a more detailed treatment of the argument in this section, see Sargent, "Zurich Reformation," 325–42.

18. "Acts of the Convention," 1.47–48.

Zwingli's view of perspicuity was challenged, however, when other Christians read the Bible for themselves and discerned quite different ideas about the Christian life than those preached by Zwingli. The emerging Anabaptist group in Zurich saw no scriptural justification for the practice of infant baptism and they were convinced that Christians were urged in Scripture to reject the idea of private property. As a consequence, some of those who had been early disciples of Zwingli began to meet separately and some were re-baptized. This raised the question of how the single meaning of Scripture could be clear and accessible to every reader when different interpretations of the same texts existed. Zwingli's response to this question was to articulate how Scripture ought to be interpreted in order that its true meaning might be discerned in *Von dem Predig Ampt* (On the Preaching Office) in 1525. Here Zwingli argued for a grammatical and historical approach to biblical interpretation and argued that preachers ought to be schooled in the biblical languages. In addition to this, Zwingli emphasized the authority of trained preaching according to these principles, identifying the preached word of the sermon with the word of God itself. Also in 1525, the Zurich Prophezei school was founded to teach preachers the literary and linguistic skills needed to interpret the Bible in accordance with Zwingli's hermeneutical principles. This interest in the humanist return *ad fontes* had long been an element within Zwingli's approach to the Bible: at the disputations, Zwingli insisted that the only grounds for debate were the simple text of the Bible in its original languages. Now, this interest in the languages of Scripture became the exclusive means by which one could be sure that interpretation was correct. As Zwingli argued in his 1526 *On the Christian Education of Youth*,

> But a man cannot rightly order his own soul unless he exercises himself day and night in the Word of God. He can do that most readily if he is well versed in such languages as Hebrew and Greek, for a right understanding of the Old Testament is difficult without the one, and a right understanding of the New is equally difficult without the other.... No Christian should use these languages simply for his own profit or pleasure: for languages are gifts of the Holy Ghost.

> If a man would penetrate to the heavenly wisdom, with which no earthly wisdom ought rightly to be considered, let alone compared, it is with such arms that he must be equipped. And

even then he must still approach with a humble and thirsting spirit.[19]

Later, in his anti-Lutheran treatise *A Friendly Answer* (1527), Zwingli attempted to explain the apparent tension between his earlier emphasis upon perspicuity and the sovereignty of the Spirit in interpretation and his later insistence on the importance of knowing the biblical languages. He argued that the relation between the Spirit and scholarly techniques was that of a horse to its reins. Like a horse, the Spirit provides the power needed for correct interpretation, but this sheer power needs to be restrained for it to operate effectively. The reins of linguistic and literary expertise enable this power to be controlled to the best ends. Yet, just as reins without a horse are useless, so too, knowledge of biblical language and literature is useless without the power of the Holy Spirit. This dual commitment to the seemingly opposing values of perspicuity and the necessity of scholarship was taken up by Zwingli's successor, Heinrich Bullinger, after Zwingli's death at the battle of Kappel in 1531. Bullinger had, up to this point, been a keen disciple of Zwingli's as dean of Bremgarten. When Bremgarten was forcibly re-catholicised, Bullinger fled to Zurich and was soon appointed to Zwingli's former position as Leutpriestertum at the Grossmünster. In his *Decades*, Bullinger affirmed the need for clergy to be well-acquainted with the biblical languages in order to interpret Scripture correctly.

> First of all, that God's will is to have his word understood of mankind, we may thereby gather especially, because that in speaking to his servants he used a most common kind of speech, wherewithal even the very idiots were acquainted. Neither do we read that the prophets and apostles, the servants of God and interpreters of his high and everlasting wisdom, did use any strange kind of speech: so that in the whole pack of writers none can be found to excel them in a more plain and easy phrase of writing. Their writings are full of common proverbs, similitudes, parable, comparisons, devised narrations, examples, and such other like manner of speeches, than which there is nothing that doth more move and plainly teach the common sorts of wits among mortal men. There ariseth, I confess, some darkness in the scriptures, by reason of the natural property, figurative ornaments, and the unacquainted use of the tongues. But that

---

19. Bromiley, *Zwingli and Bullinger*, 108–9.

difficulty may be easily helped by study, diligence, faith, and the means of skilful interpreters.[20]

Bullinger worked to make the Zwinglian biblical hermeneutics embodied in the syllabus of the Prophezei school part of the definition of Reformed faith. He was largely responsible for the writing of the Second Helvetic Confession, which claims in 2.1 that true scriptural meaning is limited to that which agrees with the study of biblical languages and the origins of the text.

> The apostle Peter has said that the Holy Scriptures are not of private interpretation (2 Pet 1:20), and thus we do not allow all possible interpretations. Nor consequently do we acknowledge as the true or genuine interpretation of the Scriptures what is called the conception of the Roman Church, that is, what the defenders of the Roman Church plainly maintain should be thrust upon all for acceptance. But we hold the interpretation of Scripture to be orthodox and genuine which is gleaned from the Scriptures themselves (from the nature of the language in which they were written, likewise according to the circumstances in which they were set down, and expounded in the light of unlike passages and of many and clearer passages) and which agree with the rule of faith and love, and contributes much to the glory of God and man's salvation.[21]

Again, this humanist-inspired grammatical and historical approach to the single meaning of Scripture is not anti-theological. According to Bullinger, Scripture can be understood purely because God wills it to be understood. The claim of single meaning is not here a claim to realism and rational objectivity. Bullinger's reading of Scripture is still very much theological in technique: he insists that a true reading of Scripture with be coherent with "the rule of faith and love" and he is not

---

20. Harding, *Decades of Henry Bullinger*, 71.

21. Scripturas Sanctas, dixit Apostolus Petrus, non esse interpretationis privatæ. Proinde non probamus interpretationes quaslibet; unde nec pro vera aut genuina Scripturarum interpretatione agnoscimus eum, quem vocant sensum Romanæ ecclesiæ, quem scilicet simpliciter Romanæ ecclesiæ defensores omnibus obtrudere contendunt recipiendum: sed illam duntaxat Scripturarum interpretationem pro orthodoxa et genuina agnoscimus, quæ ex ipsis est petita Scripturis (ex ingenio utique ejus linguæ, in qua sunt scriptæ, secundum circumstantias item expensæ, et pro ratione locorum vel similium vel dissimilium, plurium quoque et clariorum expositæ), cum regula fidei et caritatis congruit, et ad gloriam Dei hominumque salutem eximie facit.

averse to reading Scripture typologically.²² While the Zurich Reformation anticipates some of the hermeneutical emphases of modernity, it would be unwise to claim that this is where the determinate meaning of historical criticism begins.

Single Meaning in the English Reformation

Biblical interpretation does not appear to have been an issue that attracted a great deal of discussion during the English Reformations. As indicated in the previous chapter, there could be said to have been something of a tradition of English Antiochene biblical interpretation through figures such as Theodore of Tarsus, Aldhelm of Malmesbury, Richard of St. Victor, and Herbert of Bosham. Yet reformation thought in England was largely dependent upon continental reformers and, indeed, Edwardian continental imports such as Martin Bucer and Peter Martyr Vermigli.²³ Indeed, the most significant writer on biblical interpretation in the early English Reformation wrote from a place of exile: William Tyndale. In his *Obedience of a Christian Man*, Tyndale rejects the polysemy of the *Quadriga*, arguing instead for the exclusive status of the literal sense of Scripture.

> They divide the scripture into four senses, the literal, tropological, allegorical, anagogical. The literal sense is becoming nothing at all. For the Pope hath taken it clean away and hath made it his possession. He hath partly locked it up with the false and counterfeited keys of his traditions, ceremonies and feigned lies. And partly driveth men from it with violence of sword. For no man dare abide by the literal sense of the text, but under a protestation, if it shall please the Pope. The tropological sense pertaineth to good manners (say they) and teacheth what we ought to do. The allegory is appropriate to faith, and the anagogical to hope and things above. Tropological and anagogical are terms of their own feigning and altogether unnecessary. For they are but allegories both two of them and this word allegory comprehendeth them both and is enough.... Thou shalt understand therefore that the scripture hath but one sense which is the literal sense. And that literal sense is the root and ground of all, and the anchor that never faileth whereunto if thou cleave

---

22. Petersen, "Bullinger's Prophets," 254–55.
23. Trueman, "Theology of the English Reformation," 162.

> thou canst never err or go out of the way. And if thou leave the literal sense thou canst not but go out of the way.[24]

Tyndale's assertion here is not as simple as it seems. As a scholar who subscribed to many of the aims and values of renaissance humanism and was well-versed in Greek and literary analysis, Tyndale recognized that Scripture itself employs proverbs and allegories, such as the "I am" sayings of John's Gospel.[25] He also understood that literal meaning could be ambiguous and that reading needed to be attentive to detail and engaged in comparison with other scriptural texts.[26] Allegorical interpretation was still a possibility, as far as Tyndale was concerned, but its role was limited to the task of explaining and illustrating the Bible in preaching. It is legitimate to employ allegorical interpretation to use biblical events to illustrate the Gospel message, even if that is not the obvious intent of a biblical passage, Tyndale argued. Tyndale gave the example of reading the cutting and healing of Malchus's ear in Matt 26:51 (and parallels) as offering the potential to say that the law cuts, but Christ heals. But allegories such as this are not to be confused with the true meaning of the passage itself, he argued.

> This allegory proveth nothing neither can do. For it is not the Scripture, but an example or a similitude borrowed of the scripture to declare a text or a conclusion of the scripture more expressly, and to root it in the heart.... Moreover, if I could not prove with an open text that which the allegory doth express, then were the allegory a thing to be jested at and of no greater value than a tale of Robin Hood.[27]

Much of Tyndale's work is polemical, including his notorious debates with Thomas More, and his use of Scripture is characteristic of the employment of single meaning as a hermeneutical assumption in such writing.[28] The claim that the literal meaning is the single meaning of Scripture is also found in Martin Bucer's commentary on the Psalms. Bucer was German, a former Dominican who had served as an intermediary between Luther and Zwingli in their disagreement over the presence of Christ in the Eucharist. He was later offered refuge in England by Thomas

---

24. Tyndale, *Obedience of a Christian Man*, 156
25. Werrell, *William Tyndale's Theology*, 62–81.
26. Tyndale, *Obedience*, 158.
27. Ibid., 158–59.
28. Pineas, "William Tyndale's Polemical Use," 65–78.

Cranmer and came to serve as the Regius Professor of Divinity at the University of Cambridge. He argued that biblical interpretation ought to follow the literal meaning alone and gave three reasons for doing so: that this approach alone commands respect from Jews; that the literal sense is the only sense that can provide the basis of disputation and finally that the literal sense is the agreed source of Christian doctrine.[29] Yet Bucer also saw Scripture as theologically orientated towards the Church: that it was intended for Christians, not simply a witness to the past.[30] Bucer's understanding of the literal meaning as the single meaning was founded upon a theological conception of who and what Scripture was for.

The formularies of the Elizabethan settlement appear also to have assumed the hermeneutical emphases of renaissance humanism, though this is rarely ever explicit. Article IX of the Thirty-nine Articles of Religion refers rather peculiarly to the Greek phrase *phronema sarkos* ("mind of the flesh"). Article XXII as refers to the doctrine of purgatory as "repugnant to the word of God," most probably assuming a grammatical plain-sense reading of the appropriate texts. The canonical interpretation of Scripture, as well as the sense in which Scripture is a self-interpreting and self-contained unit, is expressed in the injunction in Article XXI that the Church may not "so expound one place of Scripture, that it be repugnant to another." It is interesting that the most significant hermeneutical statement in the *Book of Common Prayer* in its current form in relation to the Articles of Religion is the declaration from Charles I in 1628 that a Christian "shall not put his own sense or comment to be the meaning of the Article, but shall take it in the literal and grammatical sense." The sermon "An Exhortation to the Reading of Holy Scripture" in the *First Book of Homilies*, adopts a view similar to that of Zwingli's *Die Klarheit und Gewissheit*: that the weakness of human reason makes correct biblical interpretation possible without the work of the Holy Spirit.

> And in another place Chrysostom saith, that a man's human and worldly wisdom, or science, is not needful to the understanding of Scripture; but the revelation of the Holy Ghost, who inspireth the true meaning unto them that with humility and diligence do search therefore. He that asketh shall have, and he that seeketh shall find, and he that knocketh shall have the door opened.

---

29. Hobbs, "How Firm a Foundation," 477–91.
30. Müller, *Martin Bucers Hermeneutik*, 142–44.

For Cranmer, the single meaning of a scriptural text is perspicuous to the humble and devout reader. This is not because of the nature of enquiry as a natural grammatical task, but because the understanding of Scripture is a result of spiritual revelation. It is worth noting that Cranmer uses Matt 7:7 as the proof for his statement about perspicuity: a text frequently quoted by Zwingli at the introduction of many of his works to the same effect. Another homily ("An Information of them which take offence at certain places of Holy Scripture") from the *Second Book of Homilies*, thought to be written by John Jewel. The purpose of the homily, like the previous exhortation, is to encourage popular reading of the Bible, in this case by challenging the objection that parts of Scripture are immoral, ridiculous or confusing and thus Scripture itself is not worth reading. Again, the problem is not the text but the mind of the reader.

> Thus, if ye will be profitable hearers and readers of the Holy Scriptures, ye must first deny yourselves, and keep under your carnal senses, taken by the outward words, and search the inward meaning: reason must give place to God's Holy Spirit; you must submit your worldly wisdom and judgement unto his Divine wisdom and judgement. Consider that the Scripture, in what strange form soever it be pronounced, is the word of the living God.

The primary interest in this homily is to encourage the humility of the reader of Scripture when faced with problematic or offensive passages. Behind this exhortation is a dualism of divine and human reason and a belief in Scripture as direct divine discourse, albeit couched in human language which may provide difficulties in interpretation. The homily itself, as it attempts to deal with problematic passages, resorts to a range of specific grammatical and historical solutions, such as explaining the significance of the Hebrew term translated "horn" in Ps 75:12. Again, though the grammatical tools for biblical interpretation anticipate the biblical interpretation of modernity, the fundamental conception of Scripture under which they are used is wholly theological.

Conclusion

The nature of biblical interpretation was one of the most significant themes in Renaissance and Reformation controversy. The decisions to create a critical edition of a biblical text, to criticize the Church or, indeed, break away from it, were decisions that rested upon ideas about biblical meaning: where and how meaning could be found and the kind of authority it had when found. Such decisions were indeed aided by a sense that Scripture had a single meaning. When Erasmus looked at the Church, single meaning meant that biblical texts offered an urgent and unavoidable critique. When Ronsard contemplated the evangelical reform movements in France, it was clear to him that they had mishandled Scripture and denied its true meaning. Having encouraged popular interpretation of Scripture with his preaching on its perspicuity, Zwingli could not embrace his own interpretation with that of the Anabaptists in a single polysemic view of meaning: there could only be one true meaning and it could only be decided upon through the exercise of linguistic and literary learning. Yet the renewed clarity with which some Renaissance and Reformation writers assumed and articulated theories of the single meaning of Scripture is not an historical anomaly. As argued above, the hermeneutical imperatives of the period are simply medieval and patristic ideas given a new prominence and, in some cases, made exclusive. The ideas of single meaning in this period have strong theological foundations: it is not as though the emergence of humanism makes the reading of Scripture somehow secular, as the now contemporary use of the term is taken to mean.

Cranmer's collect for the second Sunday of Advent, written for the 1549 Prayer Book, is based upon the epistle reading for the day, Rom 15:4ff.

> Blessed Lord, who hast caused all holy Scriptures to be written for our learning: Grant that we may in such wise hear them, read, mark, learn, and inwardly digest them, that by patience and comfort of thy holy Word, we may embrace and hold fast the blessed hope of everlasting life, which thou hast given us in our Saviour Jesus Christ. Amen.

The prayer testifies to an important element in the hermeneutical revolution that the Reformations represent: a desire for biblical interpretation to be what it has always been when performed with faithfulness. Cranmer's repetition of the language of the epistle reading claims its perceived value for biblical interpretation for the Church for whose learning Scripture was written.[31] It simply cannot be claimed that the biblical hermeneutic

---

31. Sargent, *Day by Day*, 21.

brought to the fore in this period witnessed any kind of prejudice against theology and the theological interpretation of Scripture.

5

Written for Them
Single Meaning in Modernity

Modernity is, of course, difficult to define. Certainly, in relation to biblical interpretation, the hermeneutical approaches that come to the fore in the sixteenth century dominate much of the use of Scripture in the Protestant Churches and their universities until the nineteenth century. Much biblical interpretation in Reformed, Lutheran, Catholic, and Orthodox settings continued as though the Renaissance did not happen at all. The ideas that saw the historical and grammatical interpretation of the Renaissance and the Reformations develop into what might now be called historical criticism were marginal and certainly do not characterize the whole of the period discussed in this chapter (roughly the seventeenth to twentieth centuries). One only needs to consider a figure such as the seventeenth-century Leiden Hebrew scholar and Federal theologian Johannes Cocceius, who argued for spiritual meaning as something distinct from the literal meaning, to see this. Perhaps more representative of the Reformed and Puritan theological tradition, emphasizing single meaning along the lines of the Second Helvetic Confession, is the English Puritan divine William Ames. For Ames, single meaning is also related to perspicuity.

> Hence there is only one meaning for every place in Scripture. Otherwise the meaning of Scripture would not only be unclear

and uncertain, but there would be no meaning at all—for anything which does not mean one thing surely means nothing.[1]

Again, Ames approach to single meaning is theological, reflecting the very earliest traditions of ecclesiological interpretation, as in his commentary on the Petrine epistles from which he draws the following hermeneutical maxim:

> We must understand all these things so, as if they were directly written unto us. This is directly gathered from these words, *Hath written unto us* [1 Pet 3:15].... Because such was the wisdom of God, which spake in these holy men, that they wrote these things which do belong unto us as well as unto those that lived at that time ... because God would have the Scripture to be the publick instrument of the Church, not of one age only, but of all ages.[2]

Likewise, Jonathan Edwards, "America's Theologian," well-acquainted with some of the trends in European Enlightenment thought, employed an approach to the Bible that was remarkably pre-critical, particularly in its emphasis upon symbolism and typology.[3] For Edwards, typological interpretation should also be applied to the interpretation of the natural world.[4] In many ways, Edwards barely seems to have belonged to the modern world at all. Edwards saw multiple levels of meaning in Scripture but argued that the spiritual meaning of a text was of primary importance. His view of literal meaning was of something multifaceted, embracing grammatical, lexical, historical and prophetic meaning, and in this he agreed with the dominant view of literal meaning from Hugh of St. Victor onwards. But Edwards also drew a spiritual and fleshly distinction within the literal meaning, perhaps more representative of Jacques Lefèvre d'Étaples. Edwards's *Religious Affections* contains this distinction.

> Edwards' emphasis upon the necessity of spiritual understanding did not eliminate the need for the literal sense. The communicative role carried out by the latter remains indispensable to the effective use of the Bible as a means of grace because a person cannot obtain a spiritual sense of the excellency of Christ without such a notion being conveyed to the mind through

1. Ames, *Marrow of Theology*, 188.
2. Ames, *Analytical Exposition*, 249–50.
3. As referred to by Jenson, *America's Theologian*.
4. Cherry, "Symbols of Spiritual Truth," 263–71.

speculative knowledge. Although the Scripture is a "dead letter" apart from the Spirit of God, nevertheless it is the interaction of *Word* and Spirit that produces spiritual understanding.[5]

This chapter will not attempt to offer a complete survey of determinate meaning in the modern period. Its interest is primarily those interpreters of Scripture whose work is foundational to the development of what would become historical criticism. It will be suggested that many of these interpreters were motivated, not by a hatred of Christian doctrine and the hermeneutical claims the Church made about itself, but by a desire to discern the true voice of the Spirit of God in the text. This desire must be understood as a development of the hermeneutical aims of elements within the European Reformation. The concerns of the radical Seventeenth and Eighteenth Century biblical interpreters whom we now see as forerunners of historical criticism were wholeheartedly theological. Spinoza sought a common approach to biblical interpretation as a means of Christian unity in a civilized society, following the devastation of the Thirty Years War. Gabler's desire for a single and unchanging biblical theology derived from an apparently scientific hermeneutic was likewise motivated by a desire for Christian unity as well as a desire for Christians to be aware of the literal meaning of Scripture. Robert Lowth and Johann Gottfried Herder sought a determinate literary reading of the Hebrew Scriptures on the basis of theological assumptions about the Hebrew language itself and about primitive human experience. Schleiermacher's redefinition of biblical hermeneutics, arguably of the greatest significance for the development of historical criticism, was so theological that it took religious experience as its starting point. It may be, as Milbank argues, that the hermeneutics of modernity and historical criticism were premised upon a denial of a particular view of immanence and participation, but the aims and theory of these interpreters of the Bible is far from hostile to Christian theology per se. While it would be difficult to maintain that these the thoughts of these interpreters represent the mainstream of Christian theology from the historical periods to which they belong, it would be similarly difficult to characterise them as being outside the broad range of Christian theological positions regarding the inspiration and interpretation of Scripture.

---

5. Stein, "Quest for the Spiritual Sense," 105.

Benedict de Spinoza

While many recent commentators, writing from the post-liberal or theological interpretation of Scripture perspectives for example, regard Spinoza as the enemy of traditional Christian interpretation of the Bible, this analysis is somewhat unfair.[6] Spinoza's aim was not anti-Christian: even if he did wish that biblical interpretation would provide a challenge to the authoritative hermeneutic of the Roman Catholic Church. Instead, Spinoza appears to have genuinely believed that reading Scripture is a theological enterprise. He views Scripture as inspired by the Holy Spirit. He fostered a "scientific" approach to interpretation because he believed that it would bring Christians of all persuasions into contact with the true meaning of Scripture: Spinoza was inspired by a desire for the Church's unity. More than that, Spinoza believed what Zwingli first believed: that the Bible could be interpreted by all Christian people: biblical interpretation was not to be exclusively undertaken by hierarchy of the Church. Because the Bible could be interpreted like any other historically contingent text, it could also be interpreted by anyone. It is somewhat ironic, then, that the hermeneutical and methodological ideas that Spinoza would inspire have never broken out of the similarly exclusive environment of the biblical scholar. The following extract from *Tractatus Theologico-Politicus* (Theological-Political Treatise) witnesses the nature of Spinoza's anti-clerical, but not anti-theological motivation.

> To extricate ourselves from such confusion and to free our minds from theological prejudices and the blind acceptance of human fictions as God's teaching, we need to analyse and discuss the true method of interpreting Scripture. For if we do not know this, we can know nothing for certain regarding what the Bible or the Holy Spirit wishes to teach. To formulate the matter succinctly, I hold that the method of interpreting Scripture, does not differ from the [correct] method of interpreting nature, but is rather wholly consonant with it. The [correct] method of interpreting nature consists above all in constructing a natural history, from which we derive the definitions of natural things, as from certain data. Likewise, to interpret Scripture, we need to assemble a genuine history of it and to deduce the thinking of the Bible's authors by valid inferences from this history, as from certain data and principles. Provided we admit no other criteria

---

6. Milbank, *Theology and Social Theory*, 22; Legaspi, *Death of Scripture*, 23–25; Green, "In the Arms of the Angels," 201–3; Webster, *Holy Scripture*, 19.

or data for interpreting Scripture and discussing its contents than what is drawn from Scripture itself and its history, we will always proceed without any danger of going astray.[7]

Here, Spinoza differs somewhat from Thomas Hobbes, with whom he is often associated. Hobbes was similarly anticlerical and his biblical hermeneutics similarly sought to make the Bible subject to the norms of general hermeneutics, but authority in interpretation was still needed: and this role was to be taken by the anointed monarch as head of state.[8] Spinoza conceives of the text of Scripture here as the medium through which the Holy Spirit speaks to readers. The purpose of reading the Bible, he assumes, is to hear God speak. His aim to distance biblical interpretation from theological prejudice and human teaching is related to a desire for pure access to the text, but is still a theological aim in itself. Like many after him, Spinoza thought that correct biblical interpretation through shared hermeneutical theory could be a source of Christian unity. Spinoza perceived Christian disunity in Europe as ultimately a conflict of biblical interpretations. A scientific approach to the Bible, he argued, could do much to end this disunity. What particularly distinguishes Spinoza from the theological interpretation of the Reformed tradition at this point is the claim that the Bible ought to be studied in a manner similar to that of the natural sciences since the Scripture, as a human creation, belongs properly to the natural world. But Spinoza also criticized biblical literature in a way that also departs from the Reformed tradition with which, as is argued below, his approach to Scripture is very similar. For example, Spinoza critiqued the theology of the New Testament as being too influenced by Jewish views of divine causality: the intervention of God into events which otherwise appear natural. He saw this causality as the reason why the gospels contain so much of the miraculous. This critique created a sort of distantiation, hitherto unknown, between the world of the text and contemporary interpreters of the text. Yet this is far from a de-theologizing of Scripture as is often assumed. Spinoza simply sought the outworking of the reformation principle of the clarity or perspicuity of Scripture and the related view that the Bible could be interpreted by anyone. Whereas these ideas had become problematic for the magisterial reformation, as seen in Zurich, Spinoza aimed to provide a hermeneutical means by which perspicuity could be realized. As in Reformation

---

7. Spinoza, *Theological-Political Treatise*, 98.
8. Reventlow, *Authority of the Bible*, 213.

Zurich, the clear meaning of Scripture was seen by Spinoza to reside in its human contingency, accessed through language and history. As Roy A. Harrisville and Walter Sundberg argue, Spinoza's biblical hermeneutic represents a further "Protestantization" of biblical interpretation, aiming to give readers unmediated access to the true meaning of Scripture, without the guiding hand of Church or established doctrine.[9]

Of course, Spinoza's ideas were not without precedent. Indeed, the Arminian theologian Hugo Grotius (1583–1645) makes use of several of Spinoza's most famous insights much before Spinoza. In his *Annotata ad Vetus Testamentum*, Grotius argues that the Bible should not be read with a special hermeneutic which assumes inspiration; rather, it should be read as any other text, with special attention to issues of philology and historical context. According to Grotius, the aim of biblical interpretation ought to be the primary sense of biblical texts. This reading may disagree with traditional doctrinal readings. Grotius famously argues that some prophecy from the Old Testament, received as Christological in orientation in the New Testament is not, in fact, so. For example, Grotius rejects sixteen centuries of Christian interpretation of the servant song on Isaiah 53 by arguing that it needs to be understood as relating to Isaiah's own ministry. Of course, as has been seen, this radical use of single literal meaning to question traditional theological interpretation is not new in this period: one only need consider the similar approaches to the psalter taken by Diodore of Tarsus and Andrew of St. Victor. Grotius' exegetical interest was in the historical context of a text and he saw less need to explain the Old Testament with reference to the New Testament, wanted the Old Testament to be heard with its own voice. Like many Christian theologians influenced by the approaches of renaissance humanism, Grotius aspired (with relative success) to a knowledge of Hebrew and rabbinic interpretation: this was a contributing factor towards his historicism.[10] In his *Annotata*, Grotius argued that the right interpretation of some prophetic claims could be found with reference to events in the prophetic books themselves: Isa 7:14 is about one of Isaiah's sons; Jer 23:5 about Zerubbabel; and that the Old Testament itself was primarily about the History of Israel, not the Church or Christ. Similarly, in his Song of Songs commentary, Grotius contends that the book is primarily about

---

9. Harrisville and Sundberg, *Bible in Modern Culture*, 44–45. Cf. Levine, "Spinoza's Bible," 93–142.

10. Reventlow, "Humanistic Exegesis," 175–91 and Rosenberg, "Hugo Grotius as Hebraist," 62–90.

sexual love. Like Spinoza after him, Grotius wanted to avoid confessional priorities forcing the hand of biblical interpretation and also wanted the Bible to be the source of Christian unity.[11] Grotius held that the focus of Old Testament Judaism and the Gospels was tropological, urging the love of God and neighbor: the New Testament reproduces and extended the moral teaching of the Old Testament.[12] However, these historical and tropological emphases did not stop Grotius interpreting Scripture typologically, albeit as a vague reflection of other events within the same literal history of Israel and the Church. As H. J. M. Nellen notes,

> Grotius described the literal meaning of certain events in the history of Israel and then explained how these events showed a particular God-given structure which denoted other events, for instance events in the life of Christ. But in Grotius' exegesis this second, typological meaning lost all concrete value; it was no more than a vague theological justification or adumbration of the redemption by Christ.[13]

While arguing that historical knowledge was essential to a proper understanding of the Scripture, Thomas Hobbes also employed typological interpretation. Like Spinoza, Grotius was also sceptical about the truthfulness of biblical miracles, such as Joshua keeping the sun still in Josh 10:13 (in *Opera omnia theologica* I.106A), though he did not go so far as to claim a normative "scientific" way of reasoning about Scripture and the natural world. In a manner that anticipated late eighteenth-century rationalistic explanations of the miracles of Jesus, Grotius speculated that God could have caused a reflection of the sun in the clouds, so as to make it seem to be present after it had set. Spinoza departed from the radical hermeneutics of Grotius in a number of important ways, however. For example, Spinoza drew a distinction between the meaning of a biblical text and its truthfulness. Such a distinction is quite alien to biblical interpretation prior to Spinoza. Even interpreters who reject the truthfulness of an apparent literal reading of a text, such as Origen, assume that it is not the divinely intended meaning of text. Other interpreters might similarly regard a text to be historically untrue while theologically true, though such a distinction really only gains ground some time after Spinoza. Of

---

11. Nellen, "Hugo Grotius," 809–10.

12. Rabbie, "Hugo Grotius and Judaism," 99–120; de Jonge, "Grotius' View of the Gospels," 65–74; and de Jonge, "Hugo Grotius," 97–115.

13. Nellen, "Grotius," 814.

course, Spinoza was interested in the meaning of texts, rather than their truthfulness. This is due to the overriding political interest with which he approaches biblical interpretation. Spinoza is interested in fostering interpretation on which people can agree in order to create a harmonious society. P. J. Lambe argues that there is a sharp distinction between the "criticism" of Grotius, Simon and Louis Cappel and that of Spinoza, Isaac de la Peyrère and Voltaire.[14] The former sought to serve Christian doctrine confessionally, the latter sought political and controversial aims. Lambe argues for a distinction between criticism and scepticism: that Grotius employed criticism whereas Spinoza employed scepticism, understood as a questioning of received authority.

> Protestants were particularly vulnerable to overtones of scepticism which accompanied eighteenth-century ideas of criticism, because they had in principle rejected ecclesial structure of authority such as the Roman church represented. Ideas of individualism, though not at this stage entirely developed, were more easily stimulated by the "think-for-yourself" popularism encouraged by the Enlightenment. This vulnerability became built into Protestant theology and produced a peculiarly Protestant characterisation of the development of biblical criticism. It is by no means clear that things could have evolved any differently. The seventeenth-century environment transposed negative aspects onto criticism, even without a thoroughgoing scepticism. The dialectic base that evolved within Protestantism was part of a wider recasting of intellectual perceptions, subject to the commercial forces of the press and to religious considerations. Controversy was endemic to the period, as was popularism. In the eighteenth century Protestantism gradually interiorised this spirit, as its own defensive scholasticism crumbled.[15]

But this argument forces a false distinction between a committed confessional approach to Scripture and a non-theological philosophical and political approach to Scripture. As has been shown, the approach Spinoza takes to Scripture is an expression of a particular view of the relation of Christian doctrine to Scripture and features a development of the "plain sense" idea of meaning that achieved dominance through the European Reformation.

---

14. Lambe, "Critics and Skeptics," 271–96.
15. Ibid., 296.

New Approaches to Single Meaning in the Eighteenth Century

While is has been popular to conceive of the emerging intellectual trends of the eighteenth century as a single movement, "the Enlightenment," the reality is much more complex, especially as related to biblical hermeneutics. While some followed Spinoza in asserting the primacy of historical contingency and method inspired by the universal claims of the natural sciences, others saw Scripture as a witness to something in the past that needed to be recovered, whether an age of holiness (Michaelis), the purity of an original inspired language (Lowth), or primal religious experience (Herder and Schleiermacher). To some extent, all of these approaches share Spinoza's aim to create a "natural history" of what lies behind the text and assume an historical distantiation between the text, that to which it bears witness in the past, and the reader in the present. Yet none of these approaches can be described as dismissing the theological nature and purpose of biblical interpretation. Indeed, Michaelis, Lowth, Herder, and Schleiermacher all proceed from theological assumptions about the past which are, in some cases, quite profound.

Spinozan Approaches

Hermeneutics of the most historicist and rationalist flavour, following Spinoza most closely and before the historical focus of romanticism shifted attention in biblical interpretation towards a particular feature of history (language or experience), can be seen in the work of Chladenius, Eichhorn, Ernesti and Gabler. Johann Martin Chladenius (1710–1759), in his *Introduction to the Correct Interpretation of Reasonable Discourses and Writings* argued that correct interpretation is consistent with what an historical author intends as the purpose of their writing.[16] The correct interpretation of a history book written with the purpose of drawing moral lessons is to identify those lessons, rather than simply recognising the text as a description of past events, Chladenius argued. However, Chladenius' concern was principally general hermeneutics. He describes biblical hermeneutics as subject to its own special hermeneutical rules, and biblical interpretation as dependent upon revelation rather than reason. Johann Gottfried Eichhorn (1752–1827), a pupil of Michaelis,

---

16. Chladenius, *Einleitung zur richtigen Auslegung.*

used and developed "myth" as an interpretive category, offering rational explanations of the miracles of Jesus and distancing the question of the historical truthfulness of the text from its value as myth. This was an interpretive possibility contained within Spinoza's suggestion of the need to create a natural history of the events supposedly witnessed in Scripture to accompany interpretation of its texts and "to deduce the thinking of the Bible's authors by valid inferences from this history."[17] Eichhorn pushed Spinozan distantiation between historical truth, the text and the reader to new levels of alienation and is perhaps a good example of an "historical critical" biblical interpreter who really did have a prejudice against theology as well as against Scripture itself.

Spinoza's hostility to Christian doctrine as an influence upon biblical interpretation is reflected in the work of Johann August Ernesti (1707–81) who argued that the Old Testament should be considered on its own terms, without reference to the New Testament. Ernesti's *Institutio Interpretis Novi Testamenti* argues for the application of linguistic and grammatical techniques to biblical interpretation and limits the role of the rule of faith. What is perhaps most remarkable about Ernesti is the seeming lack of philosophical or theological basis to his biblical hermeneutics. He suggested that biblical interpretation is more a matter of practice than it is of theory: it is simply something one does without a question of how it is that what one considers good interpretation really is good interpretation. Good interpretation, Ernesti asserted, is simply a matter of the exercise of natural powers of intelligence and diligence. The single meaning of Scripture is assumed throughout Ernesti's work as the goal of interpretation and is associated with authorial intention: "hermeneutics are the science of attaining clearness, both in comprehending and explaining the sense of any author; or of discovering and explaining clearly what is the meaning of any sentence."[18] The closest Ernesti comes to hermeneutical theory is his distinction between the natural polysemy of words and determinate meaning of words when employed in a sentence.

> Therefore, though custom has by degrees attached more than one meaning to a term, in order that the difficulty of learning languages might not be increased by the infinite multiplication of words; yet, in practice, while the subject, the mode, and the place of speaking, remain unchanged, it only attaches one meaning to each word; and, upon the whole, arranges so, that

17. Spinoza, *Theological Political Treatise*, 98.
18. Ernesti, *Principles*, 11.

> whatever addition is made to the ordinary sense, may be understood from the whole style of speaking, or from the accompanying words.[19]

Yet, for all its lack of theological foundation, Ernesti's approach to biblical interpretation is still motivated by theological concerns. He claims that the interpretation of Scripture is the greatest and most responsible task and he claims the heritage of the Renaissance and Reformation as his own, suggesting that the hermeneutical developments of the period led to the rediscovery of truth lost since the sixth century.[20]

Like Spinoza, J. P. Gabler argued for a distinction between biblical theology and doctrinal theology. According to Gabler, biblical theology was fixed and unchanging, based on the authentic meaning of biblical literature. Doctrine ought to be derived from biblical theology but may change or develop. Again, like Spinoza, Gabler optimistically hoped that as Christians approached Scripture free from dogmatic bias, through methods inspired by the natural sciences, they would encounter a meaning of Scripture that they could all agree on. Once they had seen what Scripture actually said and once traditional doctrinal readings had been found wanting, there would be agreement and Christian unity. For Gabler, the meaning of Scripture was determinate and simple: once Christians were exposed to it there could be no more disagreement.

> Thus, as soon as all these things have been properly observed and carefully arranged, at last a clear sacred Scripture will be selected with scarcely any doubtful readings, made up of passages which are appropriate to the Christian religion of all times. These passages will show with unambiguous words the form of faith that is truly divine; the *dicta classica* properly so called, which can then be laid out as the fundamental basis for a more subtle dogmatic scrutiny. For only from these methods can those certain and undoubted universal ideas be singled out, those ideas which alone are useful in dogmatic theology.[21]

As Frei argues, early modern biblical interpreters, following some of the imperatives valued by Spinoza, moved beyond the Reformation in relation to the question of textual meaning and historical truthfulness.[22]

---

19. Ibid., 18.
20. Ibid., 6–7.
21. Sandys-Wunsch and Eldridge, "J. P. Gabler," 140.
22. Frei, *Eclipse of Biblical Narrative*, 51–64.

But it would be wrong to claim that Spinoza and those who followed him departed completely from the traditions of theological interpretation in favor of some secular and scientific way of reading Scripture. The exclusive focus upon literal meaning and biblical language is a mark of continuity with ways of reading Scripture that had gone before. The aim of seeing the Church reformed and unified by the voice of Scripture standing over and against tradition and the teaching of the Church is a theological aim resembling the hopes of William of Ockham and the European Reformers and Humanists, amongst others.

Johann David Michealis

Johann David Michaelis's intent was to establish biblical criticism as a discipline much more akin to classics in terms of the relation of the scholar to the subject matter. Biblical interpretation, he argued ought to investigate the history of Israel behind the text as a past to be revered and learned from in the present. Just as classicists make the assumption that the classical period represents something of the best of human culture, so to biblical scholars should recognize the contemporary spiritual potency of studying Israel's past.

> In turning to the poets of Israel's Golden Age, Michaelis hoped to encounter what he called the "Near Eastern Muses" (*die morgenländischen Musen*). He claimed that to read the Bible profitably and to appreciate its "sublime and beautiful poetry," one had to be aided by the Muses. Not only does this show Michaelis's debt to classical thought, it also indicates what was at stake in the appropriation of a classical Israelite literature. It was not a Greek Muse or a universal human Muse that Michaelis identified, but *Near Eastern Muses*. To understand the Bible, then, one had to reckon with the particular genius of the Orient. For Michaelis, it is this conception of a classical, ancient Near Eastern Israel, and not the churchly construct of an exceptional, suprahistorical race, that ultimately opens the literature of the Hebrew Bible to the interpreter.[23]

The goal of biblical interpretation then, as with Spinoza, is the creation of a single reliable account of Israel's history. The text of Scripture has a single meaning as it witnesses to a golden age. But this method, as employed by Eichorn, denied such a reverential reimagining of Israel

---

23. Legaspi, *Death of Scripture*, 103–4.

who considered that Michaelis had not gone far enough to demonstrate the relative cultural strangeness of ancient Israel.[24] As Michael Legaspi argues, Michaelis's hope that Israel's past could be studied as an inspiration for the present contributed to the development of an historical disjuncture between a remote and alien oriental past and a sophisticated present. Legaspi contends that Michaelis's orientalist redefinition of Israel's past also contributed to the development of the curiosity that is the "academic" Bible, stripped of any theological authority. Of course, this was never Michaelis's intention.

Robert Lowth and Johann Gottfried Herder

While Michaelis had sought to affirm the theological value of the history of Israel behind the text of Scripture, Robert Lowth, professor of Poetry at the University of Oxford between 1741–1752, held that it was the Hebrew language itself and its poetic form that was theologically instructive. In *De Sacra Poësi Hebraeorum* (translated into German by Michaelis), Lowth explored the nature of Hebrew poetry, claiming that it represents an elemental and pristine witness to humankind at its closest relation to God and the world. Hebrew poetry conveys a natural religion of the sublime, argued Lowth, a view possibly influenced by his reading of Horace.[25] While Lowth's approach to Scripture depends upon a theory of history behind the text, his turn to language and poetry represents a return to the text itself as inspired apart from its status simply as a witness to history. This was a new form of historicism: the meaning of Scripture was firmly located in the way it represented something pure in the past, rather than the way it reflected something still to come. For this reason, Lowth was hostile to typological and Christological interpretation. The spiritual power of the text was related to its poetic expression and the effect it could have upon hearers and readers.[26] This certainly necessitated a reading of the Old Testament in Hebrew as the best way in which to feel its authorially intended poetic force. The discernment of this sense is the task of the translator and commentator.

> The first and principal business of a translator, is to give the plain literal and grammatical sense of his author; the obvious

24. Sheenan, *Enlightenment Bible*, 219.
25. Bultmann, "After Horace," 62–82.
26. Legaspi, *Death of Scripture*, 110–11.

> meaning of his words, phrases, and sentences; and express them in the language into which he translates, as far as may be, in equivalent words, phrases, and sentences. Whatever indulgence may be allowed in other respects; however excusable he may be, if he fail of attaining the elegance, the spirit, the sublimity of his author ... want of fidelity admits of no excuse, and is entitled to no indulgence.[27]

Lowth made a series of judgements about Hebrew poetry and comparisons with other poetry which facilitated his theological account of the value of the medium. Hebrew poetry was most inspired primarily because Lowth understood it to be the oldest extant human poetry. As Anna Cullhead argues, this demonstrates that scriptural Hebrew poetry was judged in terms of other poetry by the professor of poetry: Lowth simply concludes that Hebrew poetry is most inspired of any poetry because of its greater antiquity with the aid of a theology of primitive innocence.[28] This is interesting because, though Lowth seeks to elevate Hebrew poetry, he does so in terms of its qualitative comparison to other ancient poetry. Hebrew poetry is judged and interpreted on the basis of poetic comparison, not on the basis of a special theological hermeneutic. But that is not to suggest that his location of scriptural meaning within the poetic impact of its original language is not theological in inspiration or aim.

Lowth's work was of immense importance in the development of form criticism and its accompanying hermeneutical imperative that the calculated *Sitz im Leben* of a text defined what that text meant on the basis of how it was used. In this respect, as well as in the nature of his interest in Hebrew poetry, Lowth had a strong influence upon Johann Gottfried Herder.[29] In his *Briefe, das Studium der Theologie betreffend* (1780–81), Herder argued that biblical interpreters must strive for historical meaning and reference as the true meaning of the text.

> One must read the Bible in a human way: for it is a book written by human beings for human beings: human is the language, human are the outer means with which it was written and preserved; human, in the end, is indeed the sense with which it can be grasped, every means that serves its interpretation, as

---

27. Lowth, *Isaiah*, XLII.
28. Cullhead, "Original Poetry," 25–47.
29. Witte, "Die literarische Gattung," 93–123; and Bultmann, "Herder's Biblical Studies," 233–34.

well as the entire purpose and use to which it is supposed to be put.[30]

The view here resembles the Spinozan location of the Bible within the natural world of cause and effect: the purely human and contingent. Yet in Herder's *On the Spirit of Hebrew Poetry* the spiritual significance of Scripture is seen in Hebrew poetry's naturalistic and elemental inspiration, reflecting something of a proto-romantic ideal. Like Michaelis, Herder thought that Hebrew poetry should be seen as just as inspired as classical poetry. Like Lowth, Herder's biblical criticism was focused upon creating translations which accurately convey the original impression of the Hebrew poetry. Because of this, Herder was interested in the literary and cultural context of biblical writing. That context was very much influenced by Herder's perception of biblical Hebrew. Herder regarded Hebrew as primitive in the best sense, reflecting the most elemental and pure human experience. Hebrew, he argued is rurally poetic (*ländlichpoetische*) and un-philosophical. Herder understood this character as a consequence of the direct descent of Hebrew from the earliest human language and experience of the *Morgenland*. Because of this, the revelatory value of biblical literature was closely related to its poetic language as an expression of pure experience, uncorrupted by too much analysis and philosophical abstraction. In this, Herder seems to develop ideas about the expressive function of poetry explored by Johann Georg Hamann.[31] But what must be noted here is that the exclusive historicism of Herder's view of inspiration is embedded within a theological narrative of original innocence. While this theological perspective on history may be at odds with some more dominant Christian theological accounts of history, one cannot dismiss it as anti-theological or anti-Christian in intent.

F. D. E. Schleiermacher

Schleiermacher developed the emerging association of inspiration and antiquity away from the literary and linguistic focus of Lowth and Herder and towards the idea that the inspiration of the biblical text was closely related to the spiritual experience of its author, as it were, behind the text. In Schleiermachian terms, the consciousness of absolute dependence of

---

30. *Briefe, das Studium der Theologie betreffend* 145 as translated in Bultmann, "Herder's Biblical Studies," 237.

31. Ibid., 239.

the scriptural author is mediated through the text he creates in response to this consciousness. Hence the task of biblical interpretation is to capture that moment of inspiration behind the text, as witnessed, however imperfectly, within the text. Because of this, the historical quest for the authenticity of biblical literature has hermeneutical significance.

> Hence what is here spoken or done can be described as inspired in a much stricter and more definite sense. On the other hand, we should recklessly break up the unity of life characteristic of these apostolic men if, in order to bring out emphatically the inspiration of the Holy Scriptures, we were to assert that they were less animated and moved by the Holy Spirit in another parts of their apostolic office than in the act of writing, or in the composition of writings (also concerned with the service of the churches) which were not destined to be included in the Canon; or again that they enjoyed His aid very much more in the public addresses or parts of addresses which were eventually preserved in the Acts of the Apostles than at any other time; or that this difference, with or without their knowledge, was to be explained by the fact that over and above their immediate purpose these writings were meant to have a bearing on all subsequent ages. Thus the peculiar inspiration of the Apostles is not something that belongs exclusively to the books of the New Testament.[32]

Here Schleiermacher expresses his lack of particular interest in verbal inspiration. The written text of Scripture, never intended to be received as such, is just one expression of the piety of the apostles: their heightened consciousness of absolute dependence resulting from their acquaintance with the one in whom that consciousness was absolute, according to Schleiermacher. Because the writing of Scripture is just one monument to the apostles' personal inspiration, the inspiration of texts cannot be regarded as something specific to Scripture. Any writing from someone whose piety is comparable to the apostles could in theory be as valuable a witness to true religion as Scripture. Because of this, Schleiermacher does not see the need for a special scriptural hermeneutic. Like Spinoza, the human contingency of Scripture means for Schleiermacher that it can be read as any other text. Since any inspiration of the text of Scripture is derived from the piety of its author, the reading of Scripture ought to begin with an understanding of that author.

---

32. Schleiermacher, *Christian Faith*, 599.

> This means, first, that all inquiries intended to ascertain the authors of the books we have, and the genuineness or the reverse of particular passages, must pursue an unhampered course, and that no doubts which may arise should either be accepted by unfriendly prejudice or rejected without scrutiny. Not only is this a part of a complete knowledge of Scripture; it is not without influence on the interpretation and the use of individual passages. It means, secondly, that we refuse to be perverted from the purest hermeneutical methods, as would be the case if we knowingly preferred to put an artificial interpretation on a passage rather than construe it in a sense suggestive of a less pure view of Christian faith.[33]

Schleiermacher argues that Christians ought to impartially consider the authenticity of biblical texts, because a sure knowledge of the text's author is an essential component of the best hermeneutics. For Schleiermacher, correct interpretation reflected the nature of discourse as consisting of two elements: the universal element of language and the personal element of the specific message. Language in itself is not communicative outside of its particular use in personal discourse by, in the case of written texts, an author.[34] Consequently, interpretation consists of two elements: the grammatical and the psychological.[35] On a grammatical level, interpretation identifies the interpretive possibilities of the words themselves on the basis of shared language. On a psychological level, interpretation limits grammatical possibility through consideration of the author and his or her intentions. These two elements function as a constantly interacting and self-correcting cycle aimed at identifying the true meaning of the text. While Ricoeur notes the that Schleiermacher tends towards a universal general hermeneutics, embracing both Scripture and other texts, it must not be forgotten that there is a special significance of the author in Schleiermacher's scriptural hermeneutics, vis-à-vis the author's expression of a consciousness of absolute dependence.[36] Again, this is a theological understanding of the manner in which Scripture relates to divine revelation and how interpretation ought to aim to disclose an utterly theological experience behind the text.

33. Ibid., 605.
34. Corliss, "Schleiermacher's Hermeneutic," 364.
35. Schleiermacher, *Hermeneutics*, 21–40. Cf. Thiselton, *New Horizons*, 206; and Schleiermacher, *Hermeneutics and Criticism*, 194.
36. Ricoeur, "Schleiermacher's Hermeneutics," 181–97. Cf. Iser, *Range of Interpretation*, 41–42.

In Vanhoozer's analysis of the history of biblical interpretation in modernity, the nature of Schleiermacher's interest in authorial intention is the reason behind the ultimate dismissal of determinate meaning in post-structuralism.[37] For Vanhoozer, Schleiermacher transformed the metaphysics of authorship by relating meaning primarily to the consciousness of the author. Schleiermacher argued that biblical interpretation ought to seek to recover the thoughts of the author to which the text gives expression. According to Vanhoozer, this meant that authorial intention became a subjective and psychological concept, rather than a rational one, as it had been for Spinoza. As a result of this new understanding of the value of the author in interpretation, psychological questions relating to the existence and nature of intention, as well as to whether or not it can be successfully recovered by another person, made authorial intention impossibly elusive. Because of this, those who wanted to maintain a sense of determinate meaning in written texts, began to explore the structural nature of language as a basis for grounding meaning. In time, structuralism too proved an inadequate basis for determinate meaning as attention in hermeneutical philosophy began to emphasise the interpretive significance of the reception of texts by readers. For Vanhoozer, determinate meaning is rooted in communicative intention: this was lost as a result of Schleiermacher's romantic understanding of authorial intention. But the ultimate rejection of determinate meaning was never Schleiermacher's purpose. For Schleiermacher, biblical interpretation has a single meaning as its ultimate goal, defined in relationship to an author, regardless of how unobtainable that goal might be in practice.

Yet, with Schleiermacher, the Romantic historical disjuncture between the text and the experience of the author begins to replace the Enlightenment disjuncture between the text and the pure history of the event behind the text. Schleiermacher's most notable theological and hermeneutical idea, the relation of the text to an historic experience, was employed by Wilhelm Martin Leberecht de Wette. De Wette understood biblical narrative as "myth": an attempt to grasp the absolute through the medium of story.[38] This enabled de Wette to develop an approach to biblical criticism which saw reason's role as determining the historical experience of the absolute which gave rise to the biblical text, more often to be understood as expressing mythological rather than historical priorities. Like Herder's

---

37. Vanhoozer, *Meaning*, 25–26.
38. Bartholomew, "Uncharted Waters," 8. Cf. Rogerson, *W. M. L. de Wette*, 27.

association of poetry and *Geist*, the mythological was inescapably linked to the nature and style of Hebrew language and writing, as argued by de Wette in *Aufforderung zum Studium der hebräischen Sprache und Literature*. Again, while this approach differs significantly from perhaps more traditional understands of inspiration and the location of theological meaning within the text, it cannot really be termed anti-theological.

Historical Criticism on Nineteenth Century Public Stage

As the predominantly Germa hermeneutical and critical developments of the eighteenth and early nineteenth centuries began to influence scholars and clergy in Great Britain, interesting and often quite public debates on the interpretation of Scripture took place. Amongst the most important of these was the publication of *Essays and Reviews* (1860) and the ensuing response to it. As Mark A. Noll observes, both *Essays and Reviews* and the conservative responses to its articles tended to share a similar view of the nature of biblical scholarship and the nature of meaning as determinate.[39] The book itself can be seen as part of a cultural debate over the purpose of higher education.[40] *Essays and Reviews*, and Jowett's essay in particular, reflected the view that the Bible should be taught as part of a scientifically conceived "religious studies" within a broader liberal arts education. This was a direct challenge to the ecclesiastical tradition in which the study of the Bible existed primarily as a feature of "theological studies" for Christian ministry. The distinction is important, because what was at stake was the nature of reading the Bible as though it had theological strings attached. In its place was the romantic and historicist notion of the Bible as a witness to religion. Jowett's essay was an important step towards the acceptance of historical criticism in the English-speaking world. Yet it is hard to escape from the intensely theological understanding of criticism that Jowett has and, indeed, his reiteration of some hermeneutical concepts which would have made some sixteenth-century Reformers proud. Jowett argues that previous readers of Scripture including the Fathers, the medieval mystics and the Reformers interpret in such a way that their meaning "overflows the meaning of the text." Instead, Jowett argues that the true meaning of biblical texts will be discerned when the Bible is ap-

---

39. Noll, *Between Faith and Criticism*, 65.
40. Hill, "Religion and the University," 183–207.

proached critically, in the same manner as works of classical literature are approached, pointing out that in such disciplines as employ historical criticism there is comparatively little disagreement over the meaning of texts.

> *Interpret the Scripture like any other book.* There are many respects in which Scripture is unlike any other book; these will appear in the results of such an interpretation. The first step is to know the meaning, and this can be done in the same careful and impartial way that we ascertain the meaning of Sophocles or of Plato. The subordinate principles which flow out of this general one will also be gathered from the observation of Scripture. No other science of Hermeneutics is possible but an inductive one, that is to say, one based on the language and thoughts and narrations of the sacred writers. And it would be well to carry the theory of interpretation no further than in the case of other works. Excessive system tends to create an impression that the meaning of Scripture is out of our reach, or is to be attained in some other way than by exercise of manly sense and industry. Who would write a bulky treatise about the method to be pursued in interpreting Plato or Sophocles?[41]

Again, as with Spinoza, one can see in Jowett a desire to maintain something of the perspicuity of Scripture as a feature of its determinate meaning. Scripture, however complicated it might be, yields its meaning just as any other text does. For Jowett, this reading requires learning, particularly of biblical languages, but only inasmuch as is required for an ancient text. While Jowett undoubtedly sees a greater sense of historical distanciation between the text and the modern reader, there is little in this hermeneutical principle that disagrees, for example, with Zwingli's *Von der Predig Ampt*, or with Grotius and certainly not with Ernesti.[42] Furthermore, Jowett understands critical interpretation of the Bible to be a Christian moral and theological duty, other than which there is no higher calling.

> First, it may be laid down that Scripture has one meaning—the meaning which it had to the mind of the prophet or evangelist who first uttered or wrote, to the readers or hearers who first received it. Another view may be easier or more familiar to us, seeming to receive a light and interest from the circumstances

---

41. Jowett, "On the Interpretation of Scripture," 504.
42. Childs, "Sensus Literalis," 89.

of our own age. But such accommodation of the text must be laid aside by the interpreter, whose business it is to place himself as nearly as possible in the position of the sacred writer... The interpreter needs nothing short of "fashioning" in himself the mind of Christ. He has to be born again into a new spiritual or intellectual world, from which the thoughts of this world are shut out. It is one of the highest tasks on which the labour of a life can be spent, to bring the words of Christ a little nearer to the heart of man.[43]

Jowett goes on to say that there is language "which penetrates the individual soul, and embraces all the world in the arms of its love, in the same manner as that of Christ Himself."[44] For Jowett, biblical interpretation aims towards a single meaning of Scripture because that single, pure, and original meaning is more spiritually potent than any other meaning that might be substituted for it. Furthermore, like Gabler, Jowett articulates the ideal that critical biblical interpretation will foster Christian unity.[45] However naïve this may seem, it is a theological goal, theologically conceived and well within the mainstream of Christian theological aspiration. As Barr argues, what troubled Jowett was the use of biblical ideas in theology that distorted their meaning within the Bible as a literary work. Yet Jowett's reading is also theological: one needs a "vision and faculty divine" to interpret it faithfully. The Bible, though it should be read like any other book, is not for Jowett like any other book.[46]

It is interesting to note that the conservative reaction to such seemingly radical assertions of a particular form of determinate meaning did not strive to undermine the principle of determinate meaning, nor is historicist definition. This can be seen in the responses to *Essays and Reviews*. But perhaps one of the most interesting conservative reactions to historical criticism, from both a hermeneutical and theological perspective, is Edward Bouverie Pusey's response to the Daniel scholarship of Samuel Davidson. While Jowett was Regius Professor of Greek at the University of Oxford, Pusey was Regius Professor of Hebrew. Pusey was particularly concerned about the Second Temple dating of Daniel given by Davidson, which denied the prophetic nature of much of the material

---

43. Jowett, "Interpretation," 505–6.
44. Ibid., 526.
45. Ibid., 531–32.
46. Barr, "Jowett and the 'Original Meaning,'" 433–37; Barr, "Jowett and the Reading of the Bible," 1–44.

in Daniel. Pusey employs the same argument employed by Jowett against Davidson: preconceived ideas about what the scriptural text means cloy a true historical vision of what it really means.

> But nothing is gained by a mere answer to objections, so long as the original prejudice, "there cannot be supernatural prophecy," remains. Be the objections ever so completely removed, unbelief remains unshaken, because these objections are put forward to delude others, scarcely to blind itself; for they who believe not, know well that the ground of their unbelief rests on their conceptions of God and of His relation to man, not on history.[47]

What Pusey never questions is that it is the historical and grammatical, historically-grounded and determinate meaning of Daniel that is under discussion. Pusey's argument is that the problem with the unbelief in prophecy of Davidson and the German scholars upon whom he draws, is not that it is heretical, but that it lacks historical evidence. Pusey's problem is not so much the method of historical criticism as applied by Davidson, but the principles which govern his use of it and the conclusions he consequently reaches. It is worth noting the extent to which Pusey uses his expertise in Semitic languages to demonstrate that the alleged Aramaisms of Daniel do not indicate a late dating, as argued by Davidson. The meaning and significance of Daniel is determined solely by the factors considered important by Davidson himself. This is interesting, since *Daniel the Prophet* was intended to be a popular book and was indeed so. Pusey could well have challenged Davidson in a manner that would have convinced many of his audience, without employing the same historical critical methodology with which his audience would be largely unfamiliar. Yet, for Pusey, historical criticism is understood within a matrix of more traditional theological concerns. As Christopher R. Seitz concludes about Pusey's treatment of Daniel,

> Theology is not a doctrine about God as the Old Testament discloses this, in the primary sense, but a discipline arising from core, unimpeachable religious truths concerning prophecy, Jesus, the believing heart, and the New's hearing of the Old Testament as determinative and totalizing. In other words, Daniel's theological truth had to cohere with a wide range of religious conceptions imported from the New Testament, or it failed as Christian Scripture to be a reliable vehicle of God's truth. Pusey

---

47. Pusey, *Daniel the Prophet*, xiii.

felt he was arguing in defence of the literal sense of Daniel, but there was much more on the table.[48]

This was essentially a debate about the literal meaning of Daniel. Pusey had a different and more theological understanding of what literal meaning was, but both sides take for granted a single meaning of the text which precludes the conclusions of their opponents. Pusey was extremely hostile to developments in German biblical criticism which, during his career, he saw hold an increasing degree of influence over British scholarship. This hostility can be seen in his 1828 monograph, *Historical Enquiry into the Probable Causes of the Rationalist Character Lately Predominant in the Theology of Germany*.

What is notable about Pusey (and is quite remarkable considering his significance as a leader of the conservative Oxford Movement) is that Pusey does not seek a return to the pre-critical and polysemic scriptural interpretation of the medieval church. What is often forgotten about Pusey is that, though he had an intense scholarly interest in early Christianity and Patristic interpretation of Scripture, he was quite quickly left behind by his fellow Tractarians. Pusey, for example, never fully adopted the ritualism of the later movement, though he supported friends in their legal battles over the use of ritual. His interpretation belongs to the reformed tradition of historical-grammatical reading limited and contained by responsibility to the biblical canon and to the faith of the Church. Similarly, the relatively conservative scholarship of F. A. J. Hort, B. F. Westcott, and J. B. Lightfoot appropriated biblical criticism for orthodox Christian purposes, encouraging other conservative scholars also to employ German methods.[49] Lightfoot himself became involved in a dispute with Walter Richard Cassels, whose anonymous book *Supernatural Religion: An Inquiry into the Reality of Divine Revelation* (1874) espoused Tubingen theology and hermeneutics for a popular audience. Lightfoot's response was not a doctrinal critique of the book, but a thoroughly modern rejection of the theory of history and revelation behind the text: a claim to philosophical bias and lack of scholarly neutrality. Lightfoot assumed the same essential historical-critical assumptions of historicism, authorial intent and determinate meaning as the Tubingen school and questioned it on its own terms: its aim to reflect the best scientific analysis of the historical data.[50]

48. Seitz, "Scripture Becomes Religion(s)," 45.
49. Noll, *Faith and Criticism*, 67.
50. Ibid., 70.

Into the Twentieth Century

It hardly needs to be stated that the accounts of single meaning offered in the various expressions of historical criticism dominated much of twentieth-century biblical scholarship. Even in more theologically conservative parts of the Christian Church, historical criticism grew to a position of dominance. Within Evangelicalism, this can be seen in the establishment and success of institutions like Tyndale House in Cambridge, and in Roman Catholicism in the research of the Pontifical Biblical Institute and the prominence and advocacy of historical critical scholars such as Joseph Fitzmyer.[51] For the most part, the philosophical and hermeneutical foundations of biblical criticism were assumed as normative, so much so that the advent of theological interpretation as well as hermeneutics influenced by continental philosophy were, and still are, often perceived as scandalous: an anti-historical, anti-scientific, unscholarly and subjective hermeneutical series of developments.[52] Perhaps one of the most illustrative scholarly debates is that between James Barr and Brevard Childs and others on the possibility and nature of biblical theology as a single narrative theology seen to be formed by the whole of Scripture. Barr's contention with biblical theology is that forces biblical authors to say what they could never have intended to say by seeing them as part of a body of literature they might never have been aware of.[53] For Barr, the only real meaning of the biblical text is its historical meaning, conditioned by authorship and setting. This problem is that of theological interpretation generally. For example, Barr claims that Karl Barth's Romans commentary is not really a commentary because the issue of what Paul actually thought is lost.[54]

> It seems to me that commentaries provide the best material for biblical theology when they concentrate on what the *writers/redactors/readers/audience* thought: what was their idea-world, their background, their sense of an opposition? For them to go further and seek to make regulative theological judgements in the sense of what the reality is, of what should be believed and

---

51. Fitzmyer, *Interpretation of Scripture*.

52. As in, for example, Aichele, Miscall, and Walsh, "Elephant in the Room," 383–404; and Barton, *Nature of Biblical Criticism*. Cf. Bartholomew, "Unchartered Waters," 1–34.

53. Barr, "Trends and Prospects," 265–82.

54. Barr, *Biblical Theology*, 57.

done, can be done only be the importation of dogmatic arguments. Thus commentaries are, though often not in an obvious way, and certainly in varying degree, a form of expression that may belong to biblical theology.[55]

Barr depends here on a typically post-enlightenment dichotomy between "dogmatic arguments" and other ways of thinking that are untainted by ideological bias, principally historical study of a text's origins and earliest reception. For Barr, it is easier to discuss the text in relation to the past than it is to discuss the text in relation to the present, as though historical distantiation is only problematic in one direction: bringing the past to the present, rather than making sense of the past from the present. Yet it would be wrong to regard Barr as naively historicist. Barr attacked the scholarly tradition of etymological explanation of biblical words and was one of the first to champion some degree of synchronic meaning, contending that the past does not adequately explain the present state of the text and that knowledge of the past does not help answer questions of a text's truthfulness.[56] Similarly, Barr recognises that historical investigation can only ever be hypothetical: historical investigation is not neutral and may be shaped by ideological factors.[57] Barr considers the irony that Childs argues against him using an essentially historicist approach, outlining the history of interpretation from the Enlightenment to deride Barr's historical criticism.[58] Barr argues that the Enlightenment really has little to do with historical criticism, in that Descartes and Rousseau and other thinkers wanted to use reason alone to understand the world, not history, and accuses Childs of epochalism: discrediting something because of its association with an historical period. Barr ultimately seems to come around to the idea of biblical theology in some form, though is clear that it cannot proceed from a view that the Bible has a central message or theology as a totality. His solution to the desire for biblical theology is dialogical: readings of the Bible ought to be involved in the way Christians think about contemporary issues, alongside and in dialogue other learning.[59]

---

55. Ibid., 58.
56. Barr, *Semantics of Biblical Language*.
57. Barr, "Allegory and Historicism," 105–20.
58. Noble, "Jowett, Childs, and Barr," 1–23.
59. Barr, *Biblical Theology*, 603–5.

Conclusion

> The idea of reading the Bible critically is not derived from an interest in history, even though in the nineteenth century there was a (contingent) alliance between the two concerns; it is linked with the Reformation insistence on the authority of the Bible, freely read, over the Church. Christian believers, according to reformation principles, have the right to ask whether the Bible really means what the Church says it means. In that sentence lies the whole development of biblical criticism in germ. Faced with an ecclesiastical interpretation of this or that text, the biblical critic does not automatically accept that the magisterium of the Church guarantees that the meaning proposed is the true one, but reserves the right to apply rational principles of criticism.[60]

That the dominant historicist hermeneutics of modernity assume and articulate determinate meaning did not need to be demonstrated here. The purpose of this chapter, as with this book more generally, was to draw attention to the sheer variety of theological bases for assuming some kind of single meaning. Spinoza argued that the single meaning of Scripture could be discerned when theological prejudice was put aside in favour of a "natural history" of what lies behind the text. But this is not the same as Michaelis belief that it was the history behind the text itself, to which the single literal meaning of the text bears witness, which is theologically and spiritually instructive. Likewise, Michaelis differs from Schleiermacher for whom the author and his consciousness of absolute dependence provides the basis for single meaning. As has been argued often, the hermeneutics of post-Enlightenment modernity can be seen as the extension of the theological hermeneutics of the Renaissance and Reformation. For many moderns, this theological allegiance is explicit. It will not do to assume that the biblical hermeneutics of modernity and historical criticism in its various forms contain within them a prejudice against theology, just as it will it do to claim determinate or single meaning as simply a product of this period.

---

60. Barton, "Historical-Critical Approaches," 16.

6

Written at All?
Single Meaning after Modernity

Today, as modernity has seemingly been drawing to a close and the hegemony of historical criticism has begun to fade, new (and in some cases, old) hermeneutical theory has been offered. Our new period witnesses to a distrust of any kind of all-explaining narrative or philosophy, whether modern or ancient, and it is perhaps not surprising that determinate meaning rarely features in recent biblical hermeneutics. As George Aichele, Peter Miscall, and Richard Walsh lament,

> Historical criticism ... comprises the congeries of well-known methods such as source criticism, form criticism, grammatical studies, and archaeology, and it attempts to combine them in ways that will produce assured and agreed-on interpretations of the biblical text, whether these be understood as the author's intention, the understanding of the original audiences, or reference to actual historical events. Postmodernism is characterized by diversity in both method and content and by an anti-essentialist emphasis that rejects the idea that there is a final account, an assured and agreed-on interpretation, of some one thing.... What unites this methodological jumble is agreement that no final or essential interpretation of the text is being produced. Other readings are always possible, and often invited.[1]

---

1. Aichele, Miscall, and Walsh, "Elephant in the Room," 383.

The hermeneutics of "Postmodernity," as varied as they of course are, tend to share an assumption of the importance of polysemic meaning. From the early to mid-twentieth century onwards, the hermeneutical canons of historical criticism were increasingly questioned and rejected. Even Rudolph Bultmann, to many the archetypal historical critic rejected historical criticism's exclusive historical understanding of determinate meaning, positing the need for existential encounter with the text in the present in addition to historical study. In 1949 René Welleck and Austin Warren popularized a critique of the exclusivity of authorial intention in general hermeneutics and within a decade William K. Wimsatt and Monroe C. Beardsley had coined the phrase, "intentionalist fallacy."[2] In theology, Henri de de Lubac opened up the question of the antiquity of multiple spiritual meaning, Bruce Longenecker showed that apostolic Christianity was in the business of extending meaning to new situations, and Raymond Brown popularized the notion that the New Testament authors created an additional *sensus plenior* to the Scriptures of Israel.[3] At the same time, many biblical scholars rejected the supposed neutrality of historical criticism and forged explicitly committed ideological interpretations of Scripture: liberationist, feminist, environmentalist, and queer approaches, amongst others. Even within the quite traditional and modern environment of the Society of Biblical Literature, the need to recognise variety in method and polysemic meaning was recently asserted in the presidential address of Fernando F. Segovia.[4] Segovia contends that the vocation of biblical scholars is to be public intellectuals, speaking to the world. The problem with biblical scholarship is that it has focused on a discourse that is private to the world of biblical scholars, but it is impossible to escape the political and social demand of the interpretive context in front of the text. The necessary engagement with the world in front of the text includes a diverse set of approaches to the Bible: making public the history of biblical literature as well as traditions of its interpretations and the relation of texts to various interpretive contexts.

A good example of theological interpretation that articulates the necessity of polysemic meaning is that of James K. A. Smith, a prominent post-liberal theologian influenced, to some extent, by Radical Orthodoxy. Smith argues that multiplicity of interpretation is an aspect of

2. Welleck and Warren, *Theory of Literature*; Wimsatt and Beardsley, "Intentionalist Fallacy," 4–18.

3. Olsen, "Spiritual Sense(s) Today," 116.

4. Segovia, "Criticism in Critical Times," 6–29.

human creativity. Christian faith involves seeing more than the obvious, as did Paul on the road to Damascus.

> Given the phenomenological constraint of the world (that which is interpreted) and the pneumatological criterion in the fundamental guidance of the Spirit as rooted in a primordial trust, a hermeneutical space is opened that invites our creation, that beckons us to heed the call and accept the gift and risk of human be-ing in its creatureliness, refusing both the metaphysical dream of immediacy and the differential narrative of violence. A creational-pneumatic hermeneutic is a hermeneutic that celebrates humanity, but it is one that also mourns its rupture and roots its lament precisely in its belief in a good creation. The heart of a creational-pneumatic hermeneutic is a space, a field of multplicitous meeting in the wild spaces of love ... where there is room for a plurality of God's creatures to speak, sing and dance in a multivalent chorus of tongues.[5]

The argument of this chapter is that while polysemic meaning now dominates the interpretation of Scripture in the practice of Christian Theology, determinate or single meaning has not gone away. Some theological hermeneutics, even when they theoretically affirm polysemy, tend in practice towards single meaning. Often, ideological interpreters of Scripture who reject determinate meaning in theory also assume its existence in the meaning they seek to undermine. At the same time, some theological interpreters of Scripture argue for such limitations on meaning that the pure subjective polysemy often featured in postmodernity is denied.

Ideological and Literary Interpretation

John Barton contends that much of biblical interpretation aimed at offering different insights into the meaning and value of the Bible, though apparently asserting the polysemic nature of meaning through the offering of another perspective, tends to support the idea of meaning as determinate. This happens in a number of ways. Some minority perspective views offer a critique of the text from their own perspective. For example, early feminist biblical scholars that sought to critique views on gender within Scripture worked on the basis that texts have a single misogynistic or women-affirming meaning to be exposed. The same scholars

---

5. Smith, *Fall of Interpretation*, 184.

also drew attention to misogynistic interpretation of texts whose single meaning does not permit such interpretation.

> ... the Feminist case ... depends on the reader's being able to make a judgement about what the texts mean, on the basis of which he or she can go on to criticize biblical scholars either for the moral failing of not dissociating themselves from a misogynistic Bible or for the exegetical failing (which is surely also a moral one) of reading misogynistic meanings into texts that lack them.... Feminist criticism, so far from denying determinate meaning to texts, actually requires it if it is to be coherent. The feminist case is that the text will not support the misogynistic use being made of it; it is not simply that misogyny is unacceptable, which is true but is not a point about biblical interpretation.[6]

This interest in explicating what the Bible actually says is a feature of Phyllis Trible's scholarship. While offering something of a new perspective, Trible's claim is that interpreters have got the meaning of the Bible wrong. In highlighting such wrong and patriarchal interpretation which defies clear aspects of certain scriptural texts and language, Trible depends upon a singularity of meaning.

> Although the OT often pictures Yahweh as a man, it also uses gynomorphic language for the Deity. At the same time, Israel repudiated the idea of sexuality in God. Unlike fertility gods, Yahweh is neither male nor female; neither he nor she. Consequently, modern assertions that God is masculine, even when they are qualified, are misleading and detrimental, if not altogether inaccurate.[7]

Trible's literary and ideological approach is itself a quest for the true meaning of Scripture, a meaning obscured by patriarchal tradition.

> ... Such an approach characterises these essays. It interprets stories of outrage on behalf of their female victims in order to recover a neglected history.... In telling sad stories, a feminist hermeneutic seeks to redeem the time. Joining this perspective is the methodology of literary criticism. As practiced here, this involves an intrinsic reading of the text in its final form.... To elicit understanding, analysis brings conventions to literature.[8]

---

6. Barton, *Biblical Criticism*, 160–61.
7. Trible, "Departriarchalizing," 34.
8. Trible, *Texts of Terror*, 3.

Trible uses language long associated with historical criticism as she seeks to "recover a neglected history" and to gain "understanding" of the text of Scripture. The same can be said for some other minority readings which attempt to offer another perspective on biblical texts: in some cases they represent attempts to expose the true meaning of a text which has so far gone un-noticed or has been forgotten. Jeffrey John, for example, in his analysis of Scripture as part of an argument for the acceptance of stable same-sex sexual relationships by the Church also assumes a very modern view of historical meaning and historical distantiation.[9] In John's case, Scripture presents problematic texts that he does not choose to reinterpret theologically, but to hold at a distance from Christian theology and sexual ethics. In a manner more akin to that of Trible, many of the essays in *The Queer Bible Commentary* claim to reveal the true story of the text, often as homoerotic, affirming of a same-sex relationship or identifying with the experience of being gay.[10]

The same is true for many who adopt a literary approach to the Bible. Even within reader-response criticism, seen by some as the most subjective and unscholarly form of literary criticism, the hermeneutics of historical criticism are often assumed. For example, Lyle Eslinger's examination of possible reader-response to the Samaritan woman at the well in John 4:1–42 aims not to supply an additional level of meaning but attempts to expose what would have been heard by the initial target audience of the text, a hearing created through the literary craft of the author. This form of reader-response criticism explores the literary experience of the initial audience to articulate what might have been heard with a particular passage. So, for example, Lyle Eslinger suggests that the initial audience of the Gospel of John would have been familiar with a betrothal type scene from the Hebrew Scriptures in which a man meets a woman at a well (Gen 24:10–61; 29:1–20; and Exod 2:15b–21).[11] Eslinger argues that this familiarity would have influenced an ancient Jewish reader's reception of John 4:1–42. According to Eslinger, allusion to the scriptural type scene is intended by John, who subverts the expectation of betrothal as the woman meets Jesus at the well. This is literary reading that assumes determinate meaning as something defined by literary inheritance and the authorial intention behind the expected response of the reader to the text.

---

9. John, *Permanent, Faithful, Stable*.
10. Guest et al., *Queer Bible Commentary*.
11. Eslinger, "Wooing of the Woman," 167–83.

The relation of literary approaches to the Bible to the hermeneutics of modernity is also observed by Stephen D. Moore and Yvonne Sherwood who argue that early theory-inspired approaches to biblical criticism failed to depart from broad aims of historical criticism. Rather than offering new alternatives to historical criticism, literary criticism in its various forms was simply an extension of the "project of the Enlightenment Bible."

> In the event, biblical literary critics, the principal translators of Theory into biblical scholarship, did not succeed in straying very far from historical criticism. Reader-response criticism, for instance, made a bigger splash in biblical studies than almost any other development in literary theory, precisely because it could be assimilated surprisingly easily to the historicist ethos of the discipline. Since its arrival in biblical studies, reader-oriented theory has tended to assimilate automatically with the discipline's inbred obsession with the historical author and the historical reader, who, even when ceremoniously renamed the Implied Author and the Implied Reader, are still implicitly shackled to their hypothetical contexts, causing reader-response criticism in biblical studies to become and exercise in historical criticism performed in a wig and dark sunglasses.[12]

Indeed, as Thiselton argues, the literary and linguistic approaches inspired by the New Criticism were not a frontal assault on interpretation as attempting to understand the meaning and purpose of texts, nor were they the antithesis of historical critical approaches which had sought the same type of meaning, albeit through exploration "behind the text." In short, these approaches were also ways of understanding what the text was created to mean or achieve.

> Little attention was given to the fact that Ransom, Wellek and Warren, and most of the "new" critics, were concerned with those specific *literary* and *poetic* devices and forces which genuinely shed light on texts of a particular genre. We may suggest, by way of example, that to view the book of Jonah as a virtually *self-contained satire* on incoherent self-centred theoretical theistic belief is more "to the point" than speculating about its possible authorship and origins. However, to fail to look "behind" the text of 1 Corinthians, or "behind" *as well as* "within" the world of the Gospels would fatally detach text from the extra-textual world of reality.[13]

12. Moore and Sherwood, *Invention of the Biblical Scholar*, 101–2.
13. Thiselton, "'Behind' and 'In Front Of,'" 100.

Single Meaning in General Hermeneutics

Modernity sought to close the gap between the special hermeneutics of biblical interpretation and the general hermeneutics of other texts and communication itself: to read the Bible as any other book. In many ways, this methodological and hermeneutical closeness has endured inasmuch as posited replacements for historical criticism have often been inspired by general hermeneutics. Because of this, it is important to examine the echoes of determinate meaning in general hermeneutics as much as specifically biblical hermeneutics, the dividing line between which is usually blurred. A good example of this is in the work of Frank Kermode, not a theologian but certainly interested in the interpretation of the Bible. Frank Kermode's analysis of the seemingly polysemic latent and manifest meanings in narrative literature fail to escape from a determinative authorial paradigm. Kermode reflects on the purpose of the parables in Mark's Gospel, seemingly both to reveal truth to insiders While concealing it from outsiders.[14] For a secular point of comparison, Kermode describes the novel *Party Going* by Henry Green. The narrative of *Party Going*, Kermode argues, is so bland and seemingly trivial that it demands reflection upon a latent or secret meaning. Crucially, this conclusion is supported by Kermode's reflection that Green is regarded as a serious author who would not otherwise have created such an uneventful and inconclusive narrative. Kermode's interpretation of one of the characters as representing the god Hermes is presented as a plausible interpretation upon this basis. Even if Mark and *Party Going* require interpretation of their hidden meaning, they do so because their authors intend readers to do just this. This cannot then be regarded as indeterminate meaning. In this case, the manifest meaning discerned by outsiders is simply not the true meaning of the text.

From the same era, Roland Barthes while formally rejecting modern ideas of determinate meaning, gives to texts a sense of agency akin to some Patristic theological understanding of Scripture. Regardless of the imagination of the reader, the text can have its way and create the meaning or experience it was intended to produce.

> Text of pleasure: the text that contents, fills, grants euphoria; the text that comes from culture and does not break with it, it is linked to a *comfortable* practice of reading. Text of bliss: the text that imposes a state of loss, the text that discomforts (perhaps

---

14. Kermode, *Genesis of Secrecy*, 2–11.

to the point of a certain boredom), unsettles the reader's historical, cultural, psychological assumptions, the consistency of his tastes, values, memories, brings to a crisis his relation with language.[15]

This gives to certain texts a sense of inescapable power, meaning and value which cannot be avoided. The power of such texts is, Barthes claims, a feature both of their language and their authorship.

> With the writer of bliss (and his reader) begins the untenable text, the impossible text. This text is outside pleasure, outside criticism, unless it is reached through another text of bliss; you cannot speak "on" such a text, you can only speak "in" it, in its fashion, enter into a desperate plagiarism, hysterically affirm the void of bliss.[16]

A similar idea of textual agency is seen in Gadamer's metaphor of interpretation as *play*.[17] Just as playing a game calls players out of the normal concerns of everyday life and renders their behaviour contingent upon the rules of play, so the text exercises a kind of agency upon the reader, limiting her interpretation of the text. Interpretation operates within the confines of what the words of the text appear to permit to the reader. Of course, in Gadamer's terminology, the horizons of the text can be extended beyond the confines of plain grammatical sense, but these new horizons are determined and limited by the text as encountered by the reader. This is also a kind of determinate meaning, albeit one which bears little resemblance to determinate meaning within historical criticism.

From the other side of the Atlantic and the other side of the continental and analytic philosophical divide, American literary pragmatism also formally rejects determinate meaning while offering interpretive practice that assumes a functional single meaning. Proceeding from Alistair MacIntyre's description of linguistic communities and linguistic rationalities, utterly distinct from one another yet utterly meaningful within themselves, Richard Rorty and Stanley Fish note the total contingency of meaning upon interpretive context. This contingency is such that texts cannot be said to "mean" anything outside the interpretive context or community.

---

15. Barthes, *Pleasure of the Text*, 14. Cf. Barthes, "Third Meaning, 319.
16. Barthes, *Pleasure of the Text*, 22.
17. Gadamer, *Truth and Method*, 91–92.

> [Reading] may be so exciting and convincing that one has the illusion that one now sees what a certain text is really about. But what excites and convinces is a function of the needs and purposes of those who are being excited and convinced. So it seems to me simpler to scrap the distinction between using and interpreting, and just distinguish between uses by different people for different purposes.[18]

Likewise, Fish contends that in the interpretive community of shared values and aspirations, reading will appear to be an objective enterprise.

> This, then, is the explanation for the stability of interpretation among different readers: they belong to the same community. Disagreements ... can be debated in a principled way, not because of a stability in texts, but because of a stability in the makeup of interpretive communities.[19]

While the meaning which commands assent here can never be universal because of the diversity of different interpretive communities, within a particular community texts can and should be experienced as though they have a single clear meaning. This meaning is that which relates best to the values of the particular community.

Single Meaning in Theological Interpretation of Scripture

As with some ideological interpretation of Scripture, recent theological interpretation of Scripture often assumes single meaning, though it is formally and theologically denied.[20] Such is the case with Stephen E. Fowl. Others, such as Kevin Vanhoozer and Francis Watson, seem to try to provide theological foundations to some of the hermeneutical values of historical criticism, including determinate meaning.

Fowl is among the most interesting and innovative theological interpreters of Scripture, with his hermeneutic broadly inspired by the pragmatism of Fish and Rorty. As noted in the introduction here, Fowl's offers a detailed rejection of determinate meaning on theological and philosophical grounds. Rather than seeking universal meanings of

---

18. Rorty, *Philosophy and Social Hope*, 144.
19. Fish, *Is There a Text*, 171.
20. For a more detailed treatment of determinate meaning in recent theological interpretation, see Sargent, *Written to Serve*, 170-94.

Scripture, which are to be considered true at all times and to every person, Fowl argues that Scripture is necessarily as polysemic as any other text because interpretation takes place in unique communities with their own values and their own criteria for what makes successful interpretation. The best thing that an interpreter can seek to do is interpret Scripture in such a way as supports and encourages the values of the specific interpretive community in which and for which interpretation takes place.[21] Of course, to members of a community, readings supporting the values that are precious to them will appear to be obvious and correct, even if such a reading seems to differ from an initially difficult reading of the text. For example, a text that appears initially to say something negative about homosexual sex or the role of women in church leadership, might be explained in such a way that denies these things are being said at all. This explanation might refer to cultural or linguistic factors that enable the text to be interpreted as though it clearly doesn't mean things that disagree with cherished views within the interpretative community. This is, in a sense, a rejection of the polysemic meaning of Scripture: Scripture can only mean what is good for the community. Interpretation within the community will always appear to be determinate, even though the persuasive reading within one group will certainly differ from that within another group. A similar focus upon the *practice* of reading Scripture theologically within the context of a worshipping community, not as a supplement to historical criticism is taken by Angus Paddison. Paddison contends that biblical interpretation cannot be abstracted from the life of the Church "as if to imply that Scripture's status in the purposes of God is an optional extra for the work of theology," but is something that is simply *done*, as in pragmatism.[22]

Of course, it was never Fowl's intention to offer a new framework in which meaning can be received as determinate, but it may be that assumptions about Scripture's clarity and single meaning are difficult to escape within an interpretive community that holds the Bible to be Scripture, to some extent written for their learning. Francis Watson, however, explicitly defends the idea of determinate meaning fully conscious of how unfashionable it has become. Like Nicholas Woltersdorff who argues for the possibility of a separation between historical meaning and actualization of Scripture as "divine discourse," Watson is influenced to some extent

---

21. Fowl, *Engaging Scripture*, 7.
22. Paddison, *Scripture*, 6.

by speech-act theory.[23] When the text is understood as an interpersonal communicative act, its meaning cannot be dissolved into pure polysemy: it must in theory mean something intended and particular.

> It may not be possible to isolate the "single sense" of the text as a whole, or to state it in definitive form, or to eliminate its ambiguities and complexities; but the notion of the "single sense," for all its difficulties, is valuable in preserving the insight that the text as a communicative act ultimately intends one thing and not another.[24]

Kevin J. Vanhoozer does more than this, inasmuch as he offers a clear theological expression of determinate meaning. Vanhoozer reads John 5:39 ("you search the Scriptures because you think that in them you have eternal life: but it is they that testify to me") as a witness to the possibility of getting meaning wrong. The Jews of John's Gospel had a certain aim in reading Scripture, but this aim seems to be misplaced. Rather than directly offering life, the Scriptures testify to Jesus Christ, the divine Word in whom there is life. Vanhoozer suggests here that it is not the responsibility of the interpreter to multiply meaning. The creation of meaning is the responsibility of the author who in this case intends Scripture to be a witness to Christ. Reflecting further on Johannine literature, Vanhoozer notes that the earliest Christians were accountable to the historical circumstances of the life of Jesus Christ (1 John 1:1), but were not free to create their own meaning for these events seen as historically fixed: interpreters should be "bound to what has already been said and done" in Scripture.[25]

> If I profess and practice determinate interpretation, then, it is not because of some general hermeneutical theory but because I believe that the ultimate purpose of Scripture is to witness to what God has done in Jesus Christ. Determinacy is a function of the specific content of the Gospel; if the interpreter-witness is not able to exhaust the meaning of divine discourse, it is not because it is unstable or indeterminate, but because "the world itself could not contain the books that would be written." Theological interpretation, then, is ultimately a martyrological act.[26]

23. Wolterstorff, *Divine Discourse*.
24. Watson, *Text and Truth*, 71-72.
25. Vanhoozer, "Four Theological Faces," 132.
26. Ibid. 132-33.

For Vanhoozer, it is the relation of Scripture to the historical Jesus, the Jesus of apostolic testimony, the Jesus whose value is not polysemic, that provides a theological rartionale for determinate meaning. But this does not mean that interpretation is straightforward. Vanhoozer notes that the theological determinacy of meaning in Scripture does not equate to unambiguous interpretation: interpretation remains a dialogue between all the dimensions of the text, along with its readers and authors as discussed by Ricoeur, who perhaps has the greatest influence on Vanhoozer's hermeneutics.[27]

Conclusion

The purpose of this chapter was to demonstrate that determinate or single meaning has endured the apparent end of modernity. Indeed, in some cases it is assumed still by those who have explicit rejected it as a feature of the hermeneutics of modernity. While it would be a mistake to claim that ideas of determinate meaning are alive and well in contemporary Christian theology, it is clear that they have not gone away, even when severed from the theologies that sustained them in the past.

---

27. Vanhoozer, "Imprisoned or Free?" 51.

Conclusion
Single Meaning and Theological Interpretation

The aim of this study was modest: to attempt to demonstrate something of the diverse range of biblical interpretation within Christian theology that has operated upon an assumption of single meaning. These ways of reading Scripture could be said to belong to the margins of historical theology, rather than representing the mainstream. At times, the assumption and articulation of Scripture's single meaning has been a feature of sectarian ecclesiology. At other times, it has been the result of intellectual changes within society. The theological frameworks in which single meaning becomes a hermeneutical principle are varied. In addition to this, even when single meaning is held to, there are a variety of views as to the type of reading needed to access this single meaning: for some it is allegorical, for others it is historical-grammatical. The determinate meaning of Scripture in Christian theology is the limitation of meaning to a single sense (with or without additional significance) on the basis of (a) eschatology and ecclesiology, (b) a metaphysical theory about the nature of divine discourse, (c) a theology of history and the historical particularity of language, (d) the needs of an interpretive community or (e) the perceived injustice or apostasy to which polemic and satire are the appropriate responses. Discussion of determinate meaning ought to recognise that the basis of determinism or meaning-limitation, as far as theological interpretation of Scripture is concerned, is varied.

The case cannot be made, though, that the single meaning of Scripture, or determinate meaning, is a concept alien to Christian theology. Nor can it be said that it is dependent on a single, anti-theological worldview.

Single meaning has been assumed for a variety of different reasons within a variety of theological frameworks. Indeed, the earliest Christian uses of single meaning are derived not from a theory of literature or of written communication or the contingency of texts upon historical process, but on the basis of unapologetically theological accounts of salvation history and ecclesiology. In 1 Peter, for example, Scripture is applied to the Christian diaspora because they, and only they, stand at the climax of salvation history to which the prophets themselves bore witness. They, and only they, are those for whom the prophets of Israel's past wrote to serve. Whilst one might not sympathise with such a radically sectarian view of salvation history today, one can hardly fail to describe it as providing a theological account of Scripture which makes possible a particular understanding of single meaning. In contrast, Origen's insistence on a single allegorical meaning is formed through a theology of the divine Word and theological problems of literal meaning. All of this is quite different from the exclusive grammatical and literary interests of the Schools of Antioch and St. Victor, or the polemics of William of Ockham, Rabelais, and Ronsard. Even in the modern period, there is a vast difference between the types of historical meaning claimed by Spinoza and Michaelis, or the focus of meaning for Lowth or Schleiermacher. The baby of determinate meaning cannot be thrown out with the bath water of historical criticism. Readings which proceed from an assumption of single meaning properly belong within the spectrum of theological interpretation.

Determinate meaning may indeed be problematic to modern readers for a variety of factors other than a particular view of its origins. Determinate meaning often depends upon exclusive claims about the nature or locus of meaning or exclusive claims about readers and their insight into texts. It may seem to belong to quite alien views of the world and of the meaning of written texts. But determinate meaning cannot be dismissed as something which has no place with Christian theology. There is nothing particularly anti-theological within the claim that scriptural texts have a single meaning. Indeed, quite the opposite is the case. At the same time, a case can be made for determinate meaning as something able to make a positive contribution to theological interpretation.

Determinate or single meaning offers a great deal to the theological interpretation of the Bible. The act of reading itself can become more spiritually and theologically challenging when a text is approached with the assumption that it has a single meaning: a meaning which may be hidden or obscured by historical or theological distance: a meaning which may require hard work before it is made clear. Determinate meaning can enable meaning to have a greater degree of otherness than might otherwise be the case. Of course, the great promise of biblical interpretation in early modernity was a similar thought that the single meaning of Scripture would stand as a corrective to doctrine. Such a claim, depending as it often does upon a claim to interpretive neutrality, may seem implausible. Yet the proliferation of meaning available when it is assumed that meaning is polysemic, can result is the dilution of authority of meanings. Interpretations simply become possibilities of meaning, easily dismissed if not to the reader's taste. With so much possibility, it is difficult for a challenging reading of a text, if one is available, to be seen to stand over and against the reader. With so much possibility, challenging readings are easily dismissed. Polysemic meaning provides an easy escape from the threat that might be posed by a text, as well as difficult questions that might arise from that threat. The discussion of apparently difficult biblical texts understood to relate to issues of human sexuality over the last few decades is a case in point. From an historical critical perspective, armed with a sense of historical distantiation, these texts are not really "difficult" at all: they are simply homophobic and should be rejected as having no contemporary relevance or moral authority. Despite some imaginative historical critical exegesis to the contrary, the historically contingent and earliest meaning of these texts must be understood as "homophobic" in the now contemporary sense of that term: they either forbid or condemn homosexual sexual intercourse. The difficulty from this perspective is not what the texts mean as such, but how they ought to be appropriated. A very demanding choice is presented: either the text is right and authoritative and must be adhered to in the face of a society for whom such ideas are abhorrent, or else the text is wrong and must be condemned. The latter decision may require a complete reassessment of theological ideas concerning the authority of Scripture. The demanding choice, however, is completely dissolved whenever these texts are regarded as polysemic. Reading Scripture with the aim of discerning a single meaning enables interpretation to be the dangerous activity it really ought to be. As Paul Joyce claims regarding historical criticism,

> There is . . . a spiritual dimension for me in being confronted by the "other" of the text as laid bare by historical criticism. The text is not me, it is not my projection or an extension of my

own psychology; rather it challenges me from beyond myself in a way that commands humility.[1]

Yet the spiritual potency of the alterity of Scripture is lost if its voice of *otherness* remains no more than one possible meaning among many. Without a framework in which meaning can be determinate, the voice of Scripture, however discerned, can only ever be heard as an option for meaning. Without the possibility of single meaning, Scripture loses much of its ability to challenge and to inspire.

While the Enlightenment vision of scientific biblical criticism as a catalyst for Christian unity appears naïve and simplistic now, the hope that an affirmation of the indeterminate meaning of Scripture can provide unity is equally misplaced. Scriptural Reasoning, for example, can offer positive recognition of difference on the basis of interpretive openness. However, this form of dialogue provides little more than the rehearsal of different viewpoints and interpretations. It is very limited in its ability to foster a common purpose that goes beyond mutual understanding.[2] The same can be said for approaches to discussions of human sexuality which encourage mutual recognition of the validity of contrasting interpretations of Scripture in relation to sexuality. The friendly discussion which can emerge when those with differing views hold to this assumption of indeterminacy is desirable. However, the possibility of unity and agreement is ruled out by the hermeneutic assumption and real debate is avoided. Biblical interpretations relating to sexuality assume the status of cherished and unquestionable religious belief, somehow safe from real scrutiny. The result is that dialogue about sexuality can only serve to enforce difference and create mutually exclusive interpretative communities. The prospect of determinate meaning holds out the possibility, however fleeting and remote, that interpretation and debate might yield a result on which people who previously held differing views can agree. Determinate meaning encourages the possibility of that someone might be persuaded to change their mind.

---

1. Joyce, "Proverbs 8," 95.
2. Sargent, "Proceeding beyond Isolation," 819–30.

Bibliography

Aichele, George, Peter Miscall, and Richard Walsh. "An Elephant in the Room: Historical-Critical and Postmodern Interpretations of the Bible." *JBL* 128.2 (2009) 383–404.
Albright, W. F., and C. S. Mann. *Matthew: A New Translation with Introduction and Commentary*. ABC 26. New York: Doubleday, 1971.
Ames, William. *An Analytical Exposition of both the Epistles of the Apostle Peter, Illustrated by Doctrines out of Every Text, and Applied by their Uses, for a Further Progress in Holiness*. London: E. G. for John Rothwell, 1641.
———. *The Marrow of Theology*. Translated by John D. Eusden. Boston: Pilgrim, 1968.
Aune, David E. "Justin Martyr's Use of the Old Testament." *BETS* 9.4 (1966) 179–97.
Bacher, Wilhelm. "Seventy-Two Modes of Exposition." *JQR* 4.3 (1892) 509.
Balla, Peter. "2 Corinthians." In *Commentary on the New Testament Use of the Old Testament*, edited by G. K. Beale and D. A. Carson, 753–84. Grand Rapids: Baker, 2007.
Banks, R. J. *Jesus and the Law in the Synoptic Tradition*. SNTSMS 28. Cambridge: Cambridge University Press, 1975.
Barthes, Roland. *The Pleasure of the Text*. Translated by Richard Miller. New York: Noonday, 1975.
———. "The Third Meaning: Research Notes on Some Eistenstein Stills." In *A Barthes Reader*, translated by Stephen Heath, edited by Susan Sontag, 316–33. London: Jonathan Cape, 1982.
Bartholomew, Craig G. "Uncharted Waters: Philosophy, Theology and the Crisis in Biblical Interpretation." In *Renewing Biblical Interpretation*, edited by Craig G. Bartholomew, Colin Greene, and Karl Möller, 1–39. SHS 1. Grand Rapids: Zondervan, 2000.
Barr, James. *The Concept of Biblical Theology: An Old Testament Perspective*. London: SCM, 1999.
———."Jowett and the 'Original Meaning' of Scripture." *Religious Studies* 18 (1982) 433–37.
———. "Jowett and the Reading of the Bible 'Like Any Other Book.'" *Horizons in Biblical Theology* 4:2—5:1 (1983) 1–44.
———. *The Semantics of Biblical Language*. London: Oxford University Press, 1961.
———. "Trends and Prospects in Biblical Theology." *JTS* 25:2 (1974) 265–82.
Barrett, C. K. *The First Epistle to the Corinthians*. London: A. & C. Black, 1968.

———. *The Gospel According to St John: An Introduction with Commentary on the Greek Text.* London: SPCK, 1967.

———. "The Old Testament in the Fourth Gospel," *JTS* 48 (1947) 155–69.

Barton, John. "Historical-Critical Approaches." In *The Cambridge Companion to Biblical Interpretation*, edited by John Barton, 9–20. Cambridge: Cambridge University Press, 1998.

———. *The Nature of Biblical Criticism*. Louisville: Westminster John Knox, 2007.

Bateman, Herbert W. "Psalm 110:1 and the New Testament," *BSac* 149 (1992) 438–53.

Bauckham, Richard. *The Climax of Prophecy: Studies on the Book of Revelation*. Edinburgh: T. & T. Clark, 1993.

———. *James: Wisdom of James, Disciple of Jesus the Sage*. New Testament Readings. London and New York: Routledge, 1999.

———. *Jude, 2 Peter*. WBC 50. Nashville: Thomas Nelson, 1983.

Beale, G. K. *John's Use of the Old Testament in Revelation*. JSNTSup 166. Sheffield: Sheffield Academic Press, 1998.

———. "Questions of Authorial Intent, Epistemology, and Presuppositions and their Bearing on the Study of the Old Testament in the New: A Rejoinder to Steve Moyise," *IBS* 21 (1999) 152–80.

———. "A Response to John Paulien on the Use of the Old Testament in Revelation." *AUSS* 39 (2001) 23–34.

Beale, G. K. and McDonough, Sean M. "Revelation." In *Commentary on the New Testament Use of the Old Testament*, edited by G. K. Beale and D. A. Carson, 1081–161. Grand Rapids: Baker, 2007.

Belleville, L. L. *Reflections of Glory: Paul's Polemical Use of the Moses-Doxa Tradition in 2 Corinthians 3.1–18*. JSNTSup 52. Sheffield: Sheffield Academic Press, 1991.

———. "'Under Law:' Structural Analysis and the Pauline Concept of Law in Galatians 3.21–24.11." *JSNT* 26 (1986) 53–78.

Bénétreau, Samuel. "Évangile et Prophétie: Un Texte Original (1 P 1, 10–12) Peut-il Éclairer un Texte Difficile (2 P 1, 16–21)?" *Bib* 86 (2005) 174–91.

Bennett, Mary Jane. "Erasmus and the Hermeneutics of Biblical Literature." *Renaissance Quarterly* 49 (1996) 542–72.

Best, Ernest. *1 Peter*. NCBC. Grand Rapids, MI: Eerdmans, 1971.

———. "1 Peter II:4–10: A Reconsideration." *NovT* 11 (1969) 270–93.

———. "Spiritual Sacrifice: General Priesthood in the New Testament." *Int* 14 (1960) 280–90.

Betz, Hans Dieter. *The Sermon on the Mount*. Hermeneia. Minneapolis: Fortress, 1995.

Black, M. "The Christological Use of the Old Testament in the New Testament," *NTS* 18 (1971–1972) 1–14.

Blomberg, Craig L. *Interpreting the Parables, 2nd Ed.*. Downers Grove: IVP Academic/ Nottingham: Apollos, 2012.

———. "Matthew." In *Commentary on the New Testament Use of the Old Testament*, edited by G. K. Beale and D. A. Carson, 1–110. Grand Rapids: Baker, 2007.

Blomberg, Craig L., and Mariam J. Kamell. *James*. ZECNT 16. Grand Rapids: Zondervan, 2008.

Bock, Darrell L. "Single Meaning, Multiple Contexts and Referents: The New Testament's Legitimate, Accurate, and Multifaceted Use of the Old." In *Three Views on the New Testament Use of the Old Testament*, edited by Stanley N. Gundry, Kenneth Berding, and Jonathan Lunde, 125–29. Grand Rapids: Zondervan, 2008.

Boehmer, J. "Tag und Morgenstern? Zu II Petr i 19." *ZNW* 22 (1923) 228–33.
Boring, Eugene M. "Narrative Dynamics in 1 Peter: The Function of Narrative World." In *Reading First Peter with New Eyes: Methodological Reassessments of the Letter of First Peter*, edited by Robert L. Webb and Betsy Bauman-Martin, 7–40. LNTS 364. London: T. & T. Clark, 2007.
Bowers, R. H. "A Middle English Treatise on Hermeneutics: Harley Ms. 2276, 32v–35v." *PMLA* 65.4 (1950) 590–600.
Bowker, J. W. "Speeches in Acts: A Study in Proem and Yelammedenu Form." *NTS* 14.1 (1967) 96–111.
Boyarin, Daniel. *Border Lines: The Partition of Judeo-Christianity*. Philadelphia: University of Pennsylvania Press, 2004.
Brashler, James. "From Erasmus to Calvin: Exploring the Roots of Reformed Hermeneutics." *Int.* 63.2 (2009) 161–66.
Bray, Gerald. *Biblical Interpretation: Past and Present*. Downers Grove, IL: InterVarsity, 1996.
Bromiley, G. W., ed. *Zwingli and Bullinger*. Library of Christian Classics. Philadelphia: Westminster Press, 1953.
Bultmann, Christoph. "After Horace: Sacred Poetry at the Centre of the Hebrew Bible." In *Sacred Conjectures: The Context and Legacy of Robert Lowth and Jean Astruc*, edited by John Jarick, 62–82. LHBOTS 457. New York: T. & T. Clark, 2007.
Bultmann, Christoph. "Herder's Biblical Studies." In *A Companion to the Works of Johann Gottfried Herder*, edited by Hans Adler and Wulf Köpke, 233–46. New York: Camden, 2009.
Burger, Christoph. *Jesus als Davidssohn: Eine traditionsgeschichtliche Untersuchung*. FRLANT 98. Göttingen: Vandenhoeck & Ruprecht, 1970.
Cabaniss, A. "Wisdom 18, 14f: An Early Christmas Text." *VC* 19 (1956) 97–102.
Caird, G. B. *The Gospel of St. Luke*. Harmondsworth: Penguin, 1963.
Callan, Terence. "A Note on 2 Peter 1.19–20." *JBL* 125.1 (2006) 265–70.
———."Pauline Midrash: The Exegetical Background of Gal. 3:19b." *JBL* 99 (1980) 549–67.
Carson, D. A. "2 Peter." In *Commentary on the New Testament Use of the Old Testament*. edited by G. K. Beale and D. A. Carson, 1047–62. Grand Rapids: Baker, 2007.
———. *The Gospel According to John*. Grand Rapids: Eerdmans, 1991.
———. "James." In *Commentary on the New Testament Use of the Old Testament*, edited by G. K. Beale and D. A. Carson, 997–1014. Grand Rapids: Baker, 2007.
Cavallin, H. C. C. "The False Teachers of 2 Pt as Pseudo-Prophets." *NovT* 21 (1979) 263–70.
Cherry, C. "Symbols of Spiritual Truth: Jonathan Edwards as Biblical Interpreter." *Int* 39 (1985) 263–71.
Childs, Brevard. "The Sensus Literalis of Scripture: An Ancient and Modern Problem." In *Beitrage zur alttestamentliche Theologie: Festschrift für Walter Zimmerli*, edited by H. Donner et al., 80–94. Göttingen: Vandenhoeck and Ruprecht, 1977.
———. "Toward Recovering Theological Exegesis." *Pro Ecclesia* 6 (1997) 16–26.
Chladenius, Johann Martin. *Einleitung zur richtigen Auslegung vernünftiger Reden und Schriften*. Düsseldorf: Stern, 1969.
Ciampa, Roy E. "Deuteronomy in Galatians and Romans." In *Deuteronomy in the New Testament*, edited by Steve Moyise and Maarten J. J. Menken, 99–117. LNTS 358. London: T. & T. Clark, 2007.

———. *The Presence and Function of Scripture in Galatians 1 and 2.* WUNT II 102. Tübingen: Mohr Siebeck, 1998.
Ciampa, Roy E., and Brian S. Rosner. "1 Corinthians." In *Commentary on the New Testament Use of the Old Testament*, edited by G. K. Beale and D. A. Carson, 695–752. Grand Rapids: Baker, 2007.
Cohn-Sherbok, D. "Paul and Rabbinic Exegesis." *SJT* 35:2 (1982) 117–32.
Collier, G. D. "'That We Might Not Crave Evil:' The Structure and Argument of 1 Corinthians 10:1–13." *JSNT* 55 (1994) 55–75.
Collins, C. John. "Coherence in James 1:19–27." *Journal of Translation and Textlinguistics* 10 (1998) 80–87.
Conzelmann, Hans. *1 Corinthians.* Hermeneia. Philadelphia: Fortress, 1975.
Corliss, Richard L. "Schleiermacher's Hermeneutic and its Critics." *Religious Studies* 26.3 (1993) 363–79.
Cranfield, C. E. B. *A Critical and Exegetical Commentary on the Epistle to the Romans, vol I.* ICC. London: T. & T. Clark, 2001.
Cranfield, C. E. B. *A Critical and Exegetical Commentary on the Epistle to the Romans, vol II.* ICC. London: T. & T. Clark, 2002.
Cullhead, Anna. "Original Poetry: Robert Lowth and Eighteenth-Century Poetics." In *Sacred Conjectures: The Context and Legacy of Robert Lowth and Jean Astruc*, edited by John Jarick, 25–47. Library of Hebrew Bible/Old Testament Studies 457. London: T. & T. Clark, 2007.
Cullmann, Oscar. *The Christology of the New Testament.* trans. Shirley C. Guthrie and Charles A. M. Hall. London: SCM, 1959.
Curran, John T. "The Teaching of II Peter 1.20: On the Interpretation of Prophecy." *TS* 4 (1943) 348–59.
Daly-Denton, Margaret. "The Psalms in John's Gospel." In *The Psalms in the New Testament*, edited by S. Moyise and M. J. J. Menken, 119–37. London: T. & T. Clark, 2004.
Daniélou, J. "Les divers sens de l'Ecriture dans la tradition chrétienne primitive." *Ephemerides Theologicae Lovanienses* 24 (1948) 119–26.
Daniélou, Jean. *Origène.* Paris: Table Ronde, 1948.
Davies, W. D. *Paul and Rabbinic Judaism: Some Rabbinic Elements in Pauline Theology.* London: SPCK, 1955.
Davies, W. D. and Dale C. Allison. *A Critical and Exegetical Commentary on the Gospel According to Saint Matthew: Vol I.* ICC. London: T. & T. Clark, 2000.
de Jonge, H. J. "Grotius' view of the Gospels and the Evangelists." In *Hugo Grotius Theologian: Essays in Honour of G. H. M. Posthumus Meyjes*, edited by H. J. M. Nellen and E. Rabbie, 65–74. SHCT 55. Leiden: Brill, 1994.
———. "Hugo Grotius: exegete du Nouveau Testament." In *The World of Hugo Grotius (1583–1645): Proceedings of the International Colloquium . . . Rotterdam 6–9 April 1983.* 97–115. Amsterdam: Amsterdam University Press, 1984.
Dempsey, G. T. "Aldhelm of Malmesbury and the Paris Psalter: A Note on the Survival of Antiochene Exegesis." *JTS* 38 (1987) 368–86.
de Lubac, Henri. *Exégèse médiévale: Les quatre sens de l'Écriture, Vol. 2.1.* Paris: Aubier, 1964.
Derrida, Jacques. "Différance." In *Margins of Philosophy*, translated by Alan Bass, 3–27. Chicago: University of Chicago Press, 1982.

Di Mattei, Steven. "Paul's Allegory of the Two Covenants (Gal. 4.21–31) in Light of First-Century Hellenistic Rhetoric and Jewish Hermeneutics." *NTS* 52 (2006) 102–22.

Diodore of Tarsus. *Commentary on the Psalms 1–51*. Translated by Robert C. Hill. Atlanta: Society of Biblical Literature, 2005.

Docherty, Susan E. *The Use of the Old Testament in Hebrews: A Case Study in Early Jewish Bible Interpretation*. WUNT II 260. Tubingen: Mohr Siebeck, 2009.

Dodd, C. H. *According to the Scriptures: The Sub-structure of New Testament Theology*. London: Collins, 1965.

Dove, Mary. "Literal Senses in the Song of Songs." In *Nicholas of Lyra: The Senses of Scripture*, edited by Philip D. W. Krey and Lesley Smith, 129–46. Leiden: Brill, 2000.

Dunn, James D. G. *The Partings of the Ways between Christianity and Judaism and their Significance for the Character of Christianity*. London: SCM, 2006.

———. *Romans 9–16*. WBC 38b. Nashville: Thomas Nelson, 1988.

Eliav, Yaron Z. "'Interpretive Citation' in the Epistle of Barnabas and the Early Christian Attitude towards the Temple Mount." In *The Interpretation of Scripture in Early Judaism and Christianity: Studies in Language and Tradition*, edited by Craig A. Evans, 353–62. JSPSup 33. Sheffield: Sheffield Academic, 2000.

Elliott, J. H. *1 Peter: A New Translation with Introduction and Commentary*. AB 37B. New Haven: Yale University Press, 2000.

———. *The Elect and the Holy: An Exegetical Examination of 1 Peter 2.4–10 and the Phrase βασίλειον ἱεράτευμα*. NovTSup 12. Leiden: Brill, 1966.

Ellis, E. Earle. "How the New Testament Uses the Old." In *New Testament Interpretation: Essays on Principles and Methods*, edited by I. Howard Marshall, 199–219. Grand Rapids: Eerdmans, 1977.

———. *Paul's Use of the Old Testament*. Edinburgh: Oliver & Boyd, 1957.

Enns, Peter. "Fuller Meaning, Single Goal: A Christotelic Approach to the New Testament Use of the Old in its First-Century Interpretive Environment." In *Three Views on the New Testament Use of the Old Testament*, edited by Stanley N. Gundry, Kenneth Berding, and Jonathan Lunde, 167–217. Grand Rapids: Zondervan, 2008.

Erasmus, Desiderius. "The Enchiridion." In *The Library of Christian Classics: Vol. XIV: Advocates of Reform*, edited by Matthew Spinka, translated by Ford Lewis Battles, 295–379. London: SCM, 1953.

———. *The Praise of Folly*. Translated by John Wilson. New York: Cosimo, 2010.

Ernesti, Johann August. *Principles of Biblical Interpretation, Translated from the Institutio Interpretis, Vol 1*. Translated by Charles H. Terrot. Edinburgh: Thomas Clark, 1832.

Eslinger, Lyle. "The Wooing of the Woman at the Well: Jesus, the Reader and Reader-Response Criticism." *JLT* 1:2 (1987) 167–83.

Evans, Gillian Rosemary. *The Language and Logic of the Bible: The Road to Reformation*. Cambridge: Cambridge University Press, 1985.

Fillmore, Charles J., and Beryl T. S. Atkins. "Describing Polysemy: The Case of 'Crawl.'" In *Polysemy: Theoretical and Computational Approaches*, edited by C. Leacock, 91–110. Oxford: Oxford University Press, 2000.

Firey, Abigail. "The Letter of the Law: Carolingian Exegetes and the Old Testament." In *With Reverence for the Word: Medieval Scriptural Exegesis in Judaism, Christianity, and Islam*, edited by John Dammen McAuliffe, Barry D. Walfish, and Joseph W. Goering, 204–24. Oxford University Press, 2010.

Fish, Stanley. *Is There a Text in this Class? The Authority of Interpretive Communities.* Cambridge, MA: Harvard University Press, 1980.

———. "Why No One's Afraid of Wolfgang Iser." *Diacritics* 11.1 (1981) 2–13.

Fishbane, Michael. *Biblical Interpretation in Ancient Israel.* Oxford: Clarendon, 1985.

———. "The Qumran Pesher and Traits of Ancient Hermeneutics." In *Proceedings of the Sixth World Congress of Jewish Studies 1*, edited by Shinan Avigdor and David Krone, 97–114. Jerusalem: Jerusalem Academic, 1977.

Fitzmyer, J. A. "'Being Therefore a Prophet . . .' (Acts 2:30)." *CBQ* 34.3 (1972) 332–39.

———. "Glory Reflected on the Face of Christ (2 Cor 3:7—4:6) and a Palestinian Jewish Motif." *Th.Stud.* 42 (1981) 630–644.

———. *The Interpretation of Scripture: In Defense of the Historical-Critical Method.* New York: Paulist, 2008.

———. "The Matthean Divorce Texts and Some New Palestinian Evidence." *Th.Stud.* 37.2 (1976) 197–226.

———. "The Son of David Tradition and Matt. 22. 41–46 and Parallels." *Conc.* 10:2 (1966) 40–46.

Ford, David F. "An Interfaith Wisdom: Scriptural Reasoning Between Jews, Christians and Muslims." *MT* 22 (2006) 345–66.

Ford, Philip John. "Biblical Imagery in Ronsard's Polemical Poetry: An Own Goal?" *Renaissance Journal* 2 (2005) 13–22.

Fowl, Stephen E. *Engaging Scripture: A Model for Theological Interpretation.* Eugene, OR: Wipf and Stock, 1998.

———. "The Importance of a Multivoiced Literal Sense of Scripture: The Example of Thomas Aquinas." In *Reading Scripture with the Church: Toward a Hermeneutic for Theological Interpretation*, 53–60. Grand Rapids: Baker, 2006.

Fraade, Steven D. "Rabbinic Polysemy and Pluralism Revisited: Between Praxis and Thematization." *AJS Review* 31.1 (2007) 1–40.

France, R. T. "The Writer of Hebrews as a Biblical Expositor." *TynB* 47.2 (1996) 245–76.

Franchet, Henri. *Le Poète et son oeuvre d'après Ronsard.* Geneva: Slatkine, 1969.

Frei, Hans. *The Eclipse of Biblical Narrative: A Study in Eighteenth and Nineteenth Century Hermeneutics.* New Haven: Yale University Press, 1974.

———. "The 'Literal Reading' of Biblical Narrative in the Christian Tradition: Does it Stretch or Will it Break?" In *The Bible and the Narrative Tradition*, edited by F. McConnell, 36–77. New York: Oxford University Press, 1986.

Gadamer, Hans-Georg. *Truth and Method.* Translated by William Glen-Doepel. London: Sheed and Ward, 1979.

Garland, D. E. *1 Corinthians.* BECNT. Grand Rapids: Baker Academic, 2003.

Garlington, D. "Role Reversal and Paul's Use of Scripture in Galatians 3.10–13." *JSNT* 65 (1997) 85–121.

Ginther, James R. "*Laudet sensum et significationem*: Robert Grosseteste on the Four Senses of Scripture." In *With Reverence for the Word: Medieval Scriptural Exegesis in Judaism, Christianity, and Islam*, edited by John Dammen McAuliffe, Barry D. Walfish, and Joseph W. Goering, 237–55. Oxford: Oxford University Press, 2010.

Godin, André. "Fonction d'Origène dans la pratique exégétique d'Erasme: Les annotations sur l'épître aux Romains." In *Histoire de l'exégèse au XVIe siècle*, edited by Olivier Fatio and Pierre Fraenkel, 17–44. Geneva: Droz, 1978.

Gombis, T. G. "The 'Transgressor' and the 'Curse of the Law': The Logic of Paul's Argument in Galatians 2–3." *NTS* 53 (2007) 81–93.

Goppelt, Leonard. *Der Erste Petrusbrief.* Meyer K. Gottingen: Vandenhoeck & Ruprecht, 1978.

———. *Typos: The Typological Interpretation of the Old Testament in the New.* Translated by Donald H. Madvig. Grand Rapids: Eerdmans, 1982.

Gordon, T. D. "A Note on ΠΑΙΔΟΓΩΓΟΣ in Galatians 3:24–25." *NTS* 35 (1989) 150–54.

Gould, Ezra P. *The Gospel According to St Mark.* ICC. Edinburgh: T. & T. Clark, 1996.

Greene, Colin J. D. "'In the Arms of the Angels': Biblical Interpretation, Christology and the Philosophy of History." In *Renewing Biblical Interpretation*, edited by Craig G. Bartholomew, Colin Greene, and Karl Möller, 188–239. SHS 1. Grand Rapids: Zondervan, 2000.

Green, Joel B. *1 Peter*. Grand Rapids: Eerdmans, 2007.

———. "Narrating the Gospel in 1 and 2 Peter." *Int.* 60:3 (2006) 262–77.

Grindheim, S. "The Law Kills but the Gospel Gives Life: The Letter-Spirit Dualism in 2 Corinthians 3.5–18." *JSNT* 84 (2001) 97–115.

Guest, Deryn, et al., eds. *The Queer Bible Commentary.* London: SCM, 2006.

Guinot, Jean-Noël. "Theodoret of Cyrus: Bishop and Exegete." In *The Bible in Greek Christian Antiquity*, edited by Paul M. Blowers, 160–69. South Bend, IN: University of Notre Dame Press, 1997.

Hafemann, Scott J. *Paul, Moses, and the History of Israel: The Letter/Spirit Contrast and the Argument from Scripture in 2 Corinthians 3.* WUNT 81. Tübingen: Mohr Siebeck, 1995.

Hagner, Donald A. "Holiness and Ecclesiology: The Church in Matthew." In *Built upon the Rock: Studies in the Gospel of Matthew*, edited by Daniel M. Gurtner and John Nolland, 178–89. Grand Rapids: Eerdmans, 2008.

———. *Matthew 1–13*. WBC 33a. Dallas: Word, 1993.

———. *The Use of the Old and New Testaments in Clement of Rome.* Leiden: Brill, 1973.

Hanson, Anthony Tyrrell. *Studies in Paul's Technique and Theology.* London: SPCK, 1974.

Hanks, Joyce Main. *Ronsard and Biblical Tradition.* Tübingen: Narr, 1982.

Hanson, R. P. C. "Notes on Tertullian's Interpretation of Scripture." *JTS* 12.2 (1961) 273–79.

Harding, Thomas, ed. *The Decades of Henry Bullinger, Minister of the Church in Zurich: The First and Second Decades.* Cambridge: Cambridge University Press, 1849.

Harkins, Franklin T. "General Introduction." In *Interpretation of Scripture: Theory: A Selection of Works of Hugh, Andrew, Godfrey and Richard of St Victor, and Robert of Melun*, edited by Franklin T. Harkins and Frans van Liere, 31–60. Victorine Texts in Translation 3. Turnhout: Brepols, 2012.

Harrisville, Roy A., and Sundberg, Walter. *The Bible in Modern Culture: Baruch Spinoza to Brevard Childs.* Grand Rapids: Eerdmans, 2002.

Hartman, Geoffrey H. *Criticism in the Wilderness: The Study of Literature Today*, 2nd Ed.. New Haven: Yale University Press, 2007.

Hays, Richard B. "Christology and Ethics in Galatians: The Law of Christ." *CBQ* 49 (1987) 268–90.

———. *The Conversion of the Imagination: Paul as Interpreter of Israel's Scripture.* Grand Rapids: Cambridge, 2005.

———. "The Conversion of the Imagination: Scripture and Eschatology in 1 Corinthians." *NTS* 45 (1999) 391–412.

———. *First Corinthians.* Interpretation. Louisville, KY: John Knox, 1997.

Heil, John Paul. *The Rhetorical Role of Scripture in 1 Corinthians.* Studies in Biblical Literature. Atlanta: SBL, 2005.

Herzer J. "Alttestamentliche Prophetie und die Verkündigung des Evangeliums: Beobachtungen zur Stellung und zur hermeneutische Funktion von 1 Petr 1, 10–12." *BThZ* 14.1 (1997) 14–22.

Hilary of Poitiers. *Commentary on Matthew.* Translated by D. H. Williams. Fathers of the Church. Washington DC: Catholic University of America Press, 2012.

———. "On the Trinity." In *Nicene and Post-Nicene Fathers, Second Series, Vol. 9.*, edited by Philip Schaff and Henry Wace, translated by E. W. Watson and L. Pullan, 40–234. Buffalo, NY: Christian Literature, 1899.

Hill, Harvey. "Religion and the University: The Controversy over Essays and Reviews at Oxford." *JAAR* 73.1 (2005) 183–207.

Hillyer, Norman. "'Rock-Stone' Imagery in 1 Peter." *TynBul* 22 (1971) 52–81.

Hines, Paul A. "Peter and the Prophetic Word: The Theology of Prophecy traced through Peter's Sermons and Epistles." *BBR* 21 (2011) 227–44.

Hirsch, E. D. *Validity in Interpretation.* New Haven: Yale University Press, 1967.

Hirschman, Marc. *The Rivalry of Genius: Jewish and Christian Biblical Interpretation in Late Antiquity.* Translated by Batya Stein. Albany: State University of New York, 1996.

Hobbs, R. Gerald. "How Firm a Foundation: Martin Bucer's Historical Exegesis of the Psalms." *Church History* 53.4 (1984) 477–91.

Hoffman, Daniel. "The Authority of Scripture and the Apostolic Doctrine in Ignatius of Antioch." *JETS* 28.1 (1985) 71–79.

Hughes, Graham. *Hebrews and Hermeneutics: The Epistle to the Hebrews as a New Testament Example of Biblical Interpretation.* SNTSMS 36. Cambridge University Press: Cambridge, 1979.

Hvalvik, Reidar *The Struggle for Scripture and Covenant: The Purpose of the Epistle of Barnabas and Jewish-Christian Competition in the Second Century.* WUNT 2.82. Tübingen: Mohr Siebeck, 1996.

Hwang, Jerry. "Turning the Tables on Idol Feasts: Paul's use of Exodus 32:6 in 1 Corinthians 10:7." *JETS* 54.3 (2011) 573–87.

Ingram, Doug. *Ambiguity in Ecclesiastes.* LHBOTS 431. London: T. & T. Clark, 2006.

Instone-Brewer, David. "1 Corinthians 9:9–11: A Literal Interpretation of 'Do Not Muzzle the Ox.'" *NTS* 38 (1992) 554–65.

Iser, Wolfgang. *The Implied Reader: Patterns of Communication in Prose Fiction from Bunyan to Beckett.* Baltimore, MD: John Hopkins University Press, 1978.

———. *The Range of Interpretation.* New York: Columbia University Press, 2000.

———. "Talk Like Whales." *Diacritics* 11.3 (1981) 82–87.

Jardine, Lisa. *Erasmus: Man of Letters.* Princeton: Princeton University Press, 1993. 55–82.

Jensen, Michael P. "Figuring Calvin: Calvin's Hermeneutics (almost) Five Centuries On." In *Engaging with Calvin: Aspects of the Reformer's Legacy for Today*, edited by Mark D. Thompson, 42–59. Nottingham: Apollos, 2009.

Jenson, Robert W. *America's Theologian: A Recommendation of Jonathan Edwards.* Oxford: Oxford University Press, 1992.

Jeremias, Joachim. *The Parables of Jesus*. Translated by S. H. Hooke. NTL. London: SCM, 1963.
———. "Paulus als Hillelit." In *Neotestamentica et Semitica: Studies in Honour of Matthew Black*, edited by E. E. Ellis and M. Wilcox, 88–94. Edinburgh: T. & T. Clark, 1969.
Jervell, Jacob. *Die Apostelgeschichte*. Göttingen: Vanderhoeck & Ruprecht, 1998.
———. *Imago Dei: Gen. 1, 26f. im Spätjudentum, in der Gnosis und in den paulinischen Briefen*. FRLANT 58. Gottingen: Vandenhoeck & Ruprecht, 1960.
Jobes, Karen H. *1 Peter*. BECNT. Grand Rapids: Baker, 2005.
———. "The Minor Prophets in James, 1 & 2 Peter and Jude." In *The Minor Prophets in the New Testament*, edited by Maarten J. J. Menken and Steve Moyise, 135–54. LNTS 377. The New Testament and the Scriptures of Israel. London: T. & T. Clark International, 2009.
John, Jeffrey. *Permanent, Faithful, Stable: Christian Same-Sex Partnerships*. London: Darton, Longman and Todd, 2012.
Joseph, Abson Prédestin. *A Narratological Reading of 1 Peter*. LNTS 440. London: T. & T. Clark, 2012.
Jowett, Benjamin. "On the Interpretation of Scripture." In *Essays and Reviews: The 1860 Text and its Reading*, edited by Victor Shea and William Whitla, 477–536. Charlottesville: University of Virginia Press, 2000.
Joyce, Paul. "Proverbs 8 in Interpretation (I): Historical Criticism and Beyond." In *Reading Texts, Seeking Wisdom: Scripture and Theology*, edited by David F. Ford and Graham Stanton, 89–101. London: SCM, 2003.
Juel, Donald. *Messianic Exegesis: Christological Interpretation of the Old Testament in Early Christianity*. Philadelphia: Fortress, 1988.
———. "Social Dimensions of Exegesis: The Use of Psalm 16 in Acts 2." *CBQ* 43 (1981) 543–86.
Kaiser, Walter C. "The Current Crisis in Exegesis and the Apostolic Use of Deuteronomy 25:4 in 1 Corinthians 9:8–10." *JETS* 21 (1973) 3–18.
———. "The Single Intent of Scripture." In *Evangelical Roots: A Tribute to Wilbur Smith*, edited by Kenneth S. Kantzer, 123–41. Nashville: Nelson, 1978.
———. "Single Meaning, Unified Referents: Accurate and Authoritative Citations of the Old Testament by the New Testament." In *Three Views on the New Testament Use of the Old Testament*, edited by Stanley N. Gundry, Kenneth Berding, and Jonathan Lunde, 45–89. Grand Rapids: Zondervan, 2008.
Hanson, R. P. *Allegory and Event: A Study of the Source and Significance of Origen's Interpretation of Scripture*. London: SCM, 1959.
Kamesar, Adam. "Hilary of Poitiers, Judeo-Christianity, and the Origins of the LXX: A Translation of 'Tractatus Super Psalmos' 2.2–3 with Introduction and Commentary." *VC* 59.3 (2005) 264–85.
Keck, L. E. "Romans 15:4—an Interpolation?" In *Faith and History: Essays in Honor of Paul W. Meyer*, edited by J. T. Carroll, C. H. Cosgrove and E. E. Johnson, 125–36. Atlanta, GA: Scholars Press, 1991.
Keith, Graham. "Justin Martyr and Religious Exclusivism." *TynBul* 43.1 (1992) 57–80.
Kelly, J. N. D. *A Commentary on the Epistles of Peter and Jude*. London: A. & C. Black, 1969.
Kermode, Frank. *The Genesis of Secrecy: On the Interpretation of Narrative*. Cambridge, MA: Harvard University Press, 1979.

———."The Plain Sense of Things." In *Midrash and Literature*, edited by Geoffrey H. Hartman and Sandford Budick, 179–94. New Haven: Yale University Press, 1986.
Kilcullen, John. "The Political Writings." In *The Cambridge Companion to Ockham*, edited by Paul Vincent Spade, 302–25. Cambridge: Cambridge University Press, 1999.
Kilpatrick, G. D. "1 Peter 1.11: TINA 'H ΠΟΙΟΝ ΚΑΙΡΟΝ." *NovT* 28 (1986) 91–92.
Kingsbury, Jack Dean. "The Title 'Son of David' in Matthew's Gospel." *JBL* 95:4 (1976) 591–602.
Knowles, Michael P. "'Everyone Who Hears These Words of Mine': Parables on Discipleship (Matthew 7:24–27//Luke 6:47–49. Luke 14:28–33. Luke 17:7–10. Matthew 20:1–16)." In *The Challenge of Jesus' Parables*, edited by Richard N. Longenecker, 286–305. Grand Rapids: Eerdmans, 2000.
Laney, J. Carl. "Deuteronomy 24:1–4 and the Issue of Divorce." *B.Sac.* 149 (1992) 3–15.
Lambe, P. J. "Critics and Skeptics in the Seventeenth-Century Republic of Letters." *HTR* 81 (1988) 271–96.
Legaspi, Michael. *The Death of Scripture and the Rise of Biblical Studies*. Oxford Studies in Historical Theology. Oxford: Oxford University Press, 2010.
Levin, Yigal. "'Son of God' and 'Son of David': The 'Adoption' of Jesus into the Davidic Line." *JSNT* 28:4 (2006) 415–42.
Levine, Nancy. "Spinoza's Bible: Concerning How It is that "Scripture, Insofar as it Contains the Word of God, Has Come Down to Us Uncorrupted."'" *Philosophy and Theology* 13.1 (2001) 93–142.
Lincicum, David. "Paul and the Temple Scroll: Reflections on a Shared Engagement with Deuteronomy." In *"What does the Scripture Say?" Studies in the Function of Scripture in Early Judaism and Christianity, Vol 2: The Letters and Liturgical Traditions*, edited by Craig A. Evans and H. Daniel Zacharias, 51–69. LNTS 470. London: T. & T. Clark, 2012.
Loader, W. R. G. "Christ at the Right Hand—Ps. CX. 1 in the New Testament." *NTS* 24 (1978) 119–217.
Löhr, Hermut. "Geschichtliches Denken im Hebräerbrief." In *Heil und Geschichte: Die Geschichtsbezogenheit des Heils und das Problem der Heilsgeschichte in der biblischen Tradition und in der theologischen Deutung*, edited by Jörg Frey, Stefan Krauter, and Hermann Lichtenberger, 443–57. WUNT 248. Tübingen: Mohr Siebeck, 2009.
Loewe, R. "Herbert of Bosham's Commentary on Jerome's Hebrew Psalter: A Preliminary Investigation into its Sources." *Bib.* 34 (1953) 44–77.
———. "The 'Plain' Meaning of Scripture in Early Jewish Exegesis." In *Papers of the Institute of Jewish Studies London 1*, edited by J. G. Weiss, 140–185. Jerusalem: Hebrew University, 1964.
Longenecker, Richard N. *Biblical Exegesis in the Apostolic Period*. Grand Rapids: Eerdmans, 1975.
———. "Early Church Interpretation." In *Dictionary of Biblical Criticism and Interpretation*, edited by S. Porter, 87. New York: Taylor & Francis, 2007.
———. *Galatians*. WBC 41. Nashville: Thomas Nelson, 1990.
———. "The Pedagogical Nature of the Law in Galatians 3:19—14:7." *JETS* 25 (1982) 53–61.
———. "'Who is the Prophet Talking About?' Some Reflections on the New Testament's Use of the Old." *Themelios* 12 (1987) 4–8.

Longxi, Zhang. "The Tao and the Logos: Notes on Derrida's Critique of Logocentrism." *Critical Inquiry* 11 (1985) 385–98.

Lowth, Robert. *Isaiah: A New Translation with Preliminary Dissertation and Notes, Critical, Philological and Explanatory*. Cambridge: James Munroe, 1834.

Lull, D. J. "'The Law was Our Pedagogue': A Study in Galatians 3:19–25." *JBL* 105 (1986) 481–98.

Luz, Ulrich. *Das Geschichtsverständnis des Paulus*. BEvT 49. Munich: Kaiser, 1968.

Malachi, Zvi. "'Creative Philology' as a System of Talmudic Exegesis: Creating Midrashic Interpretations from Multi-Meaning Words in the Midrash and the Zohar." In *Puns and Pundits: Word Play in the Hebrew Bible and Ancient Near Eastern Literature*, edited by Scott B. Noegal, 269–87. Bethesda, MD: CDL, 2000.

Martin, Matthew J. "Origen's Theory of Language and the First Two Columns of the Hexapla." *HTR* 97.1 (2004) 99–106.

Martin, Ralph P. *James*. WBC 48. Nashville: Thomas Nelson, 1988.

Martyn, J. Louis. *Galatians: A New Translation with Introduction and Commentary*. ABC 33. New York: Doubleday, 1997.

———. *Theological Issues in the Letters of Paul*. Studies of the New Testament and its World. Edinburgh: T. & T. Clark, 1997.

Matthewson, D. *A New Heaven and a New Earth: The Meaning and Function of the Old Testament in Revelation 21.1–22.5*. JSNTSup 238. Sheffield: Sheffield Academic, 2003.

Mbuvi, Andrew M. *Temple, Exile and Identity in 1 Peter*. LNTS 345. London: T. & T. Clark, 2007.

McCartney, Dan G. *James*. BECNT. Grand Rapids: Baker Academic, 2009.

McFague, Sallie. "Mother God." In *The Power of Naming: A Concilium Reader in Feminist Liberation Theology*, edited by Elizabeth Schüssler Fiorenza, 324–29. London: SCM, 1996.

McGrath, Alister E. *The Intellectual Origins of the European Reformation*, 2nd ed. Oxford: Blackwell, 2004.

McLean, B. H. *Biblical Interpretation and Philosophical Hermeneutics*. Cambridge: Cambridge University Press, 2013.

Meeks, Wayne A. "'And Rose Up to Play': Midrash and Paraenesis in 1 Corinthians 10:1–22." *JSNT* 16 (1982) 64–78.

Menken, Maarten J. J. "Genesis in John's Gospel and 1 John." In *Genesis in the New Testament*, edited by Maarten J. J. Menken and Steve Moyise, 83–98. LNTS 466. London: T. & T. Clark, 2012.

Milbank, John. *Theology and Social Theory: Beyond Secular Reason*. 2nd ed. Oxford: Blackwell, 2006.

Miller, P. C. "Pleasure of the Text, Text of Pleasure: Eros and Language in Origen's Commentary on the Song of Songs." *JAAR* 54 (1986) 241–53.

Minnis, A. J. "Material Swords and Literal Lights: The Status of Allegory in William of Ockham's *Breviloqium* on Papal Power." In *With Reverence for the Word: Medieval Scriptural Exegesis in Judaism, Christianity, and Islam*, edited by John Dammen McAuliffe, Barry D. Walfish, and Joseph W. Goering, 292–364. Oxford: Oxford University Press, 2010.

Mitchell, M. M. *Paul and the Rhetoric of Reconciliation: An Exegetical Investigation of the Language and Composition of 1 Corinthians*. HUT 28. Tübingen: Mohr Siebeck, 1991.

Moo, Douglas J. *The Epistle to the Romans*. NICNT. Grand Rapids: Eerdmans, 1996.
Moore, Stephen D. and Yvonne Sherwood. *The Invention of the Biblical Scholar: A Critical Manifesto*. Minneapolis: Fortress, 2011.
Morris, Leon. *The Epistle to the Romans*. Grand Rapids: Eerdmans, 1988.
———. *The Gospel According to Matthew*. PNTC. Grand Rapids: Eerdmans, 1992.
Moyise, Steve. "Does the Author of Revelation Misappropriate the Scriptures?" *AUSS* 40.1 (2002) 3–21.
———. "Does the NT Quote the OT Out Of Context?" *Anvil* 11.2 (1994) 133–43.
———. *Evoking Scripture: Seeing the Old Testament in the New*. London: T. & T. Clark, 2008.
———. "Intertextuality and the Study of the Old Testament in the New Testament." In *The Old Testament in the New Testament: Essays in Honour of J. L. North*, edited by Steve Moyise, 14–41. JSNTSup 189. Sheffield: Sheffield Academic, 2000.
———. "The Language of the Old Testament in the Apocalypse." *JSNT* 76 (1999) 97–113.
———. "Models for Intertextual Interpretation of Revelation." In *The Book of Revelation: Theology, Politics and Intertextuality*, edited by R.B. Hays and S. Alkier, 31–45. Waco: Baylor University Press, 2012.
———. *The Old Testament in the Book of Revelation*. JSNTSup 115. Sheffield: Sheffield Academic, 1995.
———. "The Old Testament in the New: A Reply to Greg Beale." *IBS* (1999) 54–58.
Müller, Johannes. *Martin Bucers Hermeneutik*. Vanderhoeck & Ruprecht: Guterslöh, 1965.
Myers, Alicia D. "'The One of Whom Moses Wrote': The Characterization of Jesus through Old Testament Moses Traditions in the Gospel of John." In *"What does the Scripture Say?" Studies in the Function of Scripture in Early Judaism and Christianity, Vol 2: The Letters and Liturgical Traditions*, edited by Craig A. Evans and H. Daniel Zacharias, 1–20. LNTS 470. London: T. & T. Clark, 2012.
Nellen, H. J. M. "Hugo Grotius." In *Hebrew Bible, Old Testament, vol II: From the Renaissance to the Enlightenment (1300–1800)*, edited by Magne Saebo, 809–10. Göttingen: Vandenhoeck & Ruprecht, 2008.
Neugebauer, Fritz. "Die Davidssohnfrage (Mark XII. 35–37 Parr.) und der Menschensohn." *NTS* 21:1 (1974) 91–96.
Neyrey, J. H. "The Apologetic use of the Transfiguration in 2 Peter 1:16–21." *CBQ* 42 (1980) 504–19.
Noble, P. R. "The *Sensus Literalis*: Jowett, Childs, and Barr." *JTS* 44 (1993) 1–23.
Noegal, Scott B. *Janus Parallelism in the Book of Job*. JSOT 223. Sheffield: Sheffield Academic, 1996.
———. "Polysemy." In *Encyclopedia of Hebrew Language and Linguistics, vol 3.*, edited by Geoffrey Khan, 178–86. Leiden: Brill, 2013.
Noll, Mark A. *Between Faith and Criticism: Evangelicals, Scholarship, and the Bible*. Leicester: Apollos, 1991.
Nolland, John. *Luke 1–9:20*. WBC 35a. Dallas: Word, 1989.
Obermüller, R. "Hermeneutische Themen im Jakobusbriefes." *Bib* 53 (1972) 234–44.
Olsen, Glenn. "The Spiritual Sense(s) Today." In *The Bible and the University*, edited by David Lyle Jeffrey and C. Stephen Evans, 116–38. Scripture and Hermeneutics Series 8. Grand Rapids: Zondervan, 2007.
Origen. *On First Principles*. Translated by G. W. Butterworth. London: SPCK, 1936.

———. *The Song of Songs: Commentary and Homilies*. Translated by R. P. Lawson. Ancient Christian Writers 26. New York: Paulist, 1957.
Oropeza, B. J. "Apostasy in the Wilderness: Paul's Message to the Corinthians in a State of Eschatological Liminality." *JSNT* 75 (1999) 69–86.
Orr, William F. and James Arthur Walther. *1 Corinthians: A New Translation with Introduction and Commentary*. ABC 32. New York: Doubleday, 1976.
Osborne, Thomas P. "L'Utilisation de l'Ancient Testament dans la Première Épître de Pierre." *RThL* 12.1 (1981) 64–77.
Osburn, Carroll D. "The Present Indicative in Matthew 19:9." *RQ* 24:4 (1981) 193–203.
Paddison, Angus. *Scripture: A Very Theological Proposal*. London: T. & T. Clark, 2009.
Paulien, J. "Dreading the Whirlwind: Intertextuality and the Use of the Old Testament in Revelation." *AUSS* 39 (2001) 5–22.
Paget, James Carlton. *The Epistle of Barnabas: Outlook and Background*. WUNT 2.64. Mohr Siebeck: Tübingen, 1994.
Payne, John B. "Erasmus's Influence on Zwingli and Bullinger in the Exegesis of Matthew 11:28–30." In *Biblical Interpretation in the Era of the Reformation: Essays Presented to David C. Steinmetz in Honor of His Sixtieth Birthday*, edited by David Curtis Steinmetz and Richard Alfred Muller, 63–80. Grand Rapids: Eerdmans, 1996.
Penner, Todd C. *The Epistle of James and Eschatology: Re-reading an Ancient Christian Letter*. JSNTSup 121. Sheffield: Sheffield Academic, 1996.
Perrot, C. "Les examples du desert (1 Co. 10.6–11)." *NTS* 29 (1983) 437–52.
Petersen, Rodney L. "Bullinger's Prophets of the 'Restitutio.'" In *Biblical Hermeneutics in Historical Perspective: Studies in Honor of Karlfried Froehlich on His Sixtieth Birthday*, edited by Mark S. Burrows and Paul Rorem, 245–61. Grand Rapids: Eerdmans, 1991.
Pineas, Rainer. "William Tyndale's Polemical Use of the Scriptures." *Nederlands Archief voor Kerkgeschiedenis* 45 (1962) 65–78.
Porter, Stanley E., and Pitts, Andrew W. "τοῦτο πρῶτον γινώσκοντες ὅτι in 2 Peter 1.20 and Hellenistic Epistolary Convention." *JBL* 127.1 (2008) 165–71.
Pusey, E. B. *Daniel the Prophet: Nine Lectures Delivered in the Divinity School of the University of Oxford*. Oxford: J. Parker, 1864.
Rabbie, E. "Hugo Grotius and Judaism." In *Hugo Grotius Theologian: Essays in Honour of G. H. M. Posthumus Meyjes*, edited by H. J. M. Nellen and E. Rabbie, 99–120. SHCT 55. Leiden: Brill, 1994.
Rabelais, François. *Gargantua and Pantagruel*. Translated by J. M. Cohen. London: Penguin, 1955.
Rabinowitz, Isaac, "Pesher/Pittaron: Its Biblical Meaning and its Significance in the Qumran Literature." *RevQ* 8:2 (1973) 219–32.
Ramsey, Robert L. "Theodore of Mopsuestia in England and Ireland." *ZCP* 8.1 (1912) 452–97.
Reed, Annette Y., and Adam H. Becker. "Introduction: Traditional Models and New Directions." In *The Ways that Never Parted: Jews and Christians in Late Antiquity and the Early Middle Ages*, edited by Adam H. Becker and Annette Y. Reed, 1–33. TSAJ 95. Tübingen: Mohr Siebeck, 2003.
Rendsburg, Gary A. "Word Play in Biblical Hebrew: An Eclectic Collection." In *Puns and Pundits: Word Play in the Hebrew Bible and Ancient Near Eastern Literature*. edited by Scott B. Noegal, 137–62. Bethesda, MD: CDL, 2000.

Reventlow, Henning Graf. *The Authority of the Bible and the Rise of the Modern World.* London: SCM, 1984.

———. "Humanistic Exegesis: the Famous Hugo Grotius." In *Creative Biblical Exegesis: Christian and Jewish Hermeneutics through the Centuries,* edited by B. Uffenheimer and H. Graf Reventlow, 175–91. JSOTSup 59. Sheffield: Sheffield Academic Press, 1988.

Ricoeur, Paul. *From Text to Action: Essays in Hermeneutics, II.* Translated by Kathleen Blamey and John B. Thompson. London: Continuum, 2008.

———. "Schleiermacher's Hermeneutics." *The Monist* 60.2 (1977) 181–97.

Robertson, A. and A. Plummer. *A Critical and Exegetical Commentary on the First Epistle of St Paul to the Corinthians.* ICC. Edinburgh: T. & T. Clark, 1914.

Rorty, Richard. *Philosophy and Social Hope.* London: Penguin, 1999.

Robinson, Thomas A. *Ignatius of Antioch and the Parting of the Ways: Early Jewish-Christian Relations.* Peabody, MA: Hendrickson, 2009.

Rogerson, J. W. *W. M. L. de Wette: Founder of Modern Biblical Criticism: An Intellectual Biography.* JSOTSup 126. Sheffield: Sheffield Academic, 1992.

Rorty, Richard. *Philosophy and Social Hope.* London: Penguin, 1999.

Rosenberg, A. W. "Hugo Grotius as Hebraist." *Studia Rosenthalia* 12 (1978) 62–90.

Rosner, Brian S. "Deuteronomy in 1 and 2 Corinthians." In *Deuteronomy in the New Testament,* edited by Steve Moyise and Maarten J. J. Menken, 118–35. LNTS 358. London: T. & T. Clark, 2007.

Saebo, Magne. *Hebrew Bible, Old Testament: The History of its Interpretation, vol 1.* Göttingen: Vandenhoeck & Ruprecht, 1996.

Said, Edward W. *The World, the Text, and the Critic.* Cambridge, MA: Harvard University Press, 1983.

Sanders, James A. "Paul and Theological History." In *Paul and the Scriptures of Israel,* edited by Craig A. Evans and James A. Sanders, 52–57. JSNTSup 83. Sheffield: Sheffield Academic, 1993.

Sandys-Wunsch, John and Laurence Eldridge. "J. P. Gabler and the Distinction between Biblical and Dogmatic Theology: Translation, Commentary and Discussion of his Originality." *SJT* 33:2 (1980) 133–58.

Sargent, Benjamin. "Biblical Hermeneutics and the Zurich Reformation." *EvQ* 86.4 (2014) 325–42.

———. "Chosen through Sanctification (1 Pet 1,2 and 2 Thess 2,13): the Theology or Diction of Silvanus?" *Bib* 94.1 (2013) 117–20.

———. *David Being a Prophet: The Contingency of Scripture upon History in the New Testament.* BZNW 207. Berlin: De Gruyter, 2014.

———. *Day by Day: The Rhythm of the Bible in the Book of Common Prayer.* Anglican Foundations 4. London: Latimer Trust, 2012.

———. "The Exegetical Middah דבר הלמד מעניינו and the New Testament." *NovT* 57.4 (2015) 413–17.

———. "'Interpreting Homer from Homer': Aristarchus of Samothrace and the Notion of Scriptural Authorship in the New Testament." *TynBul* 65.1 (2014) 125–39.

———. "The Narrative Substructure of 1 Peter." *ExpTim* 124.10 (2013) 485–90.

———. "Proceeding Beyond Isolation: Bringing Milbank, Habermas and Ockham to the Interfaith Table." *HeyJ* 51.5 (2010) 819–30.

———. *Written to Serve: The Use of Scripture in 1 Peter.* LNTS 547. London: T. & T. Clark.

Schäfer, P. "Nachbiblische Traditionen vom Tod des Moses." In *Josephus-Studien: Untersuchungen zu Josephus, dem antiken Judentum und dem Neuen Testament: Otto Michel zum 70. Geburtstag gewidmet*, edited by O. Betz, K. Haacker and M. Hengel, 147–74. Göttingen: Vandenhoeck & Ruprecht, 1974.

Schelkle, Karl Herman. *Die Petrusbriefe, Der Judasbrief.* HThKNT 13. Freiburg: Herder, 1961.

Schenk, Ken. "God has Spoken: Hebrews' Theology of the Scriptures." In *The Epistle to the Hebrews and Christian Theology*, edited by Richard Bauckham, et al., 321–26. Grand Rapids: Eerdmans, 2009.

Schleiermacher, F. D. E. *The Christian Faith.* Edited by H. R. Mackintosh and J. S. Stewart. London: T. & T. Clark, 1999.

———. *Hermeneutics and Criticism, and Other Writings.* Translated by Andrew Bowie. Cambridge: Cambridge University Press, 1999.

———. *Hermeneutics: The Handwritten Manuscripts.* Edited by H. Kimmerle. AAR Texts and Translations Series 1. Missoula, MT: Scholars Press, 1977.

Schlosser, Jacques. "Ancien Testament et Christologie dans la Prima Petri." In *Etudes sur la Première Lettre de Pierre*, edited by Charles Perrot, 65–93. LD 102. Paris: Cerf, 1980.

Schoedel, W. R. "Ignatius and the Archives." *HTR* 71 (1978) 97–106.

Schröter, Jens. "Schriftauslegung und Hermeneutik in 2 Korinther 3: Ein Beitrag zur Frage der Schriftbenutzung des Paulus." *NovT* 40 (1998) 231–75.

Schüssler Fiorenza, Elizabeth. *The Book of Revelation: Justice and Judgement.* Philadelphia: Fortress, 1988.

Schutter, William L. *Hermeneutic and Composition in 1 Peter.* WUNT 30. Tübingen: Mohr Siebeck, 1989.

Screech, M. A. "The Sense of Rabelais's Enigme en Prophétie (Gargantua LVIII): A Clue to Rabelais's Evangelical Reactions to the Persecutions of 1534." *Bibliothèque d'Humanisme et Renaissance* 18.3 (1956) 392–404.

Segovia, Fernando F. "Criticism in Critical Times: Reflections on Vision and Task," *JBL* 134.1 (2015) 6–29.

Seifrid, Mark A. "Romans," in *Commentary on the New Testament Use of the Old Testament*, edited by G. K. Beale and D. A. Carson, 607–94. Grand Rapids: Baker, 2007.

Seitz, Christopher R. "Scripture Becomes Religion(s): The Theological Crisis of Serious Biblical Interpretation in the Twentieth Century." In *Renewing Biblical Interpretation*, edited by Craig G. Bartholomew, Colin Greene and Karl Möller, 40–65. SHS 1. Grand Rapids: Zondervan, 2000.

Selwyn, Edward Gordon. *The First Epistle of St. Peter: The Greek Text with Introduction, Notes and Essays.* London: Macmillan, 1958.

Sheenan, Jonathan. *The Enlightenment Bible: Translation, Scholarship, Culture.* Princeton: Princeton University Press, 2005.

Shogimen, Takashi. *Ockham and Political Discourse in the Late Middle Ages.* Cambridge: Cambridge University Press, 2007.

Shotwell, Willis Allen. *The Biblical Exegesis of Justin Martyr.* London: SPCK, 1965.

Signer, Michael A. "Peshat, Sensus Litteralis and Sequential Narrative: Jewish Exegesis and the School of St. Victor in the 12th Century." In *The Frank Talmage Memorial Vol. 1*, edited by Barry Walfish, 203–16. Haifa: Haifa University Press, 1993.

Silva, Moisés. "Galatians." In *Commentary on the New Testament Use of the Old Testament*, edited by G. K. Beale and D. A. Carson, 785–812. Grand Rapids: Baker, 2007.

Simonetti, Manlio. *Biblical Interpretation in the Early Church: An Historical Introduction to Patristic Exegesis*. Translated by John A. Hughes. Edinburgh: T. & T. Clark, 1994.

Smalley, Beryl. *The Study of the Bible in the Middle Ages*. Oxford: Blackwell, 1952.

Smillie, Gene R. "Contrast or Continuity in Hebrews 1:1–2?" *NTS* 51.4 (2005) 543–51.

Smith, James K. A. *The Fall of Interpretation: Philosophical Foundations for a Creational Hermeneutic*. Downers Grove, IL: InterVarsity, 2000.

Smith, Lesley. "What was the Bible in the Twelfth and Thirteenth Centuries?" In *Neue Richtungen in der hoch und spätmittelalterlichen Bibelexegese*, edited by Robert E. Lerner, 1–15. Schriften des Historischen Kollegs Kolloquien 32. Munich: Oldenbourg, 1993.

Snodgrass, Klyne. *Stories with Intent: A Comprehensive Guide to the Parables of Jesus*. Grand Rapids: Eerdmans, 2008.

Soards, Marion L. *The Speeches in Acts: Their Content, Context and Concerns*. Louisville, KY: Westminster John Knox, 1994.

Sparks, H. D. F. "Jerome as Biblical Scholar." In *The Cambridge History of the Bible*, edited by P. Ackroyd and C. F. Evans, 510–41. Cambridge: Cambridge University Press, 1970.

Spinoza, Benedict de. *Theological-Political Treatise*. Translated by Michael Silverthorne and Jonathan Israel. Cambridge: Cambridge University Press. 2007.

Stanley, Christopher D. *Arguing with Scripture: The Rhetoric of Quotations in the Letters of Paul*. London: T. & T. Clark, 2004.

———. "'Pearls Before Swine': Did Paul's Audiences Understand his Biblical Quotations?" *NovT* 41.2 (1999) 124–44.

Stein, Stephen J. "The Quest for the Spiritual Sense: The Biblical Hermeneutics of Jonathan Edwards." *HTR* 70 (1977) 99–113.

Steinmetz, David. "The Superiority of Pre-Critical Exegesis." In *The Theological Interpretation of Scripture: Classic and Contemporary Readings*, edited by Stephen E. Fowl, 26–38. Oxford: Blackwell, 1997.

Stern, David. "Midrash and Determinacy." *Critical Inquiry* 15.1 (1988) 132–61.

———. *Midrash and Theory: Ancient Jewish Exegesis and Contemporary Literary Studies*. Chicago: Northwestern University Press, 1998.

Stockhausen, Carol Kern. *Moses' Veil and the Glory of the New Covenant*. AnBib 116. Rome: Pontifical Biblical Institute, 1989.

Strack, H. L., and P. Billerbeck. *Kommentar zum N. T. aus Talmud und Midrasch, I*. Munich, 1922.

Strauss, Mark L. *The Davidic Messiah in Luke-Acts: The Promise and its Fulfillment in Lukan Christology*. JSNTSup 110. Sheffield: Sheffield Academic, 1995.

Sweet, John. *Revelation*. London: SCM, 1990.

Syman, Edward. "The Four 'Senses' and Four Exegetes." In *With Reverence for the Word: Medieval Scriptural Exegesis in Judaism, Christianity, and Islam*, edited by John Dammen McAuliffe, Barry D. Walfish, and Joseph W. Goering, 225–36. Oxford: Oxford University Press, 2010.

Telle, Emile V. "Thélème et le Paulinisme matrimonial érasmien." In *François Rabelais, ouvrage publié pour le quatrième centenaire de sa mort, 1553–1953*, 104–19. Travaux d'Humanisme et Renaissance 7. Geneva: Droz, 1953.

Tertullian. *A Treatise on the Soul*. Translated by Peter Holmes. Edinburgh: T. & T. Clark, 1870.
Theodoret of Cyrus. *Commentary on the Psalms, 1–72*. Translated by Robert C. Hill. Fathers of the Church. Washington DC: Catholic University of America Press, 2000.
Thiselton, Anthony C. "'Behind' and 'In Front Of' the Text: Language, Reference and Indeterminacy." In *After Pentecost: Language and Biblical Interpretation*, edited by Craig Bartholomew, Colin Greene, and Karl Möller, 97–120. SHS 2. Grand Rapids: Zondervan, 2001.
———. *The First Epistle to the Corinthians*. NIGTC. Grand Rapids: Eerdmans, 2000.
———. *New Horizons in Hermeneutics: The Theory and Practice of Transforming Biblical Reading*. Grand Rapids: Zondervan, 1992.
Torjesen, K. J. "'Body,' 'Soul' and 'Spirit' in Origen's Theory of Exegesis." *ATR* 67 (1985) 17–30.
Torrance, Thomas F. *Divine Meaning: Studies in Patristic Hermeneutics*. Edinburgh: T. & T. Clark, 1995.
Trible, Phyllis. "Departriarchalizing in Biblical Interpretation." *JAAR* 61:1 (1973) 30–48.
———. *Texts of Terror: Literary-Feminist Readings of Biblical Narratives*. London: SCM, 2002.
Trigg, J. W. "The Apostolic Fathers and Apologists." In *A History of Biblical Interpretation, vol I: The Ancient Period*, edited by Alan J. Hauser and Duane F. Watson, 304–33. Grand Rapids: Eerdmans, 2003.
———. *Origen: The Bible and Philosophy in the Third Century Church*. Atlanta: John Knox, 1983.
Trueman, Carl R. "The Theology of the English Reformation." In *The Cambridge Companion to Reformation Theology*, edited by David Bagchi and David C. Steinmetz, 161–63. Cambridge: Cambridge University Press, 2004.
Trull, Gregory V. "Views on Peter's use of Psalm 16:8–11 in Acts 2:25–32." *BibSac* 161 (2004) 194–214.
Trumblower, Jeffrey A. "Origen's Exegesis of John 8:19–53: The Struggle with Heracleon over the idea of Fixed Natures." *VC* 43.2 (1989) 138–54.
Turner, Denys. *Eros and Allegory: Medieval Exegesis of the Song of Songs*. Cistercian Studies Series 156. Kalamazoo, MI: Cistercian, 1995.
Tyndale, William. *The Obedience of a Christian Man*. Edited by David Daniell. London: Penguin, 2000.
Vanhoozer, Kevin J. "Four Theological Faces of Biblical Interpretation." In *Reading Scripture with the Church: Toward a Hermeneutic for Theological Interpretation*, 131–42. Grand Rapids: Baker, 2006.
———. "Imprisoned or Free? Text, Status, and Theological Interpretation in the Master/Slave Discourse of Philemon." In *Reading Scripture with the Church: Toward a Hermeneutic for Theological Interpretation*, 51–94. Grand Rapids: Baker, 2006.
———. *Is There a Meaning in This Text? The Bible, the Reader, and the Morality of Literary Knowledge*. Grand Rapids: Zondervan, 1998.
van Unnik, W. C. "'With Unveiled Face,' An Exegesis of 2 Corinthians iii. 12–18." *NovT* 6 (1963) 153–69.
Vogelsang, E. *Die Anfänge von Luthers Christologie nach der ersten Psalmenvorlesung*. Berlin: de Gruyter, 1929.

Waszink, J. H. "Tertullian's Principles and Methods of Exegesis." In *Early Christian Literature and the Classical Intellectual Tradition*, edited by William R. Schoedel and Robert L. Wilkin, 17-31. Théologie Historique 53. Éditions Beauchesne: Paris, 1979.

Watson, Francis. *Paul and the Hermeneutics of Faith*. London: T. & T. Clark, 2004.

———. *Text and Truth: Redefining Biblical Theology*. Edinburgh: T. & T. Clark, 1997.

Weaver, Joel A. *Theodoret of Cyrus on Romans 11:26: Recovering an Early Christian Elijah Redivivus Tradition*. New York: Peter Lang, 2007.

Webster, John. *Holy Scripture: A Dogmatic Sketch*. Cambridge: Cambridge University Press, 2003.

Weimann, Robert. *Authority and Representation in Early Modern Discourse*. Edited by David Hillman. Baltimore: John Hopkins University Press, 1996.

Weiss, Johannes. *Der Erste Korintherbrief*. Göttingen: Vandenhoeck and Ruprecht, 1971.

———. *Earliest Christianity: A History of the Period AD 30-150*. New York: Harper, 1959.

Welleck, René, and Austin Warren. *Theory of Literature*. London: Penguin, 1973.

Werrell, Ralph S. *The Roots of William Tyndale's Theology*. Cambridge: James Clarke, 2013.

Wiles, M. F. "Origen as Biblical Scholar." In *The Cambridge History of the Bible*, edited by P. Ackroyd and C. F. Evans, 454-88. Cambridge: Cambridge University Press, 1970.

———. "Theodore of Mopsuestia as Representative of the Antiochene School." In *The Cambridge History of the Bible*, edited by P. Ackroyd and C. F. Evans, 489-510. Cambridge: Cambridge University Press, 1970.

William of Ockham. *A Short Discourse on the Tyrannical Government*. Cambridge Texts in the History of Political Thought. Translated by John Kilcullen. Edited by Arthur Stephen McGrade. Cambridge: Cambridge University Press, 1992.

Williams, Rowan. "Historical Criticism and the Sacred Text." In *Reading Texts: Seeking Wisdom*, edited by David E. Ford and Graham Stanton, 217-28. London: SCM, 2003.

———. "The Literal Sense of Scripture." *MT* 7.2 (1991) 121-34.

Williams, Travis B. "Ancient Prophets and Inspired Exegetes: Interpreting Prophetic Scripture in 1QpHab and 1 Peter." In *Bedrängnis und Identität: Studien zu Situation, Kommunikation und Theologie des 1. Petrusbriefes*, edited by David S. du Toit, 223-46. BZNW 200. Berlin: De Gruyter, 2013.

Willi-Plein, Ina. "Some Remarks on Hebrews from the Viewpoint of Old Testament Exegesis." In *Hebrews: Contemporary Methods—New Insights*, edited by Gabriella Gelardini, 25-35. BIS 75. Leiden: Brill, 2005.

Wimsatt, William K., and Monroe C. Beardsley. "The Intentionalist Fallacy." In *The Verbal Icon: Studies in the Meaning of Poetry*, edited by William K. Wimsatt, 4-18. Lexington: University of Kentucky Press, 1954.

Witte, Markus. "Die literarische Gattung des Buches Hiob: Robert Lowth und seine Erben." In *Sacred Conjectures: The Context and Legacy of Robert Lowth and Jean Astruc*, edited by John Jarick, 93-123. Library of Hebrew Bible/Old Testament Studies 457. London: T. & T. Clark, 2007.

Wolterstorff, Nicholas. *Divine Discourse: Philosophical Reflections on the Claim that God Speaks*. Cambridge: Cambridge University Press, 1995.

Worthen, Jeremy. "Interpreting Scripture for the Love of God: Hugh of St Victor on Reading and the Self." In *Biblical Interpretation: The Meanings of Scripture—Past and Present*, edited by John M. Court, 54–70. London: T. & T. Clark, 2003.

Wrede, William. *Vorträge und Studien*. Tübingen: Mohr Siebeck, 1907.

Wright, N. T. *The Climax of the Covenant: Christ and the Law in Pauline Theology*. Edinburgh: T. & T. Clark, 1991.

Yamasaki, Gary. "Broken Parallelism in Matthew's Parable of the Two Builders (7:24–27)." *Direction* 33 (2004) 143–49.

Young, Frances. "Alexandrian and Antiochene Exegesis." In *A History of Biblical Interpretation, vol I: The Ancient Period*, edited by Alan J. Hauser and Duane F. Watson, 334–54. Grand Rapids: Eerdmans, 2003.

Young, N. H. "*Paidagōgos*: The Social Setting of a Pauline Metaphor." *NovT* 29 (1987) 150–76.

Zwingli, Huldrych. "Acts of the Convention held in the Praiseworthy City of Zurich on the 29th Day of January on Account of the Holy Gospel." In *Selected Works of Huldreich Zwingli the Reformer of German Switzerland*, edited by S. M. Jackson, 1.47–48. Philadelphia: University of Philadelphia, 1901.

www.ingramcontent.com/pod-product-compliance
Lightning Source LLC
Chambersburg PA
CBHW031359230426
43670CB00006B/593